FREEDOM DREAMS

Other works by Robin D. G. Kelley

Three Strikes: The Fighting Spirit of Labor's Last Century
(with Howard Zinn and Dana Frank)

*Yo' Mama's Disfunktional! Fighting the Culture Wars in
Urban America*

Race Rebels: Culture, Politics, and the Black Working Class

*Hammer and Hoe: Alabama Communists during the
Great Depression*

Thelonious Monk: The Life and Times of an American Original

*Africa Speaks, America Answers: Modern Jazz in
Revolutionary Times*

FREEDOM DREAMS

THE

BLACK

RADICAL

IMAGINATION

ROBIN D. G. KELLEY

BEACON PRESS
BOSTON

Beacon Press
Boston, Massachusetts
www.beacon.org

Beacon Press books
are published under the auspices of
the Unitarian Universalist Association of Congregations.

25 24 23   8 7 6 5 4 3 2

This book is printed on acid-free paper that meets the uncoated paper
ANSI/NISO specifications for permanence as revised in 1992.

Library of Congress Cataloging-in-Publication data
can be found on page 286.

For my big sister,
MAKANI THEMBA NIXON

And in loving memory of
LISA Y. SULLIVAN
(1961–2001)
and
JOE WOOD JR.
(1964–1999)

Three dreamers who do.

CONTENTS

FOREWORD

When they say literature liberates, surely they were talking about *Freedom Dreams*.

Maybe it was love, maybe it was their dimples dancing, the way one girl rapped her words around us like a loose hug, our bodies transformed by the rhythm. Or how a few organizers lay in the hammock swaying as another's guitar dripped in calloused fingers. In the humid honey of June heat, a mango tree open-armed and waving sat deeply rooted in our Little Haiti backyard. This is where a dream became freedom. Shades of sweat gathered beneath shiny brazen green leaves, the people singing, catching the breeze like a spirit. We were timeless and no longer fighting. A premonition or an image that felt familiar came like a shoulder tap in my heart's eye. We gathered there to hang and rest after a community organizing meeting. Everyone, for more than a moment, was present and alive and forever. It was sacred ground. We weren't arguing, we weren't triggered, we weren't overwhelmed with grief. A smoke signal of possibility, a place we could feel, touch, and see. I found a new way to write a poem or as Kelley writes, a way to *transport us to another place*.

Where power seeks to obstruct and exploit language, Robin D. G. Kelley creates room for the unlanguagable. This book is a profound testament to the enduring dimension of our imaginations and the poetry of our organizing. Twenty years later, the truths revealed remain relevant and necessary especially in the thick paralyzing despair of a global pandemic. Many are disconnected from one another, a people socialized on social media constantly inundated with gross injustices all over the world and the final frontier of our movements becomes the mind. We are being initiated into the visions of those who have struggled before us: abolition, universal healthcare, global solidarity, and environmental justice. We are the dreaming. *Freedom Dreams* is a book that documents and contextualizes the political power of our shamanistic ability to feel and embody medicinal methodologies of how we resist. In the cadence of courage, these words are my belonging; it reflects the life I have made unbeknownst to me, a Blues surrealist poet marooned in the movement for our being. Fueled by the radical movements of those who came before us, Kelley conjures the legacy of Barbara Smith, Jayne Cortez, Aimé Césaire, Queen Mother Moore, Amiri Baraka, Paul Robeson, Sun Ra, and so many others.

We are what we are fighting for. Right now. As we demand presence and awareness, we are the freeing. Who are we without war, poverty, violence, police, and prisons? Who would we be if money wasn't our concern? If love was our currency, how would we distribute it? How do we value the unseen? I have spent my life traversing the tenses of time, the lettered language of the heart and mind. As our movement is busied by the struggle for our material conditions, I have obsessed over the immaterial needs of our people; poetry is where I've gone to meet the edges of myself. To touch the currents and vibrations of our experiences and perceptions. I was carved out of the flesh and blood of Black people who breathe poetry. The pain of being here and nowhere. A cause to live our most intimate lives.

We are the dreaming, an intervention organizing by way of presence. Years later, beneath the same mango tree, I watched Ntozake Shange glow back and forth in an old wicker rocking chair with a cigarette between her polished fingers like a wand. Her smile was an heirloom we all carried close. The Last Poets sipping cold brew flirting with the past, leaning in the groove of now. DJ Rich Medina spinning the soundtrack to a dream manifest conducting light in our hips and hands. The people were fed and full of imagination. Sonia Sanchez lecturing love in our living room with movement lessons. Inspired by the stories of African and Indigenous ancestors who were driven to the swamps and developed sovereign communities during the horror of American slavery, we facilitated a collective of young poets who were also organizers as we created the Maroon Poetry Festival in Liberty City, Miami. I had no idea we were rehearsing for the vision of Kelley's closing chapter. We built a temporary stage made from wood pallets in Tacolcy Park with aspirations to design a solar-powered amphitheater. Elders and young people together in harmony. The event was free and accessible, healthcare professionals on-site taking blood pressure, healing hands offering massages, morning meditation and yoga, barbers donating their skills to cut the children's hair. Tire swings roped around our trees, there was a huge flag with a North Star waving above the children's jungle gym. We built pop-up libraries, benches decorated with free books. We turned the children's workroom in the community center into an art gallery with local artists and vintage national Black treasures. We registered community members to vote in the upcoming state election and discussed the local politics of our time. We petitioned our people to help restore voting rights for 1.4 million Floridians who were formerly incarcerated. Huge banners of Emory Douglas posters billowed in the field as he discussed the revolutionary function of art with the people. It was surreal. We were more than our competing identities; we were organized in deep relationships with one another.

"Surrealism is not some lost, esoteric body of thought longing for academic recognition," Kelley writes. "It is a living practice and will continue to live as long as we dream. Nor is surrealism some atavistic romanticization of the past. Above all, surrealism considers love and poetry and the imagination powerful social and revolutionary forces, not replacements for organized protest, for marches and sit-ins, for strikes and slowdowns, for matches and spray paint."

We are one of the many echoes of Robin D. G. Kelley's words reverberating in the world. We are proof that his vision and argument are not only practical but critical to our movement's possibility and power. Here we were, *The Dream Defenders*, supported by a small group of lawyers, the Community Justice Project, workshopping the poetic language for our political vision of another Florida a few years earlier. We called our socialist vision for our people the Freedom Papers. It was an unconscious nod to the emancipation papers given to escaped Africans upon their arrival to the Spanish colony of St. Augustine. Over 250 years later, we conjured Fort Mose, the first free Black settlement in America, right in our backyard. Except, we defined freedom for ourselves—the freedom to imagine and struggle for alternatives: freedom from police, prisons, and poverty, freedom of movement, freedom of mind, freedom to be, etc. We spent many years using our literal home to facilitate workshops and nurture organizers in the efforts of decolonizing our imaginations. Language and how we use it is crucial to the vision for our lives. Kelley's book offers us our history so we can create with a clearer vision for our future. Sometimes we trip into our past as we endure the present, but freedom is always now.

While our society is hyper-focused on the technical and material developments of nation states, as we resist the patriarchy of settler colonialism, and the rising sea levels, and forests on fire, and the not enough hospital beds, and the violence of poverty, we must not lose sight of the deep emotional expressions of our heart. We are in a battle of ideas. We are in a battle for our spirits. There have been many developments and evolutions in the mechanics of our technology—Kelley reminds us, every movement demands an evolution and transformation of the heart and mind.

He writes, "*By revolution of the mind, I mean not merely a refusal of victim status. I am talking about an unleashing of the mind's most creative capacities, catalyzed by participation in struggles for change.*"

It was not easy at first to convince organizers and movement lawyers how poetry could organize our people into the revolutionary world we want to see, or that dreaming up a vision together was in fact the work we most desperately needed. But as *Freedom Dreams* demonstrates, we were not the first to struggle and we will not be the last. Poetry offers us a method and way through the world; how we organize one another shows who and what we are for. We used June Jordan's revolutionary blueprint and focused on the poetry workshop as a way to access and cultivate our radical visions. Our ability to reenvision and transform our society is what radical social movements are made of. We must return to the root, which is always love. So many of us have become victims of doubt and fear; remembering is our remedy and imagining is our inheritance. It is far more difficult to organize triggered, traumatized, and indifferent people into our liberation struggle. Therefore, our movements must lean on our radical imaginations for the strategy of social poetics to take hold.

Freedom Dreams is a dedication to the continuum. In order to create, we embody what we imagine. Freedom is not illusive. It's not beyond our reach. It is within our very hands. The capacity to dream, to cultivate and facilitate the collective as self-determined visionaries, is how we demand the alternative. This book is not an answer but an invitation to question; it is a prompt and a road map. Robin D. G. Kelley is a cartographer of a past present future. We are the poem. As we imagine, so we remember.

> Where ever we are going
> We are there
> Whoever we will be
> We have been
>
> —Aja Monet
> Fall 2021

FREEDOM DREAMS: FROM NOUN TO VERB

Fall 2021

*Over and over again, the ecstatic moment of revolt was met with
repression even greater than what we had anticipated.*

*The fissure was not a place where we could live. We could
not hold on to the new social forms we invented in the process
of revolt. The establishment leaders were sent to neutralize
the protesters. We were told to go home. We failed to make the
revolution our permanent home.*

*But the spark is kept alive,
underground, waiting for the right conditions.*

*The specter of Attica
The specter of Wounded Knee
The specter of Ferguson
The specter of Harpers Ferry
The specter of Haiti*

—Jackie Wang[1]

"Spring is coming."

—Mumia Abu-Jamal[2]

Twenty years after I delivered the lecture at Dartmouth that would become the seed for this book, the world caught fire. In the late spring of 2020, some twenty-six million people around the world took to the streets to protest the public execution of George Floyd in Minneapolis; the vigilante murder of Ahmaud Arbery in Brunswick, Georgia; the killing of Breonna Taylor, a twenty-six-year-old EMT worker gunned down in her bed by Louisville police during a "no-knock" raid. For the last decade, videos of police killing unarmed Black people in the US and Canada had become routine, but so had the protests. This was different. An unprecedented number of people risked their health and safety to face down riot police, tear gas, rubber bullets, and the COVID-19 pandemic, to demand justice and a radically different approach to public safety. Activists proposed cutting police budgets and abolishing prisons in order to fund housing, healthcare, living-wage jobs, universal basic income, green energy, and a system of restorative justice. And some cities took steps to comply. The Minneapolis city council passed a dramatic resolution to defund its police, and at least sixteen cities pledged to significantly cut expenditures on law enforcement. Los Angeles mayor Eric Garcetti agreed to cut funding to the police by $150 million. Seattle mayor Jenny Durkan promised to reallocate 50 percent of the police budget to other programs.[3]

The "Black Spring" rebellion of 2020 sparked a renewed interest in *Freedom Dreams*. I lost count of the many talks, webinars, podcasts, and conversations I was asked to do about the book and whether or not our "freedom dreams" were about to be realized. Reading groups popped up in the US, Canada, and elsewhere, sharing a free PDF version of *Freedom Dreams* and sometimes reaching out to me with questions, comments, or invitations. Interest in the book seemed to intensify as Black Spring gave way to a white winter of "wokeness fatigue," racist reaction, and liberal compromise. Protests dwindled; BLM signs were removed or power-scrubbed into oblivion, and cops kept shooting us: Jacob Blake, Dijon Kizzee, Anthony McClain, Kendrell Antron Watkins, Daniel Prude, Daunte Wright, Adam Toledo, Ma'Khia Bryant, Andrew Brown Jr., ad infinitum. After throwing a $10 million bone to a bunch of Black organizations in the name of Black Lives Matter, Amazon founder Jeff Bezos proceeded to cut employee hazard pay, spend millions to crush a union drive in Bessemer, Alabama, and launch plans to begin colonizing space.[4] Cities such as Minneapolis quietly withdrew their support for defunding their police or tried to water down their initial promises, and several Republican-dominated state legislatures passed laws expanding criminal penalties for protesting.

Meanwhile, the Democrats urged us to squash talk of defunding the police and get behind the effort to elect Joe Biden and Kamala Harris. The future of democracy depended on defeating Donald Trump. Biden prevailed with the largest vote total in history; Trump lost, with the *second* largest vote total in history. Before Biden-Harris could take office and begin deporting Haitian asylum seekers, bombing Syria, threatening war with China, and extending sanctions on Cuba, Trump's people attempted a coup d'état. On January 6, 2021, as Congress prepared to count the electoral votes and certify Biden's victory, thousands of white people, mostly white nationalists and neofascists, stormed the Capitol building in order to stop the process. The insurgents were drawn not from the suffering "white working class" but were largely middle-class entrepreneurs, paid alt-right organizers, and, especially, from the warrior class—veterans and active military personnel, and off-duty cops. In other words, leading the charge were people drawn from the ranks of the same forces who beat us back with rubber bullets, tear gas, pepper spray, and batons during the Black Spring protests; the same folks who killed, maimed, and detained Afghanis and Iraqis.

The attempted coup didn't surprise me or my friends in the movement. We knew that unless we stopped fascism and police power, these kinds of attacks were inevitable. In 2017, I wrote, "Today's organized protests in the streets and other places of public assembly portend the rise of a police state in the United States. For the past five years, the insurgencies of the Movement for Black Lives and its dozens of allied organizations have warned the country that unless we end racist state-sanctioned violence and the mass caging of Black and brown people, we are headed for a fascist state."[5] Despite polls showing that white folks now overwhelmingly believe that "Black lives matter," no one believed Black Spring smashed racism. On the contrary, the current generation of activists was already pessimistic and unsure about the future long before the Capitol insurrection.

In the face of growing pessimism, *Freedom Dreams* may come across as too hopeful and "optimistic" in these dark times. But the book is hardly optimistic; in fact, the word "optimism" never appears in the book (only "optimistic" in the title of Jayne Cortez's poem, which is a critique of being "cheerful and optimistic" in the face of catastrophe). Nor does the word "pessimism" appear, although "pessimistic" comes up once, in describing the post-emancipation generation's outlook on the future. When I use the word "hope," it does not mean wishful thinking or even dreaming. The Black radical imagination is not a kind of dream state conjured and nurtured independent of the day-to-day struggles on the ground but rather is forged in collective movements. My central point is that we cannot divorce critical analysis from social movements. The challenges of solidarity and a deep understanding of the mechanisms of oppression generate the conditions and requirements for new modes of analysis, new ways of being together. Therefore, it is not enough to imagine a world without oppression (especially since we don't always recognize the ways in which we ourselves practice and perpetuate oppression). We must also understand the mechanisms or processes that not only reproduce subjugation and exploitation but make them common sense and render them natural or invisible.

The book does not prioritize "freedom dreams" to the exclusion of "fascist nightmares." If anything, I show that freedom dreams are born of fascist nightmares, or, better yet, born *against* fascist nightmares. The very context for the book—today and twenty years ago—was the nightmare of global war, neoliberalism, and racialized state-sanctioned violence. I write these words on the eve of the twentieth anniversary of 9/11, as President Joe Biden declares an end to a war that cost $2.3 trillion and at least

170,000 lives; as Taliban forces take over Afghanistan and a defeated US military scrambles to evacuate its citizens and Afghan friends. The parallels are striking. I first proposed the book idea to my editor, Deb Chasman, on February 28, 2000, two days after three thousand of us marched down Manhattan's Fifth Avenue to protest the acquittal of the officers who killed Amadou Diallo, an unarmed Guinean immigrant shot forty-one times after police reportedly mistook his wallet for a gun. By the time I completed the manuscript, George W. Bush and Dick Cheney had stolen an election, the Department of Homeland Security was a reality, the World Trade Center was rubble, bombs were raining down on the Afghan people, Lower Manhattan was under martial law, and the US was preparing to invade Iraq.

I've had to remind readers that the movements featured here lived through much darker times than the early Bush years. The Black search for (home)land took place at the height of racist reaction, as the Bourbon South defeated Reconstruction, stripped Black men of the vote, made lynching the primary mode of discipline and punishment, and established the Jim Crow racial regime. Black Communists spread their message of liberation during the worst global economic crisis and at the height of the Red Scare. In the 1960s and '70s, a group of Black radicals envisioned the imminent collapse of the American empire just as US militarism and the national security state expanded and police violence intensified. Ida B. Wells and Anna Julia Cooper boldly asserted that genuine human freedom was impossible without the emancipation of Black women during what many historians considered to be the darkest period of African American history since chattel slavery. Angela Davis produced startlingly radical visions of freedom from a cage, and the Combahee River Collective drafted its famous statement as sexual violence and femicide against Black women was rising across the country.

These movements were fueled not by false optimism but by a deep understanding of *reality*. They were trying to sustain life by beating back the death-dealing structures of gendered racial capitalism. The only way to ensure survival for Black people was to envision a radically different future for all and fight to bring it into existence. It is in the fight that visions of the future are forged, clarified, revised, or discarded. For this reason, *Freedom Dreams* was never meant to be a manifesto or road map. It did not predict the future or present a plan of action or claim to be the catalyst for new radical insurgencies. Instead, it humbly offered a different take on histories of social movements by centering their visions of the future. This seemed important at the time because I kept encountering student activists disillusioned with both the academy and the liberalism of the Clinton era who were seeking radical alternatives. Despite what seemed to me an abundance of radical organizations in our midst, they looked nostalgically to the 1960s—especially to the Black Panther Party—for what they believed were "successful" models of revolution. But I wondered, what does "success" mean for movements committed to fundamentally transforming society? Does it mean winning campaigns? Taking state power? Passing laws that are transformative? What does it mean to "win" and why does it matter? The focus on winning was not limited to college students aspiring to become revolutionaries but had been baked into movement culture with the expanded role of the "non-profit industrial complex." Back then—and, to a large degree, even now—US social movements depended on foundations. Funders put their money behind "winnable campaigns," often undercutting the difficult and patient work of collective thinking, base building, cultivating a vision of the world activists are trying to build.[6] *Freedom Dreams* was an attempt to move beyond a bipolar understanding of social movements as either winning or losing to focus instead on the collective radical imagination that conjures and sustains visions of freedom even in the darkest times.

The start of the new millennium certainly felt like dark times. *Freedom Dreams* was written on the heels of eight years of organizing against Clinton-era neoliberalism and during the first months of the Bush era, when new movements had emerged to resist the war on drugs, the war on terror, anti-Black and anti-immigrant racism, Islamophobia, prison expansion, police violence, gendered and racialized violence against women of color and queer and trans people, and the ongoing struggle for reproductive justice. They include Critical Resistance, the Prison Moratorium Project, INCITE: Women of Color Against Violence, the James and Grace Lee Boggs Center, the Black Radical Congress, the Labor/Community Strategy Center, Miami Workers Center, Sisterfire, Malcolm X Grassroots Movement (MXGM), Sista II Sista, the Praxis Project, Los Angeles Community Action Network (LA-CAN), People Organized to Win Employment Rights (POWER), BlackOUT Arts Collective, Project South, Southerners on New Ground (SONG), Standing Together to Organize a Revolutionary Movement (STORM), School of Unity and Liberation (SOUL), Fabulous Independent Educated Radicals for Community Empowerment (FIERCE), Queers for Economic Justice, the Sylvia Rivera Law Project (SRLP), Justice for Janitors, and Black Workers for Justice, to name a few. These organizations were not without flaws or contradictions, nor were they fighting for exactly the same things. But taken together, they represent a convergence of movements that had spent years resisting state violence and neoliberalism, while cultivating abolitionist dreams of a world without oppression and exploitation; war; poverty; prisons; police; borders; the constraints of imposed gender, sexual, and ableist norms; and an economic system that destroys the planet while generating obscene inequality. They shared a vision of a future grounded in love, mutual care, cooperative economies, transformative justice, and abolition.

These are just a few of the organizations and activists that have been doing the work of imagining and fighting for a different future before, during, and long after the book came out. *Freedom Dreams* is a product of my relationship to activists and artists. Two, who are now with the ancestors, deserve special mention: revolutionary philosopher Grace Lee Boggs and poet Sekou Sundiata. Grace was the first to reach out to me about the book. She spent nearly a decade pressing me to abandon old ideas, and *Freedom Dreams* was the first encouraging sign that I had begun to listen. She agreed with the book's premise, that the catalyst for political engagement has never been misery, poverty, and oppression but the promise of constructing a new world. In June of 2002, our mutual friend historian and activist Scott Kurashige arranged a conversation between Grace and me during her visit to New York City. For over two hours, she drew out the book's key lessons but pushed me harder to read Dr. Martin Luther King's writings with greater care, especially his last Sunday sermon before his assassination in which he urged Americans "to develop new attitudes, the new mental responses" to the global revolutions in technology, warfare, and human rights.[7] Sadly, the cassette tape of our conversation was lost in the mail, but the lessons were not. Grace said it was time to leave the old protest strategies behind and focus on creating a society that promotes self-sufficiency, ecological sustainability, human interaction, and values of cooperation, mutuality, nonviolence, equality, and love. Making *revolution* meant remaking ourselves, insisting that the fundamental question facing humanity was how we "grow our souls."[8] And as I show in the epilogue, the community of organizers she helped nurture in Detroit spent the next two decades—and counting—putting this vision into practice.

The late poet Sekou Sundiata was my other chief interlocutor. His impact on both the birth and afterlife of *Freedom Dreams* has been profound. Sekou was there from conception. I titled the Dartmouth lecture that became the scaffolding for the book, "Politics and Knowledge: On the Poetry of Social Movements," precisely because my talk followed performances by poets Joy Harjo and Sekou during the long Dr. Martin Luther King Jr. holiday weekend. The title was meant to be an invitation. Tragically, Sekou never made it; on his way to New Hampshire, he got into a terrible car accident and broke his neck. Miraculously, he recovered and, fortunately for me, we both ended up back at Dartmouth in the summer of 2000, where we participated in a dialogue with a large group of students. Sekou blew my mind—his brilliance, generosity of spirit, quiet humility, and honesty turned me from fan to friend to follower. After that encounter, I rarely missed a Sekou Sundiata performance, whether with his band at the Knitting Factory or in more elaborate performances at the Aaron Davis Performing Arts Center, where his one-man show *Blessing the Boats*, about how his compadres mobilized to give him a kidney, reduced the theater to tears. We talked poetry. We talked politics. He invited me to his class at the New School to talk surrealism. And he and his wife, Maurine Knighton, invited my family and me to their home in Fort Greene, Brooklyn, for these incredible gatherings of artists, activists, and "cultural workers," in which Sekou asked hard questions about the state of the world and sought genuine answers, not bumper-sticker slogans or manifestos.

A few weeks after the twin towers came down on 9/11, we met for lunch to talk about it. He had been in the hospital during the attack but was soon released into a city of smoke, rubble, and questions for which he was not prepared. He had spent much of his life fighting things American—racism, imperialism, economic inequality, hubris, xenophobia, arrogance—and suddenly felt heartbroken for the American people. This was not the same as patriotism or national loyalty. He told me a story about a crowd of young Black men in Harlem who had cheered the attacks on the World Trade Center without considering the loss of human life. As with so many victims of American racism, vengeance came to resemble justice, prompting Sekou to ask whether love, compassion, and human solidarity are possible in these United States. His questions haunted me because I had written the chapter "Third World Dreaming" without ever questioning the romance of violent revolution, or the human costs of anti-imperialist wars. The conversation shook me to the core, in part because I witnessed the attack in real time. My talk with Sekou, more than anything else, convinced me to scrap my original epilogue—a futuristic tale of "Maroon poets" who turn a local struggle over police brutality into a revolutionary movement that takes several centuries to remake the world. I chose instead to reflect on how we might remake "Ground Zero" as a symbol of how we might remake the planet. Here is what I wrote:

> After September 11 . . . my original epilogue/dream felt uncomfortably apocalyptic. The immediate question of "where do we go from here" invaded my daydreams and dominated my

nocturnal adventures, along with the constant stench of burning metal, concrete, and Lord knows what else enveloping our
neighborhood, and the horrendous image of bombs raining
down on terrified Afghans. Where are we heading? How do we
begin to dream ourselves out of this dark place of death and
destruction and war, from this suffocating place where anyone
who is not down with the war plan could be labeled a traitor?[9]

While I stand by my decision to scrap the original text, I decided to include it in this edition, virtually unchanged. Rereading
it twenty years later, I'm struck by the extent to which the story
presaged the politics of our current moment.

Sekou turned his ruminations on 9/11 into *The America Project*,
a proposed multimedia performance piece, for which he asked
me to serve as a historical consultant. The proposal, which he
completed at the beginning of 2004, asked whether the emergence of the US as "a new kind of empire" will "cost America
its soul." Or put differently, "What does a public imagination
steeped in violence say about who we are?" He did not think the
imagination was fixed, either in violence or in utopic dreams of
revolution, but rather thought it existed in the place "where the
unthinkable is thinkable."[10] To be fair, Sekou had been thinking
about these issues before 9/11. His 1997 LP, *The Blue Oneness of
Dreams*, includes poems such as "Space," a brilliantly mad political rant in the voice of a traumatized survivor of the 1960s' war for
Black liberation, and "Bombs from Bullshit," a meditation on the
Oklahoma City bombers and the mass shooter Colin Ferguson.
At the heart of *The America Project* was a desire to find ways to
be together, to replace the nation's war mentality with the principles of love, compassion, and human solidarity. He elaborated
on these ideas in a 2004 talk in which he proposed substituting
the corporate and academic project of "diversity" with the messy
practice of democracy: "When you say 'Democracy' the discussion has to expand, it has to elevate, it has to point us towards the
purpose of 'diversity,' and the discussion has to be about more
than 'colored faces in high places.' I think that we have to insist

on linking diversity to democracy. Post 9-11 diversity conversations must have a different sense of time and place and urgency than those old, tired pre-9-11 conversations." The imagination is the portal, and artists should lead the way since, in his words, "the point is not to diversify the culture, but to change it."[11]

And this is precisely what *The America Project* set out to do. Sekou did his research, held "citizenship dinners," led community sings, organized poetry readings, and collected material, stories, and experiences to create his stunning performance piece, "The 51st (dream) State." He combined poetry, music, dance, and video projections to create not just a performance but a community-engaged, democratic experience that used personal and national stories to reimagine US citizenship and the future of humanity in the twenty-first century.[12]

Bigger Dreams

Sekou modeled what it meant to turn dream into action, to transform "freedom dreams" from noun to verb. Sadly, he passed in 2007, just eighteen months after "The 51st (dream) State" debuted. Since then, a new generation of artists has embraced "freedom dreaming" as praxis, pedagogy, and "poetic knowledge"—clearly evident in Aja Monet's stunningly beautiful, powerful foreword to this edition. Monet embodies, practices, and *transcends* everything I hoped the book might represent. She is a product of the Nuyorican Poets Café, a nurturing ground for countless radical artists such as Saul Williams, Jessica Care Moore, Magdalena Gomez, Maria Fernandez, Sarah Jones, and Jive Poetic, founder of the Insurgent Poets Society. At nineteen, Monet became the youngest poet to win the Nuyorican Grand Slam competition, but rather than pursue movie deals or big publishing contracts, she jumped headlong into movement—Dream Defenders, the Community Justice Project, Say Her Name. She cofounded the arts collective Smoke Signals Studio in Miami, managed the poetry workshop Voices: Poetry for the People, and organized its first annual Maroon Poetry Festival in Liberty City.

Chicago poet/rapper Fatimah Nyeema Warner, better known as Noname, has not only created radical, visionary works of art but chose to give up commercial fame and fortune to build a movement. In 2019, she launched Noname book clubs, where participants read and discuss critical texts on subjects ranging from colonialism, racial capitalism, revolutionary movements, Black feminism, gendered violence, the prison industrial complex, disability justice, and art and culture. From these initial gatherings, they created a books program for incarcerated people and Noname community libraries.[13]

For Freedoms, cofounded in 2016 by photographer Hank Willis Thomas and directed by abolitionist and disability justice legal scholar Claudia Peña, is precisely the sort of artist-led platform Sekou Sundiata imagined as a vehicle for authentic, "democratic" civic engagement. For Freedoms employs billboards, collaborative art projects, community gatherings, and the creative use of digital advertising platforms to provoke political engagement, reshape political discourse, and, in Thomas's words, fight "the power and exclusivity of white supremacy with the power and *inclusivity* of Black joy." "Artists are truth-tellers and storytellers," Peña explained, "and that's what we need to give us hope to prevail through these difficult times. They also offer an imagination beyond what people can see right now thus opening up a portal to new tomorrows. Solving issues requires creativity and the changing of hearts and minds. On top of which, art is healing."[14]

Tamara Singh is a Black artist dedicated to healing people and the planet. Poet, surrealist, singer, cellist, weaver, fiber artist, therapist, revolutionary, Singh is the founding director of the Paris-based Nature, the Arts Within, which provides horticultural therapy as a path to wholeness and collective well-being, reconnecting us to the earth and each other. As she explains, by "engaging directly with plants, gardens and high tactile nature arts, we cultivate sensory awareness, promoting self-awareness and self-care." To deal with the historical and contemporary trauma of racism, patriarchy, colonialism, and capitalism, she cofounded Le Collectif Psy Noires, a transnational collective of mostly Black women therapists who provide free support for people of African descent living with depression and mental illness, survivors of gendered violence, and others in need of care and immediate material aid. A genuinely abolitionist project, Le Collectif Psy Noires seeks to address "all social violence, including economic, patriarchal, medical and police violence," in part by creating networks of care outside of medical institutions, and by organizing "social justice actions."[15]

For a new generation of Black artists, the "portal to new tomorrows" is Afrofuturism. Unlike the utopian Black nationalist visions discussed in chapter 1, Afrofuturism does not pine for a romanticized African past but acknowledges our historical and ongoing catastrophe while imagining a path to liberation rooted in tradition but dedicated to limitless experimentation. Afrofuturism at its best is the braiding of surrealism and the Black radical tradition, or what writer D. Scot Miller—by way of Amiri Baraka—calls "Afrosurrealism."[16] A brilliant example is the "Black Radical Imagination," a series of short films co-curated by Erin Christovale and Amir George. The seeds for the series were planted over a decade ago, when Christovale, an artist and curator, cofounded the Los Angeles-based Black arts collective called Native Thinghood, whose slogan was "Indigenous is endogenous. Afrofuturists of tomorrowland."[17] She and Chicago-based filmmaker Amir George were "both really inspired" by *Freedom Dreams*, specifically the idea "that if it weren't for the simple fact of imagining a future that could be non-oppressive . . . then we wouldn't be in the streets or changing things within government or creative fields. That idea of the Black radical imagination really resonated with us. And this was at a time where we both were coming out of film school and feeling like representations of ourselves were highly characterized or stereotyped or non-existent."[18] For several years beginning in 2013, Christovale and George toured the country screening what could be described as Afrosurrealist visual poems and speculative films by over a dozen artists, including Jacolby Satterwhite, Cauleen Smith, Jabari Zuberi, Akosua Adoma Owusu, Cristina de Middel, and Terence Nance.[19]

Black, queer artist Lauren Halsey fashions her dreams of Afrofu-
turist utopias through "funkified," three-dimensional recreations
of her native South Central Los Angeles. She reimagined her
people's past, present, and future in signage, dioramas, figurines,
music, graffiti tags, cosmic landscapes, and modern hieroglyphs,
an archive of everyday life that proves Black existence, resistance,
resilience, and refusal to disappear. Halsey's exhibitions *we still
here, there* and *Crenshaw District Hieroglyph Project* resist not
only gentrification and erasure but the carceral architecture that
pervades South Central and Black urban landscapes everywhere:
the bulletproof glass, security cameras, police stations, pictures
of alleged shoplifters taped on store walls. Her "freedom dreams"
are not petit-bourgeois exercises of describing utopias on "Post-it"
notes from the safety of a museum or university and leaving on a
spiritual high with no obligation to struggle. She sees in everyday
people, in the Black working class, the potential to make the future by mapping where they have been, what they remember and
carry, what they discard, and how they continually struggle, survive, and create. "I'm not interested in escapism," she explained.
"I'm interested in creating legible, real representations of who
we were centuries ago or five minutes ago, and of who we can
become five seconds from now or one hundred years from now.
I'm interested [in] drawing connections among multiple histories
and collective experiences of neighborhoods to consider the here
and now, as well as past and potential futures."[20]
And she is interested in building potential futures not merely
as models to gaze upon but at human scale. The music of
Parliament-Funkadelic inspired Halsey's artistic and political vision. "Early on I was very intrigued by the space making that was
happening with P-Funk seamlessly on the scale of worlds (out-
erspace, place, Blackness, queerness, me). They beamed me up
and into their radical worlds without me ever having to leave my
bedroom. . . . That relationship to space making carries over to
my work where I remix and propose new spaces with what we
already have and who we already are, to conjure new reflections
on self-determination, affirmation, community wealth building,

love, Funk, etc."[21] Halsey initially trained as an architect, and it shows in her work and community practice. She takes inspiration from the builders of pyramids, imagining what it means to create structures "in which black people can experience themselves differently and not feel weighed down by some of the oppressive forces, or oppressive moments in architecture that one might experience living in a certain type of neighborhood depending on class."[22] Halsey realized part of her dream when she and her crew, Monique McWilliams, Korina Matyas, and others, launched the Summaeverythang Community Center, a space for young people ages six to twenty-three, offering free classes in art, printmaking, sign painting, coding, gardening, meditation, writing, literacy, resume building, prep for standardized college entrance exams, and an annual residency for selected musicians. As Halsey told one interviewer, "My interest is to not only affirm folks through my practice/the artwork but most importantly to do so with tangible results: paid jobs, transcendent programming, free resources and workshops."[23] She worked closely with the Los Angeles Black Worker Center, headed by veteran Black labor organizer Lola Smallwood Cuevas, in order to hire Black carpenters and construction workers at union wages. When COVID-19 struck on the eve of the center's opening, Halsey pivoted and transformed Summaeverythang into a community food bank. Every week she and her crew box and deliver thousands of pounds of organic, locally sourced produce to the Nickerson Gardens housing projects and other low-income families in Watts. Free. Free of pesticides, free of GMOs, free of obligation, free of stigma, free of charge.[24]

Just as the music of P-Funk inspired Lauren Halsey's radical vision, musicians have often been the greatest catalysts of social movements.[25] In May 2017, the LA chapter of the transnational feminist organization AF3IRM (formerly Gabriela Network) hosted Freedom Dreams: A Transnational Musical Dialogue, a fundraiser featuring Chilean MC Ana Tijoux, Palestinian singer and rapper Shadia Mansour, Australian-born vocalist Maya Jupiter, and Mexican-born radical "Latin rock" icon Ceci Bastida.[26] As AF3IRM organizers explained, "In the current reality, poetry and imagination help produce language and consciousness to articulate a collective vision of liberation—our freedom dreams. Who better than artists and cultural producers to engage with and create spaces for dialogue as we embark in this process? Artists have always infused movements with hope and creativity, encouraging us to dream beyond the conditions in which we are forced to live."[27] Writing in 2021, I hear a "freedom dreams" soundtrack in drummer Terri Lyne Carrington's abolition-feminist LP *The Waiting Game*; in flutist Nicole Mitchell's Afro-futurist compositions such as *Xenogenesis Suite* and *Mandorla Awakening*; in the insurgent works of pianist/composer/activist Samora Pinderhughes, whose albums *The Transformations Suite* and *Black Spring* speak to the power of Black resistance and resilience in the face of unremitting anti-Black racism; in saxophonist James Brandon Lewis's *Unruly Manifesto* and in his ongoing collaborative project with poet Thomas Sayers Ellis, "Heroes Are Gang Leaders"; in the EP *Freedom Dreams* by the Boston hardcore band "Move"; in the Zapatista-inspired soul-rock of Jose Quetzal Flores and Martha Gonzales; in the African-Indigenous-inspired Afro Yaqui Music Collective; and in the revolutionary, world-facing music of William Parker, Imani Uzuri, Vijay Iyer, Jen Shyu, Jason Moran, Jennifer Koh, Davóne Tines, Esperanza Spalding, Ambrose Akinmusire, Arturo O'Farrill, and many, many others.

Choreographer, scholar, and dancer Shamell Bell found ways to enact "freedom dreams" to disrupt power and embody the future we wish to build. A cofounder of Black Lives Matter LA, Bell introduced "street dance activism" to the movement, using co-choreographed dance to occupy and transform public space into places of dignity, community, resistance, and pedagogy for "critical social justice." Out of her organizing work, Bell developed a project she calls Collective Freedom Dreaming: Engaged Pedagogy as Praxis, which brings together a broad range of activists, scholars, cultural workers, and educators in a process of transformation that uses dance and storytelling to collectively create new visions of liberation. Her idea of "collective freedom dreaming" is premised on the idea that embodied practice, collaborative research, and solidarity in the streets and the classroom can create the conditions of possibility for transformative justice and new modes of pedagogy.[28]

Marshall Kai Green is one of the original members of Black Youth Project (BYP) 100. Founded by activist-scholar Cathy Cohen, BYP 100 practices radical inclusivity and builds Black political movement through a Black, queer, feminist, and abolitionist lens.[29] Green, a professor at Williams College, has created collaborative nonfiction literary, visual, and musical projects that situate the work of "freedom dreaming" at the intersection of trans identity, race, Black feminist thought, and antiviolence work. His course Freedom Dreams, Afro-Futures and Visionary Fictions turns the classroom into a space for collective imagining of alternative futures expressed by students and visitors through music, video, performance, and poetry/spoken word. Green's fellow BYP 100 cofounder and queer cultural worker Jonathan Lykes established Liberation House in Chicago, a space for artists engaged in "liberation praxis," and curated an extraordinary album of freedom songs and chants titled *The Black Joy Experience*. Each track features the voices of organizers beckoning us to "confront the state," embrace healing and safety and "Black joy," love ourselves and our Blackness, and keep working to build new futures while learning from our ancestors. His song "Freedom Dreams" consists of a short and simple refrain—reminiscent of a nineteenth-century spiritual—promising to "lift my palms toward freedom land" and birth new dreams. One of the tracks features BYP 100 director, Charlene Carruthers, performing a spoken-word piece titled "The Radical Imagination (Message)":

We have no choice but to fight, but to resist
And dream big
Dream big
The Black Radical Imagination lives and breathes and exists
    through us
They have called us to this moment
And we have everything that we need, and more.[30]

"Dream big," indeed. Carruthers beautifully encapsulates the central point of *Freedom Dreams*, that the Black radical imagination "lives and breathes and exists through us"— the assembly of people called to fight and resist. Besides BYP 100, the assembly includes the James and Grace Lee Boggs Center to Nurture Community Leadership, the Eastside Solutionaries Collective (Detroit), the Movement for Black Lives (M4BL), #Black Lives Matter, Dream Defenders, We Charge Genocide, BOLD (Black Organizing for Leadership and Dignity), Project NIA, UBUNTU!, Youth Justice Coalition, LA's Community Rights Campaign, Million Hoodies Movement for Justice, Dignity and Power Now, Ella's Daughters, Assata's Daughters, Black Feminist Futures Project, Good Kids Mad City, Leaders of a Beautiful Struggle, Let Us Breathe Collective, Dissenters, Millennial Activists United, Afro-Indigenous Rising, Not Another Black Life, Repairers of the Breach and the Poor People's Campaign, the Southern Workers Assembly, Cooperation Jackson, Excluded Workers Congress, The Majority, and Scholars for Social Justice, to name just a few.

Since the book's publication, movements and dreams have changed and grown, exposing the limits of my own political imagination and pointing to a wider horizon of possibility.[31] I've had the privilege of learning from literally thousands of activists, artists, students, and intellectuals who have engaged this work and advanced a vision of freedom far more expansive, more complex, more radical than what I had originally written. If I were to write this book today, here are other paths of the Black radical imagination I would examine:

QUEER AND TRANS LIBERATION. Queer futures, or what the late theorist José Muñoz called "queer futurity," hold the promise of a radically different definition of the "human" that could finally demolish the inherited, heteronormative constraints of gender and sexuality.[32] And although the LGBTQI community has always played critical organizational and leadership roles in movements, they've often had to sacrifice their public identity or face harassment, marginalization, even violence. We've witnessed a significant shift over the past two decades, as the leadership of Black radical movements has become predominantly queer, trans, and nonbinary. Many contemporary Black liberation movements, like #Black Lives Matter, the Ferguson rebellion, and BYP 100, not only have queer leadership but center queer and trans liberation in their politics. Certainly, queer and trans liberation means more than visibility or rights, or even the end of capitalism, racism, ableism, violence, and war, but new ways of being free that center joy and pleasure. In 2021, performance artist and organizer Tourmaline created "Pleasure Gardening," a New York City walking/audio tour commissioned by the Museum of Modern Art that explores the practice of "freedom dreaming" in the histories of Black queer and trans people who find fun and pleasure in between the spaces of confinement, segregation, exploitation, and violence.[33]

MUTUAL AID. My daughter, Elleza Kelley (who was eleven when the book came out), taught me to look for freedom dreams in the spaces of enclosure and fugitivity. Her scholarship explores how Black communities transformed plantations, ghettos, rooftops, prisons, and the like into commons, spaces of fugitive praxis and mutual care. She introduced me to the writings of anarchist Peter Kropotkin and first schooled me on the importance of mutual aid as a potentially radical practice of prefiguring the future we want to build. The irony, of course, is that my mother, her grandmother, modeled a practice of mutual aid and passed it down to us. I even hinted at it in these very pages when I wrote that my mother raised us "to help any living creature in need, even if that meant giving up our last piece of bread. Strange, needy people always passed through our house, occasionally staying for long stretches of time." What I understood as values or a moral duty, Elleza helped me see as political practice. Abolitionist and legal scholar Dean Spade also helped me see mutual aid as an essential ingredient for revolution, since it is fundamentally about building solidarity and practicing a culture of collective care in lieu of a neoliberal culture of individualism and the market. He explains, "Social movements that have built power and won major change have all included mutual aid, yet it is often a part of movement work that is less visible and less valued. In this moment, our ability to build mutual aid will determine whether we can win the world we long for, or whether we will dive further into crisis."[34]

DISABILITY JUSTICE: The absence of any discussion of disability in *Freedom Dreams* is a major oversight. Disability justice embraces an abolitionist framework—which is to say, it demands nothing less than the overthrow of ableism and *all* the structures that undergird it: racism, patriarchy, sexual and reproductive oppression, capitalism, imperialism, and settler colonialism. It must. Consider what it means for a disability *rights* movement to wage a successful struggle against institutionalization while leaving intact a racist, capitalist, heteropatriarchal system. Disabled people who are poor, Black, Brown, Indigenous, and gender nonconforming are more likely to end up homeless, incarcerated, or subjected to police violence. I'm especially indebted to Aurora Levins Morales, feminist writer and disability justice activist, and Rich Feldman of the Boggs Center, for helping me imagine a world without ableism. Morales, for example, has demonstrated time and again how climate justice is disability justice by drawing attention to how toxins—in the ecosystem, in our personal care products, in common solvents and cleaning chemicals—are disabling.[35] Feldman, whose son Micah has a cognitive disability, reminded me that, similar to residential schools for Native children, mental institutions were responsible for the deaths of tens of thousands of patients, many buried in unmarked graves. In the face of a genocide that is hardly acknowledged, Feldman asked, "What does it mean to be human?" The answer, he conceded, will depend on our capacity to embrace "revolutionary values."[36]

DECOLONIZATION AND INDIGENOUS THOUGHT: Although *Freedom Dreams* discusses anticolonial movements, it is silent on decolonizing Turtle Island or Black-Indigenous solidarity (outside of a brief mention of Maroon societies). Once again, I should have paid more attention to my mother's wisdom. Coincidentally, she had started a doctoral program at the University of California, Berkeley, in Native American studies just as I was completing *Freedom Dreams*. The more she shared with me, the more I came to see gaps in my own work. She made me rethink the question of land and reparations—twin themes that are central to the book. How could I reconcile the creation of all-Black towns as acts of self-determination and limited freedom when they were built on stolen land? How has the biblical story of Exodus been used to erase Indigenous inhabitants from the "promised land" of Canaan?[37] Now, when I revisit the chapter on reparations, for example, the absence of Native people and Indigenous critique is glaring. It reminds me that if we are going to think of dispossession, genocide, and slavery as inseparable pillars upholding the settler-colonial regime and its ongoing policies of extraction, we must also think about reparations and decolonization together. But is it possible to reconcile reparations for slavery and structural racism with decolonization? Only if we think about reparations, as I argue in these pages, as a project aimed at building power for social movements, eliminating all forms of oppression, and creating an economy geared toward collective needs and redistribution rather than accumulation. Unfortunately, most contemporary "plans" for reparations do not challenge the terms of racial capitalism or settler colonialism; their logic is firmly rooted in property rights, documentation (proof that one is a descendant of slaves), and compensation without transformation.[38]

At the same time, until fairly recently, decolonizing imperial North AmeriKKKa seemed out of reach, almost utopian. Then two developments helped me see that decolonization was not only possible but absolutely necessary. First, Indigenous movements at the forefront of the climate justice movement, from Idle No More to Standing Rock to the Kanaka 'Ōiwi struggle to defend Mauna Kea, have been clear: five hundred years of settler-colonial capitalism has brought the planet to the brink of ecological collapse. The choice before us is decolonization or extinction. Decolonization means ending capitalism and returning the land, not as "property" but as the source of life to be stewarded by its original inhabitants and where animals, plants, and humans can coexist and thrive together. Second, visiting South Africa and Palestine, bearing witness to existing settler colonialism and its historical legacies, and learning from radical, decolonial movements in both places really brought home Eve Tuck and K. Wayne Wang's point that "decolonization is not a metaphor."[39]

My first trip to South Africa occurred on the heels of the Rhodes Must Fall and Fees Must Fall movements, in which students rose up to demand a decolonized university, a decolonized nation, and ultimately a decolonized world free of exploitative and hierarchical relationships, free of racism, capitalism, patriarchy, free of all phobias. They exposed the "post-apartheid" state as a chimera, a neoliberal betrayal of the Freedom Charter's promise that the people shall govern, share the wealth and the land, and enjoy equal rights, security, and housing. I met with an impressive group of radical thinkers and activists—including former leaders of the student protests—who continually underscored the paramount importance of decolonization and land in the Black radical imagination.[40] I was frequently reminded of Steve Biko's observation that before the European invasion, land was held in common: "As everybody here knows, African society had the village community as its basis. . . . Hence most things were jointly owned by the group, for instance there was no such thing as individual land ownership. The land belonged to the people and was merely under the control of the local chief on behalf of the people. When cattle went to graze it was on an open veld and not on anybody's specific farm."[41]

In South Africa, as in most of the world, dispossession was ongoing. I saw it in places such as the "environmentally conscious" Shamwari Game Reserve in the Eastern Cape. My son and I briefly stayed there at a lodge named after Sarili kaHintsa, the nineteenth-century Xhosa paramount chief who followed the prophesy of a fifteen-year-old girl named Nongqawuse, who in 1856 called on the people to kill the cattle and destroy the crops in order to incite spirits that would drive out the white settlers. The owners named the lodge Sarili because it sat on Xhosa land, a fact we learned from the head of staff, who had been working for Shamwari for two decades. Recognizing where my sympathies lie, he then casually shared that he descended directly from Sarili, his family had been forced off the land and reduced to farm laborers, and that the grave sites of his ancestors had been disappeared by commercial farms and game reserves. Every African employee at Shamwari quietly disclosed their dreams of taking back the land, not as privatized wealth but as a source of livelihood, sustenance, reconstruction, and nation building. We couldn't help but notice the dilapidated shacks on the other side of the N2 highway where some of the employees of the big game reserves lived, or the irony of how the project of conserving biodiversity was deployed in the service of privatization, turned capitalists into the environmental guardians of the planet while rendering Indigenous people landless. As we were about to leave, the head of staff informed me that he might soon be out of a job: the property had just been sold to Dubai World.

I traveled to Palestine in 2012, and again in 2018, and witnessed firsthand settler colonialism and apartheid in its most brutal and direct form. Whether visiting any number of West Bank refugee camps, traveling along racially segregated highways in the shadow of a massive apartheid wall, or walking through Hebron, where settlers literally moved into Palestinian homes and regularly attacked the Palestinian souk (market) with bricks and garbage and human feces, the violence of colonialism is everywhere. In Palestine, decolonization begins with ending the occupation, guaranteeing the right of return, and restoring all stolen land and property. On my second trip, organized by Rabab Abdulhadi, I happened to spend most of my time on the bus talking to a young Diné organizer named Melissa Tso. She pointed out similarities between the occupied territories and reservations, compared the detention of Palestinian children with keeping them in boarding schools, commented on how Palestinians passing through checkpoints or living in Israel were treated like Indigenous people in settler towns situated on the edge of reservations. It was Melissa Tso who introduced me to the Red Nation.

Launched in 2014 by Indigenous scholar/activists Nick Estes (Kul Wicasa) and Melanie K. Yazzie (Diné), the Red Nation was formed in response to the murders of Allison Gorman and Kee Thompson, two houseless Diné people who were sleeping on the street in Albuquerque. Literally two weeks after Israel began its deadly assault on Gaza and three weeks before Ferguson police killed Mike Brown, protests erupted in Albuquerque demanding accountability for the murders of Gorman and Thompson and protection for unsheltered Indigenous people and those who live in what the Red Nation identified as "border towns." Border towns are municipalities surrounded by reservations—which, technically, are sovereign nations but in practice occupied territory. Border towns are products of Indigenous dispossession, relocation, and ethnic cleansing; they render Native peoples vulnerable to state and vigilante violence, precarity, and dependence on a settler-run economy; they exploit Native bodies—living and dead—to promote tourism; and as occupied territory, border towns are marked by fences, walls, and checkpoints. The Red Nation organized not for better police protection of Native peoples but against border-town oppression and, more precisely, to bring about an end to settler colonialism.

The Red Nation issued a document laying out perhaps the most extraordinary vision of a liberated future I've ever seen. More than a manifesto, *The Red Deal: Indigenous Action to Save Our Earth* is a plan for decolonization that entails eliminating all forms of oppression and violence—racism, patriarchy, ableism, capitalism, imperialism, settler colonialism, and ensuring sexual and reproductive freedom. Their demands include reinstating all treaty rights; ending disciplinary violence against all Indigenous and oppressed peoples (which ultimately means abolishing police, prisons, and the military); ending discrimination, torture, and the killing of Native women and LGBTQ2+ people; full and free access to healthcare, education, social services; ending the occupation of all Indigenous territories and abolishing all imperial borders; and Land Back. Grounded in Indigenous thought, *The Red Deal* advances a vision of freedom based not on possession or anthropocentrism but on balance, assembly, and mutuality. It makes no promise of triumph, of the "end of history," of the resolution of all contradictions and antagonisms, but instead offers a path for new ways of living and being together, where every life belongs, is valued, heard, respected, and protected under a system of justice that is nonpunitive, noncarceral, and transformative. It calls for nothing less than the reversal of colonial structures that have deliberately attempted to erase other ways of knowing through genocide.[42]

The Red Deal reflects and refracts the freedom dreams of virtually everyone discussed in this book, demonstrating once again how social movements are the great "incubators of new knowledge" and the keepers of old. The Red Nation's decolonial vision speaks to other horizons of solidarity. "We draw from Black abolitionist traditions," they write in *The Red Deal*, "to call for divestment from carceral institutions like police, prisons, the military, and border imperialism in addition to divestment from fossil fuels."[43] They carry forth another sort of Black and Red alliance absent from the book but present in the streets. Before Black Spring, Black Lives Matter activists showed up at Standing Rock, and throughout Canada, Indigenous and Black solidarity has been a fundamental feature of anti-police protests.[44] The question is, what are their shared freedom dreams? What kinds of futures are they/we imagining and creating together?

We can never really know. It should be clear by now—and will become clearer as you read this book—that the Black radical imagination does not stand still; it lives and breathes and moves with the people. The best we can do is catch a glimpse of how people in motion have envisioned the future and what they did to try to realize or enact that future. But every freedom dream shares a common desire to find better ways of being together without hierarchy and exclusion, without violence and domination, but *with* love, compassion, care, and friendship. Once again, my daughter, Elleza, who lived with this book longer than anyone besides me, grasped this core truth with astonishing clarity. When asked by an interviewer whether progressive movements can retool citizenship as a way to reproduce a culture of care, she replied:

> Better ships than citizenship include friendship, relationship, or even a pirate ship, where unauthorized, motley formations are bound together to disrupt notions of the private, of property, of wealth and its concentration. . . . I think one of the worst aspects of citizenship is that it needs authorization, or that its expression is tied to what is given by a governing (or ruling, more precisely) body. The kind of citizenship I dream of is one where we acknowledge our attachment to each other, desire to be attached to one another, in relations other than property relations. Where serving the other is a way of serving the self. It sounds very romantic, but isn't that the origin of all the things we want to make and bring into the world? The power of the love letter is that it is written without the guarantee of a response.[45]

And what are radical social movements if not love letters?

Notes for Introduction

1. Jackie Wang, *Carceral Capitalism* (Cambridge, MA: Semiotext(e), 2017), 302–3.

2. Mumia Abu-Jamal, *Have Black Lives Ever Mattered?* (San Francisco: City Lights Books, 2017), dedication.

3. Sarah Holder, "The Cities Taking Up Calls to Defund the Police," *Bloomberg City Lab*, June 9, 2020, https://www.bloomberg.com/news/articles /2020-06-09/the-cities-taking-up-calls-to-defund-the-police; Dana Goldstein, "Do Police Officers Make Schools Safer or More Dangerous?," *New York Times*, June 12, 2020, https://www.nytimes.com/2020/06/12/us/schools-police -resource-officers.html.

4. "Amazon Donates $10 Million to Organizations Supporting Justice and Equity," Amazon News, last updated July 14, 2020, https://www.about amazon.com/news/policy-news-views/amazon-donates-10-million-to -organizations-supporting-justice-and-equity; Kandist Mallett, "Jeff Bezos Is Going to Space as Climate Change Threatens Life on Earth," *Teen Vogue*, July 12, 2021, https://www.teenvogue.com/story/jeff-bezos-space-elon-musk; A. M. Gittlitz, "Billionaires in Space," *Nation*, July 23, 2021, https://www .thenation.com/article/society/branson-bezos-space.

5. Robin D. G. Kelley, "Births of a Nation: Surveying Trumpland with Cedric Robinson," *Boston Review*, January 12, 2017.

6. In 2007, organizers from Critical Resistance, All of Us or None, Cop-Watch, Youth Justice Coalition, Q-Team, and the LA Community Action Network met at the Southern California Library in South Los Angeles to discuss their "freedom dreams" and the obstacles keeping their movements from realizing them. (A passage from *Freedom Dreams* was the prompt for the conversation.) They all agreed that the funders' misplaced emphasis on "winnable" campaigns not only created unnecessary competition between organizations and organizers but undercut the important work of advancing a long-term revolutionary vision. Melissa Burch, of Critical Resistance and All of Us or None, remarked that the pressure to win "really just keeps us from being able to create what it is that we want to seek, as opposed to just fighting these short-term defensive battles all the time." Southern California Library, *Without Fear . . . Claiming Safe Communities Without Sacrificing Ourselves* (Los Angeles: SCL, 2007), 77–81. That same year, the organization INCITE! published a landmark collection of essays critiquing the nonprofit industrial complex. See INCITE!, eds., *The Revolution Will Not Be Funded: Beyond the Non-Profit Industrial Complex* (Durham, NC: Duke University Press, 2007).

7. The sermon "Remaining Awake Through a Great Revolution" can be found at the Martin Luther King, Jr. Research and Education Institute, https://kinginstitute.stanford.edu/king-papers/publications/knock-midnight -inspiration-great-sermons-reverend-martin-luther-king-jr-10.

8. Grace Lee Boggs, *The Next American Revolution: Sustainable Activism for the 21st Century* (Oakland: University of California Press, 2012), 72.

9. Robin D. G. Kelley, *Freedom Dreams: The Black Radical Imagination* (Boston: Beacon Press, 2002), 195–96.

10. Sekou Sundiata, "The America Project" (working title), proposal in my possession, ca. 2004; Robin D. G. Kelley to Sekou Sundiata, March 3, 2004; and various email exchanges between Sundiata and the author.

11. Sekou Sundiata, "Thinking Out Loud: Democracy, Imagination and Peeps of Color," keynote speech for Diversity Revisited: A Conversation of Diversity in the Arts, Pittsburgh, June 8, 2004, pp. 5–6, 14.

12. Julie Ellison, "Lyric Citizenship in Post 9/11 Performance *Sekou Sundiata's the 51st (dream) state*," in Cindy Weinstein and Christopher Looby, eds., *Aesthetics and the Politics of Freedom* (New York: Columbia University Press, 2012), 91–114; Stacy Teicher Khadaroo, "Remembering Poet Sekou Sundiata," *Christian Science Monitor*, August 13, 2007.

13. Noname Book Club, https://nonamebooks.com/About.

14. Barbara Victoria Niveyro, "For Freedoms: On Opening Up a Portal to New Tomorrows," NYXT, September 15, 2020, https://www.nyxt.nyc/blog/forfreedoms2020.

15. Tamara Singh, conversations and email exchanges with author; websites for Nature the Art Within, www.hortustherapy.com, and Le Collectif Psy Noires, https://collectifperspective.org.

16. D. Scot Miller, "Afrosurreal Generation," http://dscottmiller.blogspot.com/2013/11/black- brown-and-beige-surrealist.html; D. Scot Miller, "A Conversation with Robin D. G. Kelley," Open Space, March 30, 2017, https://openspace.sfmoma.org/2017/05/a-converstion-with-robin-d-g-kelley.

17. Native Thinghood, https://nativethinghood-blog.tumblr.com.

18. Charia Rose, "Erin Christovale Is Curating the Future Through the Black Radical Imagination," *Free the Work*, December 16, 2019, https://freethework.com/article/erin-christovale-black-radical-imagination-curating-hammer-interview.

19. See also Alessandra Raengo and Lauren McLeod Cramer, "A Conversation with Erin Christovale About 'You are mine. I see now, I'm a have to let you go,'" *liquid Blackness* 5, no. 1 (April 2021): 91–95; Avishay Artsy, "Erin Christovale: Black Radical Imagination," UCLA School of the Arts and Architecture, posted October 7, 2020, https://arts.ucla.edu/single/erin-christovale-black-radical-imagination; Erin Christovale and Amir George, eds., *Black Radical Imagination* (Los Angeles: Dominica, 2015).

20. Mark Pieterson, "We Built This City: A Conversation with Lauren Halsey," *Art in America*, June 7, 2018, https://www.artnews.com/art-in-america/interviews/built-city-conversation-lauren-halsey-56483.

21. Quoted in Taliah Mancini, "A Transcendental Storehouse for Culture: An Interview of Lauren Halsey," *Autre*, April 10, 2018, https://autre.love

/interviewsmain/2018/4/9/a-transcendental-storehouse-for-culture-an-interview
-of-lauren-halsey.

22. Mimi Zeiger, "Interview: Artist Lauren Halsey on her South-Central
Inspired Afrofuturism," *Pin-Up: The Magazine for Architectural Entertainment* 17 (2020), https://pinupmagazine.org/articles/interview-lauren-halsey
-afrofuturist-south-central-david-kordansky-mimi-zeiger.

23. Quoted in Mancini, "A Transcendental Storehouse for Culture." See
also Elleza Kelley, "Montage of a Dream[world]: Lauren Halsey's Fantasy
Architecture," forthcoming essay for Lauren Halsey's catalogue.

24. Patricia Escárcega, "Artist Lauren Halsey's Latest Project: Bringing
Beautiful Produce to Underserved Neighborhoods," *Los Angeles Times*,
July 31, 2020, https://www.latimes.com/food/story/2020-07-31/lauren-halsey
-summaeverythang-feeding-south-la.

25. Music as an expression of the Black radical imagination is treated
tangentially in *Freedom Dreams*, in part because much has been written on the subject. There are too many examples to cite, but here are a
few: Amiri Baraka, *Blues People: Negro Music in White America* (1963);
Frank Kofsky, *Black Nationalism and the Revolution in Music* (1970); Fred
Moten, *In the Break: The Aesthetics of the Black Radical Tradition* (2003);
Graham Lock, *Blutopia: Visions of the Future and Revisions of the Past
in the Work of Sun Ra, Duke Ellington, and Anthony Braxton* (1999); An-
gela Y. Davis, *Blues Legacies and Black Feminism: Gertrude "Ma" Rainey,
Bessie Smith, and Billie Holiday* (1998); Eric Porter, *What Is This Thing
Called Jazz? African American Musicians as Artists, Critics, and Activists*
(2002); Mark Anthony Neal, *What the Music Said: Black Popular Music
and Black Public Culture* (1999); Tricia Rose, *Black Noise: Rap Music and
Black Culture in Contemporary America* (1994); Ingrid Monson, *Freedom
Sounds: Civil Rights Call Out to Jazz and Africa* (2007); Scott Saul, *Free-
dom Is, Freedom Ain't. Jazz and the Making of the Sixties* (2003); Shana
Redmond, *Anthem: Social Movements and the Sound of Solidarity in the
African Diaspora* (2013); Alex Zamalin, *Black Utopia: The History of an
Idea from Black Nationalism to Afrofuturism* (2019); Michael Denning,
Noise Uprising: The Audiopolitics of a World Musical Revolution (2015);
and, of course, my own book, *Africa Speaks, America Answers: Modern Jazz
in Revolutionary Times* (2012).

26. "FM May 23: Freedom Dreams/Voices That Change the World," *Feminist Magazine*, May 5, 2017, https://feministmagazine.org/2017/05/fm-may-23;
AF3IRM, "Freedom Dreams: A Transnational Musical Dialogue," post, May 11,
2017, http://af3irm.org/af3irm/2017/05/freedom-dreams-a-transnational-musical
-dialogue.

27. AF3IRM, "Freedom Dreams: A Conversation with Shadia Mansour and
Dr. Martha Gonzalez," post, April 19, 2017, http://af3irm.org/af3irm/2017/04
/freedom-dreams-shadia-mansour-martha-gonzalez-in-conversation.

28. Shamell Bell, "Living Is Resisting: 'Rize' to 'Street Dance Activism': An Autoethnographic Memoir," PhD diss., UCLA, 2019. Full disclosure: Shamell Bell and Marshall Kai Green were former students of mine.

29. I have participated in Marshall Kai Green's class at Williams College: Freedom Dreams, Afro-Futures and Visionary Fictions.

30. *The Black Joy Experience* (Black Youth Project 100 Productions, 2018). See also Charlene A. Carruthers, *Unapologetic: A Black, Queer, and Feminist Mandate for Our Movement* (Boston: Beacon Press, 2018).

31. The questions posed by the book have inspired a few different conferences and convenings. In 2014, Barbara Ransby, the brilliant activist-intellectual, organized a beautiful conference bearing the title Freedom Dreams, Freedom Now!, which used the occasion of the fiftieth anniversary of Freedom Summer '64 to pose these questions: What does liberation look like, and what sort of future are we trying to build? Alicia Garza, veteran activist, Black Lives Matter cofounder, and founding director of Black Futures Lab, inspired the Brooklyn Museum to hold a series of events called "Freedom Dreaming: A Call to Imagine," in which artists and activists envisioned an abolitionist future without racism, sexism, homophobia, xenophobia, and classism. See Sarah Branch, "Freedom Dreaming: A Call to Imagine," Bric, June 8, 2018, https://www.bricartsmedia.org/blog /freedom-dreaming-call-imagine. In addition to the movement work I discuss in this essay, see also Bettina Love, *We Want to Do More Than Survive: Abolitionist Teaching and the Pursuit of Educational Freedom* (2019); Rujeko Hockley, "Freedom Dreaming," *Brooklyn Rail*, December 2020, https:// brooklynrail.org/2020/12/criticspage/Freedom-Dreaming; Clarence Lang, "Freedom Dreams," *Dissent* 61, no. 1 (Winter 2014): 86–90; Alan Wald, "'Triple Oppression' to 'Freedom Dreams,'" *Against the Current* 27, no. 6 (Jan.–Feb. 2013): 24–27; Ashley D. Lynch, "Emancipating Black: Black/Afrikan/ Quare/Trans* (In)visibility Liberation Aesthetics and Praxis in Contemporary African and Diaspora Art," PhD diss., Howard University, 2018; Marisol Norris, "Freedom Dreams: What Must Die in Music Therapy to Preserve Human Dignity?," *Voices: A World Forum for Music Therapy* 20, no. 3 (2020): 1–4; and SaVonne Anderson, "Radical Imagination Is a Necessary, Sustaining Force of Black Activism," *Mashable*, February 28, 2016, https://mashable .com/article/black-activism-radical-imagination.

32. José Esteban Muñoz, *Cruising Utopia: The Then and There of Queer Futurity* (New York and London: New York University Press, 2009). Here I'm indebted to Marshall Kai Green, C. Riley Snorton, Dean Spade, Cathy Cohen, Tourmaline, and many others, as well as to my NYU colleague José Muñoz, who tragically left us way too early.

33. Tourmaline, "Filmmaker and Activist Tourmaline on How to Freedom Dream," *Vogue*, July 2, 2020, https://www.vogue.com/article/filmmaker -and-activist-tourmaline-on-how-to-freedom-dream.

34. Elleza Kelley, "Sites of Inscription: Writing In and Against Post-Plantation Geographies," PhD diss., Columbia University, 2021, and "'Follow the Tree Flowers': Fugitive Mapping in *Beloved*," *Antipode* 53, no. 1 (2021): 181–99; Dean Spade, *Mutual Aid: Building Solidarity During this Crisis (and the Next)* (New York: Verso Books, 2020), 8.

35. Patty Berne, "What Is Disability Justice?," in *Skin, Tooth, and Bone: The Basis of Movement Is Our People; A Disability Justice Primer*, 2nd ed., ed. Patricia Berne and Sins Invalid (San Francisco: Sins Invalid: 2019); Mia Mingus, "Changing the Framework: Disability Justice," *Leaving Evidence*, February 12, 2011, https://leavingevidence.wordpress.com/2011/02/12/changing-the-framework-disability-justice; Marta Russell, *Capitalism & Disability: Selected Writings by Marta Russell*, ed. Keith Rosenthal (Chicago: Haymarket Books, 2019); and Aurora Levins Morales, *Kindling: Writings On the Body* (Cambridge, MA: Palabrera Press, 2013).

36. Rich Feldman to Robin D. G. Kelley, email, July 4, 2021. On Micah's journey, see Janice Fialka, *What Matters: Reflections on Disability, Community and Love* (Toronto: Inclusion Press, 2016).

37. Steven Salaita explores this question in *Holy Land in Transit: Colonialism and the Quest for Canaan* (Ithaca, NY: Syracuse University Press, 2006), and *Inter/Nationalism: Decolonizing Native America and Palestine* (Minneapolis: University of Minnesota Press, 2016).

38. See, for example, William A. Darity Jr. and Kirsten Mullen, *From Here to Equality: Reparations for Black Americans in the Twenty-First Century* (Chapel Hill: University of North Carolina Press, 2020).

39. Eve Tuck and K. Wayne Yang. "Decolonization Is Not a Metaphor," *Decolonization: Indigeneity, Education & Society* 1, no. 1 (2012): 1–40. I came around to this position thanks largely to Noura Erakat, Sunaina Mara, Magid Shihade, Neferti X. Tadiar, J. Kehaulani Kauanui, Bill Mullen, Nikhil Singh, Rana Barakat, Rabab Abdulhadi, Karma Nabulsi, Alyosha Goldstein, Amin Husain, Steven Salaita, Jodi Byrd, Mishuana Goeman, Harsha Walia, Nick Estes, Melissa Tso, Leanne Betasamosake Simpson, Glen Coulthard, Eve Tuck, K. Wayne Yang, Patrick Wolfe, and Lorenzo Veracini.

40. I am especially indebted to my encounters with Thuli Gamedze, Asher Gamedze, Brian Kamanzi, Moshibudi Motimele, Panashe Chigumadzi, Fezokuhle Mthonti, Bongani Madondo, Tendayi Sithole, Koni Benson, Leigh-Ann Naidoo, Mwelela Cele, Simamkele Dlakavu, Thando Sipuye, Mahlatse Mpya, Dinga Sikwebu, Salim Vally, Richard Pithouse, Neo Lekgotla laga Ramoupi, and Achille Mbembe, to name a few.

41. Steve Biko, *I Write What I Like: Selected Writings* (Chicago: University of Chicago Press, 1996), 43.

42. The Red Nation, *The Red Deal: Indigenous Action to Save Our Earth* (Brooklyn: Common Notions, 2021). The first iterations of the Red Deal appeared on the Red Nation website in 2019. The 2021 book is a major elaboration

of the original thirty-three-page document. See Nick Estes, "A Red Deal," *Jacobin*, August 2019, https://www.jacobinmag.com/2019/08/red-deal-green-new-deal-ecosocialism-decolonization-indigenous-resistance-environment. The shorter pamphlet can be found here: http://thered nation.org/wp-content /uploads/2020/04/Red-Deal_Part-I_End-The-Occupation-1.pdf.

43. The Red Nation, *The Red Deal*, 32.

44. Sandy Hudson, "Indigenous and Black Solidarity in Practice: #BLMTOTentCity," in *Until We Are Free: Reflections on Black Lives Matter in Canada*, ed. Rodney Diverlus, Sandy Hudson, and Syrus Marcus Ware (Regina: University of Regina Press, 2020).

45. Brian Kamanzi and Elleza Kelley, "Close Reading: Rooftops, Love Letters & the Classroom," *Pathways to a Free Education* 4 (2019): 29.

PREFACE

Freedom Dreams is a kind of crossroads for me. I spent more than half my life writing about people who tried to change the world, largely because I, too, wanted to change the world. The history of social movements attracted me because of what it might teach us about our present condition and how we might shape the future. When I first embarked on this work nearly twenty years ago, the political landscape looked much clearer: We needed a revolutionary socialist movement committed to antiracism and antisexism. Buoyed by youthful naïveté, I thought it was very obvious then. Over time, the subjects of my books as well as my own political experience taught me that things are not what they seem and that the desires, hopes, and intentions of the people who fought for change cannot be easily categorized, contained, or explained. Unfortunately, too often our standards for evaluating social movements pivot around whether or not they "succeeded" in realizing their visions rather than on the merits or power of the visions themselves. By such a measure, virtually every radical movement failed because the basic power relations they sought to change remain pretty much intact. And yet it is precisely these alternative visions and dreams that inspire new generations to continue to struggle for change.

I had been thinking about these issues when Professor Judith Byfield and Ozzie Harris, director of Dartmouth's Office of Equal Opportunity and Affirmative Action, asked me to deliver the Dr. Martin Luther King Jr. lecture at Dartmouth College in January 2000. In many ways, the opportunity to meditate on King's legacy and vision brought a lot of these issues to the surface, especially since I was feeling somewhat alienated from the same old protest politics. What had happened to the dream of liberation that brought many of us to radical movements in the first place? What had happened to socialism the way we imagined it? What had happened to our New Eden, our dreams of building a new society? And what had happened to hope and love in our politics? My lecture consisted of a series of reflections on these questions, which consequently became *Freedom Dreams*.

Dr. King constantly warned us that we would not be able to build a truly liberatory movement without the "strength to love." In his 1963 book of the same title, he wrote:

> We Negroes have long dreamed of freedom, but still we are confined in an oppressive prison of segregation and discrimination. Must we respond with bitterness and cynicism? Certainly not, for this will destroy and poison our personalities. . . . To guard ourselves from bitterness, we need the vision to see in this generation's ordeals the opportunity to transfigure both ourselves and American society. Our present suffering and our nonviolent struggle to be free may well offer to Western civilization the kind of spiritual dynamic so desperately needed for survival.

King's words became a kind of template for my lecture, indeed, for all of my thinking from that point on. How do we produce a vision that enables us to see beyond our immediate ordeals? How do we transcend bitterness and cynicism and embrace love, hope, and an all-encompassing dream of freedom, especially in these rough times?

Rough times, indeed. I was putting the final touches on *Freedom Dreams* the day the World Trade Center went down—a horrible event I witnessed from my bedroom window. And as I sent off this manuscript to my editor, bombs were raining down on the people of Afghanistan and unknown numbers of innocent people were dying, from either weapons of mass destruction or starvation. Violence will only generate more violence; the carnage has just begun. Now more than ever, we need the strength to love and to dream. Instead of knee-jerk flag-waving and submission to any act of repression in the name of "national interests," the nation ought to consider King's vision and take a cue from the movement that proved to be the source of his most fertile ideas. The civil rights movement demanded freedom for all and believed that it had to win through love and moral suasion. Those committed to the philosophy of nonviolence saw their suffering as redemptive. The very heart of the movement, the extraordinary Southern Black folks who stood nobly in the face of police dogs and water canon and white mobs and worked as hard as they could to love their enemy were poised to become the soul of a soulless nation, according to Dr. King. Imagine if that soul were to win out, if the movement's vision of freedom were completely to envelope the nation's political culture. If this were the case, then the pervasive consumerism and materialism and the stark inequalities that have come to characterize modern life under global capitalism could not possibly represent freedom. And yet, freedom today is practically a synonym for free enterprise.

Perhaps I'll be labeled a traitor for saying this, but we are not yet completely free. U.S. democracy has not always embraced everyone and we have a long history to prove it, from slavery and "Indian wars" to the 2000 presidential elections. Indeed, the marginal and excluded have done the most to make democracy work in America. And some of the radical movements I write about in the pages that follow have done awful things in the name of liberation, often under the premise that the ends justify the means. Communists, Black nationalists, Third World liberation movements—all left us stimulating and even visionary sketches of what the future could be, but they have also been complicit in acts of violence and oppression, through either their actions or their silence. No one's hands are completely clean.

And yet to write another book that either drones on about how oppressed we are or merely chronicles the crimes of radical movements doesn't seem very useful. I conceived *Freedom Dreams* as a preliminary effort to recover ideas—visions fashioned mainly by those marginalized Black activists who proposed a different way out of our constrictions. I'm not suggesting we wholly embrace their ideas or strategies as the foundation for new movements; on the contrary, my main point is that we must tap the well of our own collective imaginations, that we do what earlier generations have done: dream.

Trying to envision "somewhere in advance of nowhere," as poet Jayne Cortez puts it, is an extremely difficult task, yet it is a matter of great urgency. Without new visions we don't know what to build, only what to knock down. We not only end up confused, rudderless, and cynical, but we forget that making a revolution is not a series of clever maneuvers and tactics but a process that can and must transform us.

"WHEN HISTORY SLEEPS":
A BEGINNING

When history sleeps, it speaks in dreams: on the brow of the
sleeping people, the poem is a constellation of blood. . . .

— Octavio Paz, "Toward the Poem"

My mother has a tendency to dream out loud. I think it has something to do with her regular morning meditation. In the quiet
darkness of her bedroom her third eye opens onto a new world,
a beautiful light-filled place as peaceful as her state of mind.
She never had to utter a word to describe her inner peace; like
morning sunlight, it radiated out to everyone in her presence. My
mother knows this, which is why for the past two decades she has
taken the name Ananda ("bliss"). Her other two eyes never let her
forget where we lived. The cops, drug dealers, social workers, the
rusty tapwater, roaches and rodents, the urine-scented hallways,
and the piles of garbage were constant reminders that our world
began and ended in a battered Harlem/Washington Heights ten-
ement apartment on 157th and Amsterdam.

Yet she would not allow us to live as victims. Instead, we were a
family of caretakers who inherited this earth. We were expected
to help any living creature in need, even if that meant giving

up our last piece of bread. Strange, needy people always passed through our house, occasionally staying for long stretches of time. (My mom once helped me bring home a New York City pigeon with a broken leg in a failed effort to nurse her back to health!) We were expected to stand apart from the crowd and befriend the misfits, to embrace the kids who stuttered, smelled bad, or had holes in their clothes. My mother taught us that the Marvelous was free—in the patterns of a stray bird feather, in a Hudson River sunset, in the view from our fire escape, in the stories she told us, in the way she sang Gershwin's "Summertime," in a curbside rainbow created by the alchemy of motor oil and water from an open hydrant. She simply wanted us to live through our third eyes, to see life as possibility. She wanted us to imagine a world free of patriarchy, a world where gender and sexual relations could be reconstructed. She wanted us to see the poetic and prophetic in the richness of our daily lives. She wanted us to visualize a more expansive, fluid, "cosmos-politan" definition of Blackness, to teach us that we are not merely inheritors of a culture but its makers.

So with her eyes wide open my mother dreamed and dreamed some more, describing what life could be for us. She wasn't talking about a postmortem world, some kind of heaven or afterlife; and she was not speaking of reincarnation (which she believes in, by the way). She dreamed of land, a spacious house, fresh air, organic food, and endless meadows without boundaries, free of evil and violence, free of toxins and environmental hazards, free of poverty, racism, and sexism . . . just free. She never talked about how we might create such a world, nor had she connected her vision to any political ideology. But she convinced my siblings and me that change is possible and that we didn't have to be stuck there forever.

The idea that we could possibly go somewhere that exists only in our imaginations—that is, "nowhere"—is the classic definition of *utopia*. Call me utopian, but I inherited my mother's belief that the map to a new world is in the imagination, in what we see in our third eyes rather than in the desolation that surrounds us.

Now that I look back with hindsight, my writing and the kind of politics to which I've been drawn have more to do with imagining a different future than being pissed off about the present. Not that I haven't been angry, frustrated, and critical of the misery created by race, gender, and class oppression—past and present. That goes without saying. My point is that the *dream of a new world*, my mother's dream, was the catalyst for my own political engagement. I came to Black nationalism filled with idealistic dreams of a communal society free of all oppressions, a world where we owned the land and shared the wealth and white folks were out of sight and out of mind. It was what I imagined precolonial Africa to be. Sure, I was naive, still in my teens, but my imaginary portrait, derived from the writings of Cheikh Anta Diop, Chancellor Williams, Julius Nyerere, Kwame Nkrumah, Kwame Ture, and others, gave me a sense of hope and possibility of what a *post*colonial Africa could look like.

Very quickly, I learned that the old past wasn't as glorious, peaceful, or communal as I had thought—though I still believe that it was many times better than what we found when we got to the Americas. The stories from the former colonies—whether Mobutu's Zaire, Amin's Uganda, or Forbes Burnham's Guyana—dashed most of my expectations about what it would take to achieve real freedom. In college, like all the other neophyte revolutionaries influenced by events in southern Africa, El Salvador and Nicaragua, Cuba and Grenada, I studied Third World liberation movements and postemancipation societies in the hope of discovering different visions of freedom born out of the circumstances of struggle. I looked in vain for glimmers of a new society, in the "liberated zones" of Portugal's African colonies during the wars of independence, in Maurice Bishop's "New Jewel" movement in Grenada, in Guyana's tragically short-lived nineteenth-century communal villages, in the brief moment when striking workers of Congo-Brazzaville momentarily seized state power and were poised to establish Africa's first workers' state. Granted, all these movements crashed against the rocks, wrecked by various internal and external forces, but they left behind at least some kind of vision, however fragmented or incomplete, of what they wanted their world to look like.

Like most of my comrades active in the early days of the Reagan era, I turned to Marxism for the same reasons I looked to the Third World. The misery of the proletariat (lumpen and otherwise) proved less interesting and less urgent than the promise of revolution. I was attracted to their communism because, in theory, it sought to harness technology to solve human needs, give us less work and more leisure, and free us all to create, invent, explore, love, relax, and enjoy life without want of the basic necessities of life. My big sister Makani and I used to preach to others about the end of money; the withering away of poverty, property, and the state; and the destruction of the material basis for racism and patriarchy. I fell in love with the young Marx of *The German Ideology* and *The Communist Manifesto*, the visionary Marx who predicted the abolition of all exploitative institutions. I followed young Marx, via the late English historian Edward P. Thompson, to those romantic renegade socialists like William Morris who wanted to break with all vestiges of capitalist production and rationalization. Morris was less concerned with socialist efficiency than with transforming social relations and constructing new, free, democratic communities built on, as Thompson put it, "the ethic of cooperation, the energies of love."

There are very few contemporary political spaces where the energies of love and imagination are understood and respected as powerful social forces. The socialists, utopian and scientific, had little to say about this, so my search for an even more elaborate, complete dream of freedom forced me to take a more imaginative turn. Thanks to many wonderful chance encounters with Franklin and Penelope Rosemont, Ted Joans, Laura Corsiglia, and Jayne Cortez, I discovered surrealism, not so much in the writings and doings of André Breton or Louis Aragon or other leaders of the surrealist movement that emerged in Paris after World War I, but under my nose, so to speak, buried in the rich, Black soil of Afrodiasporic culture. In it I found a most miraculous weapon with no birth date, no expiration date, no trademark.

I traced the Marvelous from the ancient practices of Maroon societies and shamanism back to the future, to the metropoles of
Europe, to the blues people of North America, to the colonized
and semicolonized world that produced the likes of Aimé and Suzanne Césaire and Wifredo Lam. The surrealists not only taught
me that any serious motion toward freedom must begin in the
mind, but they have also given us some of the most imaginative,
expansive, and playful dreams of a new world I have ever known.
Contrary to popular belief, surrealism is not an aesthetic doctrine but an international revolutionary movement concerned
with the emancipation of thought. Members of the Surrealist
Group in Madrid, for example, see their work as an intervention
in life rather than literature, a protracted battle against all forms
of oppression that aims to replace "suspicion, fear and anger with
curiosity, adventure and desire" and "a model space for collective living—a space from which separation and isolation are ban-
ished forever."

The surrealists are talking about total transformation of society, not just granting aggrieved populations greater political and
economic power. They are speaking of new social relationships,
new ways of living and interacting, new attitudes toward work
and leisure and community. In this respect, they share much with
radical feminists whose revolutionary vision extended into every
aspect of social life. Radical feminists taught us that there is nothing natural or inevitable about gender roles, male dominance,
the overrepresentation of men in positions of power, or the tendency of men to use violence as a means to resolve conflict.
Radical feminists of color, in particular, reveal how race, gender,
and class work in tandem to subordinate most of society while
complicating easy notions of universal sisterhood or biological
arguments that establish men as the universal enemy. Like all the
other movements that caught my attention, radical feminism, as
well as the ideas emerging out of the lesbian and gay movements,
proved attractive not simply for their critiques of patriarchy but
for their freedom dreams. The work of these movements taken as
a whole interrogates what is "normal"; shows us how the state and

official culture polices our behavior with regard to sexuality, gender roles, and social relationships; and encourages us to construct a politics rooted in desire.

Black intellectuals associated with each of these movements not only imagined a different future, but in many instances their emancipatory vision proved more radical and inclusive than what their compatriots proposed.* Indeed, throughout the book I argue that these renegade Black intellectuals/activists/artists challenged and reshaped communism, surrealism, and radical feminism, and in so doing produced brilliant theoretical insights that might have pushed these movements in new directions. In most cases, however, the critical visions of Black radicals were held at bay, if not completely marginalized. Of course, there are many people still struggling to realize these dreams—extending, elaborating, and refining their vision as the battle wears on. This book is about those dreams of freedom; it is merely a brief, idiosyncratic outline of a history of Black radical imagination in the twentieth century. I don't pretend to have written anything approaching a movement history or an intellectual history, and I am not interested in explaining why these dreams of revolution have not succeeded (yet!). Rather, I simply want to explore the different ways self-proclaimed renegades imagined life after the revolution and where their ideas came from. Although *Freedom Dreams* is no memoir, it is a very personal book. It is loosely organized around my own political journey, around the dreams I once shared or still share—from the dreams of an African utopia to the surreal world of our imagination, from the communist and feminist dreams of

---

*Let me emphasize that I am interested in Black people's dreams of the new society. A fascinating book by William H. Pease and Jane Pease, *Black Utopia: Negro Communal Experiments in America,* looks at white abolitionist and liberal designs for Black communities whose main goal was to "train the Negro for complete freedom" (p. 19). Freedom was defined according to Jeffersonian values, determined of course by the white architects of these Negro villages. While most communal societies were socialist or communist oriented, the settlements created for Black people centered on enterprise, thrift, and individual accumulation—in short, their goal was to instill ex-slaves with middle-class capitalist values in order to prepare them to be productive members of the mainstream. Black people in their study are largely objects of white liberal ideology, not agents pursuing their own vision of freedom.

abolishing all forms of exploitation to the four-hundred-year-old dream of payback for slavery and Jim Crow.

My purpose in writing this book is simply to reopen a very old conversation about what kind of world we want to struggle for. I'm not the only one interested in the work of dreaming—obviously there are many activists and thinkers having this conversation right now, ranging from my sister Makani Themba-Nixon, Cornel West, and Lian and Eric Mann to Cleveland's Norma Jean Freeman and Don Freeman, Newark's Amina and Amiri Baraka, and Detroit's Grace Lee Boggs, to name but a few. For decades, these and other folks have dared to talk openly of revolution and dream of a new society, sometimes creating cultural works that enable communities to envision what's possible with collective action, personal self-transformation, and will.

I did not write this book for those traditional leftists who have traded in their dreams for orthodoxy and sectarianism. Most of those folks are hopeless, I'm sad to say. And they will be the first to dismiss this book as utopian, idealistic, and romantic. Instead, I wrote it for anyone bold enough still to dream, especially young people who are growing up in what critic Henry Giroux perceptively calls "the culture of cynicism"—young people whose dreams have been utterly coopted by the marketplace. In a world where so many youth believe that "getting paid" and living ostentatiously was the goal of the Black freedom movement, there is little space to even *discuss* building a radical democratic public culture. Too many young people really believe that this is the best we can do. Young faces, however, have been popping up en masse at the antiglobalization demonstrations beginning in Seattle in 1999, and the success of the college antisweatshop campaign No Sweat owes much of its success to a growing number of radicalized students. The Black Radical Congress, launched in 1997, has attracted hundreds of activists under age twenty-five, and so has the campaign to free Mumia Abu-Jamal. So there is hope.

The question remains: What are today's young activists dreaming about? We know what they are fighting against, but what are they fighting for? These are crucial questions, for one of the basic premises of this book is that the most powerful, visionary dreams of a new society don't come from little think tanks of smart people or out of the atomized, individualistic world of consumer capitalism where raging against the status quo is simply the hip thing to do. Revolutionary dreams erupt out of political engagement; collective social movements are incubators of new knowledge. While this may seem obvious, I am increasingly surrounded by well-meaning students who want to be activists but exhibit anxiety about doing intellectual work. They often differentiate the two, positioning activism and intellectual work as inherently incompatible. They speak of the "real" world as some concrete wilderness overrun with violence and despair, and the university as if it were some sanitized sanctuary distant from actual people's lives and struggles. At the other extreme, I have had students argue that the problems facing "real people" today can be solved by merely bridging the gap between our superior knowledge and people outside the ivy walls who simply do not have access to that knowledge. Unwitting advocates of a kind of "talented tenth" ideology of racial uplift, their stated goal is to "reach the people" with more "accessible" knowledge, to carry back to the 'hood the information folks need to liberate themselves. While it is heartening to see young people excited about learning and cognizant of the political implications of knowledge, it worries me when they believe that simply "droppin' science" on the people will generate new, liberatory social movements.

I am convinced that the opposite is true: Social movements generate new knowledge, new theories, new questions. The most radical ideas often grow out of a concrete intellectual engagement with the problems of aggrieved populations confronting systems of oppression. For example, the academic study of race has always been inextricably intertwined with political struggles. Just as imperialism, colonialism, and post-Reconstruction redemption politics created the intellectual ground for Social Darwinism and other manifestations of scientific racism, the struggle against racism generated cultural relativist and social constructionist scholarship on race. The great works by W. E. B. Du Bois, Franz Boas, Oliver Cox, and many others were invariably shaped by social movements as well as social crises such as the proliferation of lynching and the rise of fascism. Similarly, gender analysis was brought to us by the feminist movement, not simply by the individual genius of the Grimke sisters or Anna Julia Cooper, Simone de Beauvoir, or Audre Lorde. Thinking on gender and the possibility of transformation evolved largely in relationship to social struggle.

Progressive social movements do not simply produce statistics and narratives of oppression; rather, the best ones do what great poetry always does: transport us to another place, compel us to relive horrors and, more importantly, enable us to imagine a new society. We must remember that the conditions and the very existence of social movements enable participants to imagine something different, to realize that things need not always be this way. It is *that* imagination, that effort to see the future in the present, that I shall call "poetry" or "poetic knowledge." I take my lead from Aimé Césaire's great essay "Poetry and Knowledge," first published in 1945. Opening with the simple but provocative proposition that "Poetic knowledge is born in the great silence of scientific knowledge," he then demonstrates why poetry is the only way to achieve the kind of knowledge we need to move beyond the world's crises. "What presides over the poem," he writes, "is not the most lucid intelligence, the sharpest sensibility or the subtlest feelings, but experience as a whole." This means everything, every history, every future, every dream, every life form from plant to animal, every creative impulse—plumbed from the depths of the unconscious. Poetry, therefore, is not what we simply recognize as the formal "poem," but a revolt: a scream in the night, an emancipation of language and old ways of thinking. Consider Césaire's third proposition regarding poetic knowledge: "Poetic knowledge is that in which man spatters the object with all of his mobilized riches."

In the poetics of struggle and lived experience, in the utterances of ordinary folk, in the cultural products of social movements, in

the reflections of activists, we discover the many different cognitive maps of the future, of the world not yet born. Recovering
the poetry of social movements, however, particularly the poetry
that dreams of a new world, is not such an easy task. For obvious reasons, what we are against tends to take precedence over
what we are for, which is always a more complicated and ambig-
uous matter. It is a testament to the legacies of oppression that
opposition is so frequently contained, or that efforts to find "free
spaces" for articulating or even realizing our dreams are so rare
or marginalized. George Lipsitz helps explain the problem when
he writes in Dangerous Crossroads, "The desire to work through
existing contradictions rather than stand outside them represents
not so much a preference for melioristic reform over revolutionary change, but rather a recognition of the impossibility of standing outside totalitarian systems of domination." Besides, even if
we could gather together our dreams of a new world, how do we
figure them out in a culture dominated by the marketplace? How
can social movements actually reshape the desires and dreams of
the participants?

Another problem, of course, is that such dreaming is often suppressed and policed not only by our enemies but by leaders of
social movements themselves. The utopian visions of male nationalists or so-called socialists often depend on the suppression
of women, of youth, of gays and lesbians, of people of color. Desire can be crushed by so-called revolutionary ideology. I don't
know how many times self-proclaimed leftists talk of universal-
izing "working-class culture," focusing only on what they think
is uplifting and politically correct but never paying attention to,
say, the ecstatic. I remember attending a conference in Vermont
about the future of socialism, where a bunch of us got into a fight
with an older generation of white leftists who proposed replacing
retrograde "pop" music with the revolutionary "working-class"
music of Phil Ochs, Woody Guthrie, preelectric Bob Dylan, and
songs from the Spanish Civil War. And there I was, comically
screaming at the top of my lungs, "No way! After the revolution,

we STILL want Bootsy! That's right, we want Bootsy! We need the funk!"

Sometimes I think the conditions of daily life, of everyday oppressions, of survival, not to mention the temporary pleasures accessible to most of us, render much of our imagination inert. We are constantly putting out fires, responding to emergencies, finding temporary refuge, all of which make it difficult to see anything other than the present. As the great poet Keorapetse Kgositsile put it, "When the clouds clear / We shall know the colour of the sky." When movements have been unable to clear the clouds, it has been the poets—no matter the medium—who have succeeded in imagining the color of the sky, in rendering the kinds of dreams and futures social movements are capable of producing. Knowing the color of the sky is far more important than counting clouds. Or to put it another way, the most radical art is not protest art but works that take us to another place, envision a different way of seeing, perhaps a different way of feeling. This is what poet Askia Muhammad Toure meant when, in a 1964 article in Liberator magazine, he called Black rhythm-and-blues artists "poet philosophers" and described their music as a "potent weapon in the Black freedom struggle." For Toure, the "movement" was more than sit-ins at lunch counters, voter registration campaigns, and freedom rides; it was about self-transformation, changing the way we think, live, love, and handle pain. While the music frequently negatively mirrored the larger culture, it nonetheless helped generate community pride, challenged racial self-hatred, and built self-respect. It created a world of pleasure, not just to escape the everyday brutalities of capitalism, patriarchy, and white supremacy, but to build community, establish fellowship, play and laugh, and plant seeds for a different way of living, a different way of hearing. As Amiri Baraka put it in his famous essay, "The Changing Same," Black music has the potential to usher in a new future based on love: "The change to Love. The freedom to (of) Love."

Freedom and love may be the most revolutionary ideas available to us, and yet as intellectuals we have failed miserably to grapple with their political and analytical importance. Despite having spent a decade and a half writing about radical social movements, I am only just beginning to see what animated, motivated, and knitted together these gatherings of aggrieved folk. I have come to realize that once we strip radical social movements down to their bare essence and understand the collective desires of people in motion, freedom and love lay at the very heart of the matter. Indeed, I would go so far as to say that freedom and love constitute the foundation for spirituality, another elusive and intangible force with which few scholars of social movements have come to terms. These insights were always there in the movements I've studied, but I was unable to see it, acknowledge it, or bring it to the surface. I hope this little book might be a beginning.

DREAMS OF THE NEW LAND

Africa I guard your memory
Africa you are in me
My future is your future
Your wounds are my wounds
The funky blues I cook
are Black like you—Africa
Africa my motherland
America my fatherland
Although I did not choose it to be
Africa you alone can make me free
Africa where the rhinos roam
Where I learned to swing
Before America became my home
Not like a monkey but in my soul
Africa you are rich with natural gold
Africa I live and study for thee
And through you I shall be free
Someday I'll come back and see
Land of my mothers, where a Black god made me
My Africa, your Africa, a free continent to be.

—Ted Joans, "Africa"

Schoolhouse Rock didn't teach me a damn thing about "freedom." The kids like me growing up in Harlem during the 1960s and early 1970s heard that word in the streets; it rang in our ears with the regularity of a hit song. Everybody and their mama spoke of freedom, and what they meant usually defied the popular meanings of the day. Whereas most Americans associated freedom with Western democracies at war against communism, free-market capitalism, or U.S. intervention in countries such as Vietnam or the Dominican Republic, in our neighborhood "freedom" had no particular tie to U.S. nationality (with the possible exception of the Black-owned Freedom National Bank). Freedom was the goal our people were trying to achieve; *free* was a verb, an act, a wish, a militant demand. "Free the land," "Free your mind," "Free South Africa," "Free Angola," "Free Angela Davis," "Free Huey," were the slogans I remember best. Of course, "freedom" was also employed as a marketing tool to sell us things like Afro wigs, hair care products, and various foodstuffs, but even these commodities were linked in our minds to the Black struggle for independence, not just in the urban ghettos but around the world. "Freedom" even became a kind of metonym for Africa—the home we never knew, the place where we once enjoyed freedom before we were forcibly taken in chains across the sea. We drank Afro-Cola, which came in a blue can emblazoned with a map of the African continent, partly because slick marketing executives told us it contained the taste of freedom, partly because we pretended it was nectar from the motherland.

Of course, not everyone identified with Africa or associated the continent with dreams of freedom, but we were living in Harlem, of all places, during the era of the "black freedom movement." Formal colonialism had ended throughout most of Africa—the exceptions being southern Africa and the Portuguese colonies—so those who paid attention to such things were excited by the prospects of a free and independent Africa. By the time I enrolled at California State University at Long Beach, the Black Studies program there reignited my nascent, underdeveloped Pan-African vision of the world. Our professors turned diehard party people and wannabe Greeks into angry young "Afrikans." And we had good reason to be angry. After twelve years of public miseducation, reading works by pioneering Black scholars such as Eric Williams's *Capitalism and Slavery*, Cheikh Anta Diop's *The African Origins of Civilization*, George E. M. James's *Stolen Legacy*, Angela Davis's *Women, Race, and Class*, W. E. B. Du Bois's *Souls of Black Folk* and *Black Reconstruction in America*, J. A. Rogers's *World's Greatest Men and Women of African Descent*, among others, opened up a whole new world for us. We learned of the origins of Western racism, the history of slavery, the rise and fall of African kingdoms before the European invasion, the Egyptian roots of Western civilization. We were particularly obsessed with the large-scale civilizations along the Nile—Egypt, Ethiopia, Nubia—as were generations of Afrocentric scholars before us, as Wilson Moses recently pointed out in his valuable book *Afrotopia*. Indeed, the title alone explains why we junior Afrocentrists were attracted more to the powerful states of the ancient world than to the civil rights movement: We looked back in search of a better future. We wanted to find a refuge where "black people" exercised power, possessed essential knowledge, educated the West, built monuments, slept under the stars on the banks of the Nile, and never had to worry about the police or poverty or arrogant white people questioning our intelligence. Of course, this meant conveniently ignoring slave labor, class hierarchies, and women's oppression, and it meant projecting backwards in time a twentieth-century conception of race, but to simply criticize us for myth making or essentialism misses the point of our reading. We dreamed the ancient world as a place of freedom, a picture to imagine what we desired and what was possible.

Sometimes we couldn't read fast enough; other times, we were so overtaken with emotion we put our books down and wept, or fantasized about revenge. More importantly, we began to see ourselves—as earlier generations of Black intellectuals had—as part of an African diaspora, an oppressed "nation" without a homeland. Many of us gravitated to campus Black nationalist groups, imagining Africa as our true home, either as a place of eventual return or a place from which we were permanently exiled. At least in our minds, we joined a long line of Black thinkers who believed that to achieve freedom we first had to get out of Dodge.

Exodus

Few scholars or activists today take proposals to leave America and return to Africa or some other "homeland" seriously. Back-to-Africa proposals in principle are almost universally dismissed as "escapist" or associated with essentialist, romantic ideas about Black cultural unity. Critics dwell on the impracticality of such schemes, or they point to sharp cultural and class differences that keep the Black world divided. They are not wrong to do so, but any wholesale dismissal of the desire to leave this place and find a new home misses what these movements might tell us about how Black people have imagined real freedom. The desire to leave Babylon, if you will, and search for a new land tells us a great deal about what people dream about, what they want, how they might want to reconstruct their lives.

After all, the history of Black people has been a history of movement—real and imagined. Repatriation to Liberia and Sierra Leone. Flight to Canada. Escape to Haiti. The great Kansas Exodus. The back-to-Africa movements of Bishop Henry McNeil Turner and Marcus Garvey. The 49th State movement. The Republic of New Africa. The Rastafarian settlement of Shashamane, Ethiopia. I'm goin' to Chicago, baby, I can't take you along. Space is the Place. The Mothership Connection. All these travel/escape narratives point to the biblical story of Exodus, of the Israelites' flight out of Egypt. It isn't a coincidence that the stream of Black migrants who fled the South for Kansas and Oklahoma in the late 1870s were called "exodusters," or that one of the South Carolina emigration societies was called the Liberian Exodus Association. Indeed, as Eddie Glaude points out in his recent book *Exodus! Religion, Race, and Nation in Early Nineteenth-Century Black America*, the book of Exodus served as the key political and moral compass for African

Americans during the antebellum era, and it would continue to do so after the Civil War. Exodus provided Black people with a language to critique America's racist state and build a new nation, for its central theme wasn't simply escape but a new beginning.

Exodus represented dreams of Black self-determination, of being on our own, under our own rules and beliefs, developing our own cultures, without interference. Even before New World Africans laid eyes on the Bible, the fundamental idea behind Exodus was evident in the formation of Maroon societies throughout the Americas. Maroon societies were settlements of renegades from the plantation system made up primarily of runaway slaves, some indigenous people, and, in a few instances, white indentured servants who rebelled against the dominant culture. These settlements often existed on the run, in the hills or swamps just outside the plantation economy. Africans tended to dominate these communities, and many sought to preserve the cultures of their original homelands while combining different Old and New World traditions. Over time, Africans adopted elements of various Native American cultures, and vice versa, and Europeans relied on aspects of these cultures for their own survival. In the words of political scientist Cedric Robinson, these movements were inventive "rather than imitative, communitarian rather than individualistic, democratic rather than Republican, Afro-Christian rather than secular and materialist[;] the social values of these largely agrarian people generated a political culture that distinguished between the inferior world of the political and the transcendent universe of moral goods." The impulse toward separatism, defined broadly, is rooted in maroonage and the desire to leave the place of oppression for either a new land or some kind of peaceful coexistence.

The problem with modern "Egyptland" is that it claimed to be a republic, and too many Black people—slave and free—invested their own blood, sweat, and tears in building or protecting the country. Therefore, in the United States the impulse to leave conflicted with Black claims to full citizenship and full remuneration for our contribution to the nation. Prior to the adoption of the Fourteenth Amendment in 1868, the question as to whether or not African Americans were citizens of the United States had not been settled. The experiences of free African Americans during the antebellum era demonstrate that citizenship was beyond their grasp, and the Fugitive Slave Law of 1850 and the *Dred Scott* decision of 1857 denying Black people citizenship rights cleared up any ambiguity on the matter. While some Black leaders insisted on their right to citizenship during the mid-nineteenth century, others such as Mary Ann Shadd Cary, Jermain Loguen, James T. Holly, Samuel Ringgold Ward, Paul Cuffe, and Martin Delany called on Black people to find a homeland of their own. Not that they were willing to relinquish their claims to citizenship; rather, they reached a point of profound pessimism and began deeply to question their allegiance to and identification with the United States.

Whether they thought about leaving or not, the question of citizenship always loomed large, compelling some to renounce the United States altogether. Nineteenth-century Black activist H. Ford Douglass once said: "I can hate this Government without being disloyal, because it has stricken down my manhood, and treated me as a saleable commodity. . . . I can join a foreign enemy and fight against it, without being a traitor, because it treats me as an ALIEN and a STRANGER." Emigration not only rendered African Americans "transnational" people by default, but it remained at the heart of a very long debate within Black communities about their sense of national belonging. The debate was further complicated by the fact that many white people supported emigration. The American Colonization Society was formed within the U.S. House of Representatives in 1816 for the purpose of deporting free Black people to Liberia. Its leading members included Henry Clay, Daniel Webster, and Francis Scott Key, composer of the "Star Spangled Banner." During the Civil War, President Lincoln's initial program to reconstruct the nation included an elaborate plan to deport Black people, first to Liberia and later to what he believed was a more practical location—Central America.

When the prospect of enjoying real citizenship emerged on the horizon during Reconstruction, emigrationist sentiment among

African Americans ebbed and Lincoln's plan won very few adherents among Black leaders. However, despite the ratification of the Fourteenth Amendment, the question of African American citizenship had not been resolved, and with the collapse of Reconstruction and the erection of Jim Crow, the situation took a turn for the worse. In the South, Black people were denied the right to vote and hold public office, access to the public schools that they had helped established and continued to finance with their tax money, and any semblance of justice. Instead, African Americans were subjected to mob violence and "lynch law." Between 1882 and 1946, at least 5,000 people, the vast majority of whom were Black, were lynched in the United States. Black communities had to deal not only with a steady stream of lynchings but also with a constant threat of invasion by armed, murderous white mobs. In the decade from 1898 to 1908, "race riots" broke out in Wilmington, North Carolina; Atlanta; New Orleans; New York City; Phoenix; South Carolina; Akron, Ohio; Washington Parish, Louisiana; Birmingham, Alabama; Brownsville, Texas; and Springfield, Illinois; to name but a few. Historian Carter G. Woodson expressed the problem poignantly in his 1921 essay "Fifty Years of Negro Citizenship as Qualified by the United States Supreme Court": "The citizenship of the Negro in this country is a fiction."

Most Black people believed there was an order higher than the Constitution. Psalm 68, verse 31 of the Bible had promised redemption for the Black world: "Princes come out of Egypt. Ethiopia stretches forth her hands unto God." This passage was as important to Pan-Africanist and emigrationist sentiment as the book of Exodus, becoming the theological basis for what became known in the nineteenth century as Ethiopianism. Ethiopianism spread throughout the Black world, from the Americas to Africa, calling for the redemption of Africa by any means necessary. One of the earliest published examples of this doctrine was Robert Alexander Young's *Ethiopian Manifesto: Issued in Defense of the Blackman's Rights in the Scale of Universal Freedom* (1829), which predicted the coming of a new Hannibal who would lead a violent uprising to liberate the race. The Black abolitionist speaker

Maria Stewart echoed some of the ideas in Young's manifesto, drawing on scripture to argue that Africans were the "chosen people." While she identified herself as African, described America as "the great city of Babylon," and believed that Black people possessed a distinct national destiny apart from that of other Americans, she did not advocate emigration.

Because the Bible, not the specifics of our lineage or heritage, framed most nineteenth-century Black conceptions of national destiny, Ethiopia took on greater importance than any other nation or region of Africa. It was also known as Abyssinia, and Black people the world over considered it the cradle of civilization. Ethiopia has remained one of the Black Christian world's principal icons and, in some ways, might be called an African Jerusalem. As historian William Scott explained, many African Americans believed that "Ethiopia had been predestined by biblical prophecy to redeem the Black race from white rule." Its reputation as a beacon of hope and strength for Africa and the African diaspora was strengthened in 1896, after Menelik II, leader of the Amhara, united Ethiopia's princes to defeat Italy. Italy's humiliating loss to Ethiopian armies in the battle of Adwa demonstrated to the world that Europe was indeed vulnerable, and it rendered Africa's "holy land" the only independent nation on the continent. For many Black observers, it appeared as if prophesy would come to pass. Groups such as the short-lived Star Order of Ethiopia, founded by Grover Cleveland Redding, called on African Americans to move there. The Ethiopian ambassador to the United States also encouraged Black people to settle there. By 1933 the African-American community in Ethiopia numbered between 100 and 150. When Italy invaded Ethiopia again in 1935, this time successfully, the entire Black world mobilized in its defense, some volunteering for military service.*

---

*Of course, every reality is more complicated. Menelik united many local rulers in Ethiopia, but he also consolidated his power over his new allies and signed a peace treaty ceding Eritrean territory to Italy. While vindicationist "race" scholars praised Abyssinia for its ancient civilizations, its written language, its rulers' proud claim of direct lineage to Solomon and the Queen of Sheba, Black radical writers showed more

Nineteenth-century emigrationists looked upon Africa as the new promised land, a land of milk and honey where its offspring in the diaspora could return and thrive. Bishop Henry McNeil Turner of the African Methodist Episcopal (AME) Church emerged as one of the most outspoken advocates of emigration. As vice-president of the American Colonization Society (ACS), Turner supported Black emigration to Liberia during the late nineteenth and early twentieth centuries. The AME missions under his guidance promoted redemption as uplift ideology—the idea that education, modernization, and devotion to God would uplift the continent and the race. At the same time, Bishop Turner had no love for the United States, once describing the Constitution as "a dirty rag, a cheat, a libel, and ought to be spit upon by every Negro in the land." He believed that white supremacy generated Black self-hatred and that no Black man could achieve manhood unless Blacks could protect and govern themselves. Turner attracted a significant following, especially among poor workers and farmers who believed that any place was better than the Jim Crow South. One Mississippi man wrote to the ACS asking for assistance, comparing his circumstances to slavery and asking, "Oh my God help us to get out from here to Africa."

Most nineteenth-century proponents of repatriation viewed the imminent return of African Americans as a kind of civilizing mission, bringing Christianity to the heathens and technology and knowledge to the backward natives. Africa needed to be redeemed not from European colonialism but because it was a civilization in decline. Redemption translated into uplift ideology, a radically different cultural approach to "return" from the early impulse toward maroonage. By the end of the century, Africa's most vocal Negro redeemers tended to be formally educated elites who drew their ideological arsenal from Western notions of national destiny, race, progress, and civilization. Men such as Alexander

---

skepticism. On the eve of Mussolini's invasion, Ethiopia was ruled by a dying monarchy that did not believe in land reform. As one of the few regions on earth where slavery persisted well into the early 1930s, Ethiopia was hardly a land of freedom.

Crummell, Henry Highland Garnet, Bishop Turner, Edward Wilmot Blyden, and the lesser-known leaders of emigrationist organizations dreamed of turning their ancestral homeland into modern, "civilized," powerful nations where Black people could create their own wealth and rule themselves. They imagined a society patterned on the best of the West—its schools, railroads, factories, and religion—without the racism, inequality, and oppression. While they desired "Africa for the Africans," limited autonomy if not total independence, and freedom for all (at least in theory), they also wanted to participate in the international market as equals.

For the next few decades, Liberia became the model for the benefits of civilization; it was upheld by African-American intellectuals as evidence that, if left alone, Black people could develop a free and industrious nation on the basis of their own intelligence, frugality, and good planning. Liberia was to be a Black man's utopia, the land where race prejudice was a thing of the past and every person in the republic enjoyed the fruits of citizenship. Unfortunately, this is not what happened. In their haste to defend Liberia, most commentators ignored or played down the role of the United States (via the Firestone Rubber Company) as an imperialist presence in the colony and the position of Americo-Liberians as a new, exploitative ruling class. As a result, the indigenous population of Liberia was exploited and oppressed by African Americans, who had ironically returned to their ancestral homeland to escape tyranny.

Few emigration advocates during this period questioned the Western model. Edward Wilmot Blyden was among the few to propose adopting elements of traditional African culture, but only after years of study. His early works, A Voice from Bleeding Africa (1856) and The Call of Providence to the Descendants of Africa in America (1862) both argued that God allowed enslavement of Black people so that they might be converted to Christianity. It was now the manifest destiny of Black people to return to their ancestral homeland and bring the benefits of Christianity and "civilization." By the end of the century, following a thorough study of Islam, he wrote a series of articles proposing that Black people develop an African personality (as opposed to copying European culture) and defending indigenous African culture, including polygamy and traditional family practices. He argued that African cultures were naturally communal and did not allow private ownership of land, and that their emphasis on collective responsibility for the entire community rendered homelessness, poverty, and crime nonexistent. And because all adult women were in marital relationships, he argued, there were no "spinsters" or prostitutes.

Blyden's defense of traditional African culture might be one of the first explicit examples we have of what later would be called African communalism or African socialism—the idea that precolonial societies were inherently democratic and practiced a form of "primitive communism" that could lay the groundwork for a truly egalitarian society. In the shadow of the failed Paris Commune, the upsurge of working-class socialist movements throughout the Western world, and growing concern about the dangers of industrialization, Blyden's celebration of African communalism is particularly striking. Of course, we now know that African social organization ran the gamut from hunter-gatherer societies to large-scale, class-stratified societies based on agriculture, slave labor, and even limited manufacturing, and that traditional family and gender relationships were based on severe hierarchies. What is noteworthy, however, is the fact that Blyden and others imagined Africa as a place free of exploitation and believed that this model might lay the basis for a society of Black settlers. Rather than worship Western culture and modernization, Blyden at least toyed with the idea that traditional, precapitalist life might offer a superior road to freedom.

Redemption

Marcus Garvey, founder of the Universal Negro Improvement Association (UNIA)—the largest "African redemption" movement in the history of the world—promoted a vision of a New Africa that embraced certain Western ideas and technologies but transformed them to suit Black people's needs. He created African Fundamentalism, a revision of Christianity rooted in Ethiopianism, African Methodism, and a variety of religious beliefs that would eventually make their way into the Rastafarian faith. As Robert Hill points out, Garvey argued that Adam and Eve and their progeny were Black and that Cain was stricken by God with leprosy (whiteness) as punishment for the murder of his brother, Abel. The white race, in other words, began as lepers punished by God. But Garvey differed from the Ethiopianists by insisting that the Egyptians were Blacks who enslaved the Hebrews. Garvey's strong identification with the Egyptians makes perfect sense given his argument that we descended from a powerful civilization. His vision of the power of indigenous African culture was ancient, rooted in Egypt and Ethiopia, not in contemporary African culture, for he accepted Oswald Spengler's idea that African civilization was among those in decline. Only a movement for Africa's redemption could restore Africa's original glory. Interestingly, while he did not identify with the enslaved Jews of ancient times, he did identify with the modern Zionist movement. Garvey called his own movement Black Zionism, comparing the struggle for an African homeland with the Jewish movement for a homeland in Palestine. He patterned his Universal African Legion after the Jewish Legion, which came to be seen as a Jewish national guard for Palestine. He even received significant patronage from Jewish financiers such as William Ritter of the United States and Abraham Judah and Lewis Ashenheim of Jamaica.

Garvey founded the UNIA with his first wife, Amy Ashwood, in his native Jamaica in 1914. It began as a benevolent association, but when they moved to Harlem in 1916, Garvey transformed the UNIA into a mass-based, global, Black nationalist movement intent on redeeming Africa and establishing a homeland for the Black world. In some ways the UNIA resembled an army preparing for battle, which might be expected of any nationalist movement born in the midst of the greatest European nationalist conflict of all time: World War I. Yet like most race leaders at the time, Marcus Garvey was heir to an older warrior tradition rooted in the Old Testament. Redemption, after all, was a violent and bloody proposition. Betray God and He might smite your first born, take you down by sword or plague, crush you to earth or drown you. Nat Turner, leader of a bloody slave revolt in Virginia in 1831, was told by God that slavery was to be eliminated by bloodshed, even if it meant sacrificing the master's women and children. It was God's will, and the signs from heaven were clear: "I should arise and prepare myself, and slay my enemies with their own weapons." Nat Turner was not out of step with the leading Black abolitionists of the day. Besides Robert Alexander Young's prediction of a race war led by a new Hannibal, David Walker warned white people that God was prepared to take His vengeance out on them, and that when the slaves rose up and cut their throats, it was God's will. "The whites want slaves," he wrote in his *Appeal*, "and want us for their slaves, but some of them will curse the day they ever saw us. As true as the sun ever shone in its meridian splendor, my colour will root some of them out of the very face of the earth."

The UNIA never actually waged war anywhere, but World War I militarism had a profound impact on the organization's gender politics, according to the historian Barbara Bair. Garveyite parades, pageants, poetry, and songs, as well as speeches and documents, drew on metaphors of war that defined gender roles within the movement. Black men assigned to the UNIA's African Legion performed military drills, symbolizing assertiveness, readiness, and self-defense. UNIA leaders wore elaborate uniforms resembling European imperial designs, therefore reversing the dominant image of Black men as subordinate. Garveyite leadership exuded strength, dominance, and nationhood. The Black Cross nurses symbolized the nurturing role of women by ministering to the needs of soldiers and the community as a whole. They wore white habits that, likewise, reversed the dominant image of Black womanhood. Challenging stereotypes of Black women as hypersexual Jezebels, the Black Cross nurses were "angels of charity and mercy," holy sisters united in purity and devotion to their own community and to the greater redemption of Africa.

In many respects, Garvey's vision of the proper role of Black men and women in a new, liberated society differed little from those of previous generations of Black nationalists, who embraced the prevailing notion that African redemption equaled manhood redemption. The strength of the nation as a measure of manhood, after all, was a common characteristic of modern nationalism. The writings and speeches of Crummell, Edward Blyden, and even W. E. B. Du Bois described Africa as the "fatherland," and the redemption of the fatherland was almost always framed in terms of manhood rights. Not surprisingly, early Pan-Africanist and emigrationist organizations were almost entirely male affairs. While politics was considered an exclusively male domain in this era, masculinity was especially pronounced in Black nationalist politics because of its roots in the struggle against slavery. Despite the fact that abolitionism developed alongside woman suffrage, the struggle against slavery by free Blacks and even white abolitionists was cast as a struggle for manhood rights largely because servility of any kind was regarded as less than manly. Black men's inability to protect their families under slavery was considered a direct assault on their manhood, since manhood was defined in part by one's ability to defend one's home. Thus, it is not surprising that Black abolitionist appeals emphasized manhood rights and violence as strategies of liberation. Abolitionists like David Walker, John Russwurm, and Henry Highland Garnet called on slaves to "act like men" and rise up against slavery, and their appeals were frequently echoed by Black women activists. From Maria Stewart to Ida B. Wells, Black women chastised Black men for failing to fulfill their manly role as defenders of the race.

Consequently, women barely figured in most Pan-Africanist or emigrationist imaginings of what the New Land might look like, except in Garveyism. Thanks to critical scholarship by Barbara Bair, Ula Taylor, Michelle Mitchell, and others, we know that women participated at all levels in the UNIA and were central to the construction of modern Black nationalism. Garveyite women spoke, taught, organized local meetings, and wrote and edited texts (though always under the threat of male censorship), and in so doing simultaneously challenged and reinforced gender divisions and conventions in the movement. The UNIA's construction of gender in the auxiliaries extended to its conception of Africa under colonial domination, which was symbolically conceived as a benighted woman in need of salvation. *Motherland* replaced the more common nineteenth-century word *fatherland*, as representations of Africa in the Garveyite press ranged from the nursing mother whose children had been torn from her breast by slavery to the shackled woman raped by imperialist masters. Defending Africa from imperialism was tantamount to defending Black womanhood from rape; Black men were called upon to redeem this oppressed and degraded Black woman, our mother of civilization, in a bold, chivalrous act. Rape symbolism was not just a convenient metaphor but carried specific historical resonance in light of the history of sexual terrorism visited upon Black women in slavery and freedom. These themes reappear over and over again in Garveyite songs, such as "The Universal Ethiopian Anthem," "God Bless Our President," and "Legion's Marching Song":

> The Legion here will fight for Africa there,
> We are going to avenge her wrongs,
> We are coming, oh Mother Africa,
> We are four hundred millions strong. . . .
>
> No cracker will dare seduce our sister,
> Or to hang us on a limb,
> And we are not obliged to call him mister,
> Or to skin our lips at him. . . .

Clearly, the UNIA was very conservative when it came to gender. Among other things, it promoted Victorian mores, the patriarchal family, and the idea that women's primary roles centered on caregiving, domesticity, and race building by way of reproduction and education. But in the context of a racist culture that viewed Black women as immoral, licentious, and criminally inclined, or faithful but ignorant members of a servant class, placing

Black women on a pedestal to be exalted and protected radically challenged the status quo. Although the pedestal created its own limitations, both for women's autonomy and independence and for their participation within the leadership of the UNIA, Black women did exercise more power in the Garvey movement than they had in other Pan-Africanist organizations of the day. Structured along the lines of African-American churches, the UNIA elected a "male president" and a slate of male officers along with a "lady president" and women officers who oversaw the female auxiliaries and juvenile division. The Parent Body Leadership, its international body, designated one position for a woman—fourth assistant general president, which was held by Henrietta Vinton Davis, one of the UNIA's leading orators. Women who held these elected and appointed positions were more than tokens; they often used their platforms to challenge the movement's gender conventions. Amy Jacques Garvey, Marcus Garvey's second wife, used her position to write a column in the *Negro World* featuring stories about women in traditionally male professions—physicians, executives, bankers, engineers, etc.—and profiled strong, heroic Black women such as Sojourner Truth and Harriet Tubman. She covered a range of controversial issues, from birth control to women's roles in political movements, and she encouraged women's participation in the public sphere. Although her argument was based partly on the idea that women's special virtue, unique spirituality, could soften "ills of the world," Amy Jacques Garvey was just as quick to describe women as warriors. In a scathing critique of the UNIA's failure to promote more women to important leadership positions, she portrayed some male leaders as cowards who harbored "old-fashioned tyrannical feelings" and predicted that the women "will press on and on until victory is ours. . . . Ethiopia's queens will reign again, and her Amazons protect her shores and people." Likewise, Henrietta Vinton Davis called on women to be prepared for battle like their foremothers in Africa and America: "If our men hesitate, then the women of the race must come forward, they must join the great army of Amazons and follow a Joan of Arc who is willing to be burned at the stake to save her country."

Garveyism continues to exist today, but its heyday was really the 1920s. It was a movement founded in the midst of war, steeled on war metaphors, and practically destroyed by a war waged by the U.S. state and colonial governments throughout the world. Internal conflicts also destabilized the Garvey movement; corruption, theft, and bad investments (not to mention poor political judgments like Marcus Garvey's decision to meet with leaders of the Ku Klux Klan) all contributed to the collapse of the UNIA. Perhaps the outcome was inevitable. After all, the economic philosophy undergirding Garveyism was independent enterprise and entrepreneurship. In this philosophy, industries such as the Black Star Line would not only serve Black people but would also be a source of capital placed entirely in Black hands, wealth for a rising race. The problem was that Marcus Garvey trusted his lieutenants; he didn't believe they would skim wealth off the top or consider their personal desire for wealth above the greater good of the African world.

I doubt that most of Garvey's followers imagined the New Land as an African version of American capitalism, a land of entrepreneurs hawking commodities and opportunities at every turn. Instead, the Black Star Line was less a business venture than the new ark. Africa, or somewhere other than here, marked a new beginning, a beautiful, peaceful, collective life where needs were fulfilled and poverty was a thing of the past. It was not unlike the vision of the promised land radical Jews had hoped Israel would become—a socialist paradise modeled after the kibbutz. Just as the kibbutz draws on ancient ideas of how God intended men and women to live their lives, ancient Africa in the Black imagination continues to be a window on our dreams of the New Land.

Space Is the Place

What does the New Land look like? Singer-songwriter Abbey Lincoln tells us in her 1972 song "Africa," a paean to the continent, the home she had been searching for, the "land of milk and honey." She sings not about a lost past but a hopeful, glorious future; she sings of a deep longing for a place *like* Africa, for it was remembered and experienced as a world that kept us whole. Lincoln's lyrics echo a massive body of literary, visual, musical, and political texts. We read them in the writings of Countee Cullen, Claude McKay, Aimé Césaire, Suzanne Césaire, Leon Damas, Margaret Danner, Margaret Walker, Nicolas Guillén, Sonia Sanchez, Langston Hughes, Jayne Cortez, Paul Robeson, Melvin B. Tolson, Ted Joans, and Carolyn Rodgers. We see them in the paintings and sculptures of Aaron Douglass, Lois Mailou Jones, Sargent Johnson, Charles Alston, Meta Warwick Fuller, Hale Woodruff, Wifredo Lam, Betye Saar, John Biggers, Richmond Barthé, Faith Ringgold, Melvin Edwards, Jeff Donaldson, Camille Billops, and Bill Maxwell. We hear them in the music of Duke Ellington, Randy Weston, Melba Liston, John Coltrane, Dizzy Gillespie, Lee Morgan, Horace Parlan, Pharoah Sanders, Archie Shepp, Sun Ra, Max Roach, Yusef Lateef, Bob Marley, Mutabaruka, Mandrill, X-Clan, Blackstar, Harmony, Poor Righteous Teachers, and Tonton David. And I've barely scratched the surface.* The desire to pack up and leave persisted well into the late twentieth century, although it seems as though the story of Noah's ark from Genesis might have overtook the Book of Exodus as the more common analogy of flight. Increasingly, the ark has taken the form of the modern space ship, and the search for the New Land has become intergalactic. Predictions of the destruction of Earth abound. Genesis, indeed.

For at least a century, a long line of Black intellectuals and religious leaders have contemplated space travel, including the Honorable Elijah Muhammad of the Nation of Islam. One of the most famous, if not the most fascinating, Black proponents of

---

*I had planned to write more about Africa in the imagination of jazz musicians; Africa has not only been a source of musical ideas, but also a utopian dreamscape, a place of return. However, this point has been demonstrated thoroughly and persuasively in Graham Lock's *Blutopia: Visions of the Future and Revisions of the Past in the Work of Sun Ra, Duke Ellington, and Anthony Braxton*, and Norman Weinstein's *A Night in Tunisia*. There isn't much I can say that has not been said by these authors, so I refer you to these works as an extension of the general argument I am making here.

space travel was the Birmingham-born pianist/composer Herman Sonny Blount, better known as Sun Ra. As early as the 1950s, he called his band an Arkestra, and he claimed that he had left this earth only to return. He, too, looked backward to look forward, finding the cosmos by way of ancient Egypt. Critical of racism in America and elsewhere, he promoted a kind of interplanetary emigrationist movement. Dressed in metallic outfits that might best be described as ancient Egyptian space suits, Sun Ra's Arkestra played an advanced form of music that incorporated vocalists, dancers, and electronic instruments long before they became popular. He did not consider his music jazz, nor did he accept the "avant-garde" label. As he once said, "It's more than avant-garde, because the 'avant-garde' refers to, I suppose, advanced earth music. But this is not earth music." At the heart of Sun Ra's vision was the notion of alter/destiny—the idea that through the creation of new myths we have the power to redirect the future. He penned many poems and songs promoting an Alter/destiny, including "Imagination":

> Imagination is a Magic carpet
> Upon which we may soar
> To distant lands and climes
> And even go beyond the moon
> To any planet in the sky
> If we came from
> nowhere here
> Why can't we go somewhere there?

Sun Ra and his Arkestra inspired other Afrofuturists, interstellar fellow travelers, such as George Clinton, founder of Parliament/Funkadelic, Jamaica's Lee Scratch Perry, and Chicago disc jockey "Captain Sky," whose radio shows spoke metaphorically of space travel to bring attention to the conditions of Black people in the United States. Perry and Clinton, in particular, employed the image of the ark as a mode of space travel. Perry, who made dub records charting "the relationship between madness, space/time travel, the Old Testament, and African identity," called his studios The Black Ark, and made records such as *Heart of the Ark, Build the Ark,* and *Black Ark in Dub.* Clinton's ark took the form of the "Mothership," a funky flying saucer designed to take all the party people to a better place.

Not surprisingly, the most visionary strand of hip-hop culture also embraces a politics of escape not averse to interstellar time travel. During hip-hop's infancy, the pioneer Bronx disc jockey Afrika Bambaataa and his various groups—the Jazzy Five, Cosmic Force, and the Soul Sonic Force—embraced the space-age styles as well as the impulse to escape the wretchedness of daily life through dance music. Founder of the Zulu Nation —a politically conscious organization of rappers, break-dancers, graffiti artists, and others associated with 1970s hip-hop culture—Bambaataa is perhaps best known for his hit song "Planet Rock." By the early 1990s, the themes of exodus, the search for paradise, even African redemption became more pronounced in the music of groups such as Poor Righteous Teachers, Arrested Development, Digable Planets, Jungle Brothers, De La Soul, Tribe Called Quest, PM Dawn, and X-Clan, among others. More recently, artists such as Mos Def, Talib Kweli, Dilated Peoples, Afu Ra, Natural Resource, Common, Reflection Eternal, and Dead Prez, among others, have continued to explore some of these themes.

These artists might be described as modern ancients redefining freedom, imagining a communal future (and present) without exploitation; all-natural, African, barefoot, and funky. A product of many influences, from Rastafarianism and the Five-Percent Nation (a youth-oriented Islamic group) to science fiction, some of these groups advocated vegetarianism, natural hair, and a pace of life where humans were the masters of time rather than the other way around. Poor Righteous Teachers, whose notion of "pure poverty" signifies both a knowledge of the condition of Black folk and a position from which to critique forms of oppression, called for the creation of a new utopia within the city by transforming the way people live their lives. Others, like X-Clan, combined a politics of resistance with a politics of escape in songs such as

"Xodus," "Cosmic Ark," and "Arkilogical." In addition to fighting racism in their place of residence, in part by founding their own Black radical political movement called Blackwatch, they sing songs that advocate a return to "the East"—what they imagine as a peaceful, classless, oppression-free Africa. Decked out in beads, leather, ear and nose rings, big walking sticks, and a wild assortment of African garments, the men and women of X-Clan had a startling visual presence. Musically they mixed the sound of African drums with samples from Parliament/Funkadelic. And despite the serious revolutionary rhetoric, X-Clan never lost a sense of humor: Its ark was a pink Cadillac.

Songs by groups such as Digable Planets, PM Dawn, even De La Soul promoted an alternative vision to the violent and artificial realities of urban life. The tragically short-lived Arrested Development (one of the original Southern hip-hop groups, let's not forget) focused much of its music on reconstructing relationships between human beings across lines of color, gender, generation, and spirituality, and of reconnecting Black people to the natural world. These themes are especially pronounced in songs such as "People Everyday," "Mama's Always on Stage," "Children Play with Earth," "Natural," and "Dawn of the Dreads." Their wildly popular 1992 hit "Tennessee," from their debut album *Three Years, Five Months, and Two Days in the Life of . . .* captures the desire for a new space, a place in the countryside away from urban chaos, and yet it is a place with a history of pain and violence that "Speech," the lead rapper, must reckon with. It is God who tells him to "break / outta the country and / into more country":

Where the ghost of
childhood haunts me.
Walk the roads my
forefathers walked,
climbed the trees my
forefathers hung from.
Ask those trees for all
their wisdom,

they tell me my ears are
so young. . . . Home
go back to from
whence you
came. . . . Home.
. . . .
Take me to another place
Take me to another land
Make me forget all that hurts me
Let me understand your plan.

In one sense, "Tennessee" parallels the Exodus story in that God tells the singer to go find salvation, except that the new Israel is situated in Egyptland itself, after the apparent overthrow of the Pharaoh.

Another powerful but little-known example of hip-hop's vision of an earthbound utopia, free of fratricidal violence, full of natural beauty and splendor, is "Sunny Meadowz" by Oakland-based rapper Del tha Funkee Homosapien, which appeared on his 1991 debut album, *I Wish My Brother George Was Here*. That Del was produced by Ice Cube (Del's cousin) and the Lench Mob, known to most hip-hop fans for their notorious gangsta rhymes of mayhem and misogyny, makes "Sunny Meadowz" even more of a curiosity. He opens by declaring war on all the thugs and fake rappers, promising to snatch their gold chains and gold "fronts" (teeth) and return them "to the caves of the Motherland / and ride a rhinoceros back to the other land." Listen to his description of "the meadowz":

> D. E. L., the eighteen-year-old dweller of the meadow,
> It sure in the hell beats living in the ghetto.
> Things are peace and everything's settled
> With a goodnight snooze on a bed of rose petals.
> I wake up in the morning feeling happy and refreshed. . . .

Before the day is over, the singer journeys past earth, reclines on a hippo, writes "scriptures by the old wishing well," and lives a wonderful life where everything is clean and natural. Although he does have a maid in the meadowz, and in his imagination his music keeps him paid, freedom is conceived in the "Sunny Meadowz" not in terms of materialism but as a way of living, a way of being in the world that is at once intensely personal and collective. This is not the image one usually associates with the hip-hop generation, especially at the beginning of the twenty-first century. And yet it is pervasive, especially among some of the young contemporary "spoken-word artists" who are also products of hip-hop culture. Consider the following stanzas by Mariah-dessa Ekere Tallie:

> I want to walk barefoot
> in a place where barefoot has no name
> in a place where soul on Earth
> is natural
> a place where toes in soil
> is common as
> true love
> laughter
> and birth. . . .
>
> I want to walk barefoot
> in cities without streets
> where admiration is a deep silence
> and conversations are replaced by the eloquence of eyes
> barefoot in a place
> where excuses are not enforced in law books
> where there is no law
> only that which is right. . . .

The imagery has changed; even the geography has shifted from Africa to anyplace but where we are now. But the dream of Exodus still lives in those of us not satisfied with the world as we know it. It is not the only dream. There is yet another radical tradition that insists that we can all live together in peace and harmony, but only if we transform society together. For many Black radicals seeking justice, salvation, and freedom, the vision of socialism proved to be especially compelling, even if incomplete.

"THE NEGRO QUESTION": RED DREAMS OF BLACK LIBERATION

Sing a song full of the strife that the dark past has
taught us.
Sing a song full of the hope Communism has
brought us.
Facing a Red! Red! Sun of a new day begun
Let us fight on till victory is won.

—Black Communist revision of the
"Negro National Anthem," ca. 1932

We can spot 'em a mile away. They're at every political forum, demonstration, panel discussion, and cultural event, hawking their papers bearing names with *Socialist* or *Workers* or *International* in the titles, shouting people down, hogging the microphone. They sometimes come with Black, Asian, and Latino comrades, but their whiteness and often their arrogance underscore their visibility in a room full of angry Black folk. They come hard, ready to throw down the gauntlet to the bourgeois nationalists, inviting everyone to join the class struggle, all the while saving their worst invective for their adversaries on the Left. Once at the mic, they don't usually identify themselves until two-thirds into their speech and the requests to "sit yo' ass down" begin to escalate. But we always know who they are, we tolerate their presence for the most part, and some of us even buy their papers and pamphlets. I know I did and still do. My library is overflowing with texts published by International Publishers, Pathfinder Press, and assorted lesser-known revolutionary basement presses. Sometimes you can find as much about Black struggles in the leftist sectarian newspapers and broadsides as in the Nation of Islam's *The Final Call*—certainly much more than in *Ebony*, *Jet*, or *Essence*. Police killings of unarmed African Americans, conflicts in housing projects, Klan activity in North Carolina; you name it, you can find it in the *Revolutionary Worker* or the *Worker's Vanguard*. They even put out the writings of great Black intellectuals in the form of cheap pamphlets. Why go to Barnes and Noble when you can get nicely stapled Xeroxes of Frantz Fanon and Malcolm X and Sojourner Truth for a buck?

They come to Black political events to spread their respective positions and to recruit. And sometimes they succeed. During the mid-1980s, I gave two years of my life as a rank-and-file member of the Communist Workers' Party (CWP), selling *Worker's Viewpoint*, attending study groups, writing internal position papers, and helping organize demonstrations. The CWP was especially attractive because its most visible leaders were Black and Asian American. And being a self-styled intellectual, I liked the fact that CWP members read . . . and read and read. I briefly joined one study group made up almost entirely of working people in South Central Los Angeles, many of whom had earned only a high school diploma and worked full-time. My comrades were far more advanced and rigorous than most of my professors at Cal State Long Beach. They patiently walked me through Mao and modern Chinese history; introduced me to radical Pan-Africanism; critiqued my undigested Afrocentrism; and schooled me on a whole host of issues, from police repression to the relationship between local plant closings and the movement of international capital.

Even if one knows absolutely nothing of the American Left and its history, anyone with a political bone in her body recognizes its deep, unwavering interest in the plight of Black people. We have a century of Black opinion as to why: They're just using Black people to promote their agenda, or they're agent provocateurs sent in by the FBI. The less conspiracy-prone chalk it up to alienated white youths rebelling against their parental culture. Then there were those who regarded some on the Left as genuine revolutionaries willing to grapple with issues that established Negro leaders tend to ignore. Committed Black support for left-wing movements is hard to fathom after a half-century of cold war, in which the anti-Communist confessionals of Richard Wright, Ralph Ellison, George Padmore, Margaret Walker, and a host of others stood in for Black opinion. Although most of these authors chastise the communists for *not being radical enough*, they are usually read through an interpretive frame that can see Black people only as passive victims of communist conspiracy.

Of course, it is impossible to generalize about the American Left and its intentions because it has never been a singular, unified movement. Hundreds of sectarian parties have fought each other over the correct line on China or Albania, the "Woman Question," skilled versus unskilled workers, united front versus proletarian revolt, ad infinitum. Toward the top of the pyramid of political issues has been the ever-present "Negro Question." If there is one thing all the factions of the twentieth-century American Left share, it is the political idea that Black people reside in the eye of the hurricane of class struggle. The American Left, after all, was born in a society where slavery and free labor coexisted, and only skin color and heritage determined who lived in bondage and who did not. This is why the nascent Left in the United States understood the problem posed by racial divisions as the Negro Question, for these African descendants stood at the fulcrum of the nation's racial identity and political economy.

All Marxist-identified groups proposed their own answers to the Negro Question, and the best of them realized that this was no subsidiary interrogation. As one might expect, the best answers generally came from the Negroes themselves, the very objects of the question who even today are rarely given their due as radical theorists. On the one hand, their answers offered profound insights into the political economy and cultures of the United States and the West more generally—answers that could have pushed the American Left in entirely new directions. On the other hand, the very burden of racism, nourished in a capitalist economy built on the foundation of slavery and Jim Crow, weighed like a nightmare on the brains of every generation of white working people seeking emancipation. Remember that much of their identity was bound up with *not* being a "nigger," a savage, an uncivilized "beast of burden" presumably easily controlled by their capitalist enemies. The white Left's inability to understand, let alone answer, the Negro Question turned out to be its Achilles' heel. The tragedy for America, perhaps, is that these committed revolutionaries set out to save the Negro when they needed Black folk to save them.

> Labor cannot emancipate itself in the white skin where in the Black it is branded.
>
> —*Karl Marx*, Capital

The Marxist Left was officially born in 1848 with the formation of the International Workingmen's Association, or the First International. A product of the revolutions that rocked Europe that year, the ideals of the First International were carried into America by newspapers and German immigrants who had participated in the upheaval that compelled Karl Marx and Friedrich Engels to write a lengthy pamphlet called *The Communist Manifesto.* We tend to picture the 1848 revolutions and the birth of American Marxism as the story of white men in the trenches, red flag unfurled in the name of bearded and proud skilled workers. But the "colored" world remained a haunting specter in 1848: The revolution in France resulted in the abolition of slavery in its colonies, forty-four years after African descendants threw them out of Haiti and ended French slavery and colonialism there by combat. The British had abolished slavery fourteen years earlier and were still wrestling with their Negro Question: how to turn all this ex-property into willing and docile workers for Britannia. On home soil, the Negro stood at the center of U.S. politics. The American state had just taken northern Mexico by force in its quest to rule North America from coast to coast, and the burning question of the day was whether slavery would be allowed into the newly acquired Western territories.

Most of the newly arrived German Marxists knew they couldn't run away from slavery. And as natural as nigger hating was to Jacksonian democracy, the "'48ers" had not been here long enough to absorb all the lessons of American whiteness. Their communist clubs, formed in 1857—the year the Supreme Court decided in *Dred Scott v. Sanford* that Black people were not citizens of the United States—were among the few political associations in the country that required members to respect all people, regardless of race or sex, as equals. Besides, Marx and Engels' *The Communist Manifesto* recognized the color line and its role in maintaining colonialism. Even more remarkable was Marx's understanding of what the West's alleged civilizing mission was all about. In the August 8, 1853, issue of the New York *Daily Tribune*, Marx wryly pointed out, "The profound hypocrisy and inherent barbarism of bourgeois civilization lies unveiled before our eyes, turning from its home, where it assumes respectable forms, to the colonies, where it goes naked."

That barbarism rested with the purveyors of "civilization" rather than their colonial subjects went uninterrogated by white socialists (though the idea was taken up by Black radical intellectuals in the aftermath of fascism). In fact, very few members of the growing socialist movement in the United States were willing to support racial equality, especially after the Civil War destroyed the system of chattel slavery for good. White workers looked upon freed Black labor as competition willing to accept lower wages and horrible working conditions. The Socialist Labor Party (SLP), formed after the collapse of the First International in 1872, decided to organize Black workers in order to solve the problem of competition. But SLP leaders believed, as did their predecessors in the First International, that once the socialist revolution came, all race problems would disappear. SLP leader Daniel DeLeon put it succinctly: "There was no such thing as a race or 'Negro question' . . . there was only a social, a labor question . . . so far as the Socialist and labor movements were concerned."

It was an odd position to take, especially by the 1890s when lynching increased, racial segregation became law, and African-American citizens who worked so hard for the Republican Party in the days of Reconstruction were suddenly disfranchised. Of course, Black people fought back, joining unions of farmers and workers, forming armed self-defense organizations, and building religious, fraternal, educational, and political institutions that ultimately became sources of power and inspiration for the stony road ahead. A handful found hope and possibility in an interracial socialist movement. In 1901, the Socialist Party of America, the crown jewel of the Second International, was launched after the demise of the SLP. The Second International's social democratic politics proved more broad based and popular than the socialism of its predecessors, but its approach to the Negro Question remained unchanged: Racism was merely a feature of capitalism — kill the latter and the former would wither away.

The socialists limited the Negro Question largely to the Black male proletariat, leaving the struggles of Black women out of the discourse altogether. Although August Bebel's *Women under Socialism* provided a radical framework for understanding women's oppression, the Woman Question was restricted to whites only. Socialists were silent on the disproportionate numbers of Black women in the labor force, the racist character of the early birth control and suffrage movements, stereotypes of Black women's sexuality, or the ways in which race hindered women's solidarity. In fact, the most prominent Black woman radical of the late nineteenth century, Lucy Parsons, wrote eloquently about the oppression of women and the working class, but ignored race. Parsons was a member of the socialist-oriented Workingmen's Party who was also attracted to anarchism for its emphasis on cooperative organization of production without profit, eliminating the state, and direct action. She published articles in the revolutionary socialist press about lynching and the Woman Question, but she never put the stories together. Lynching, in her view, was merely a class question; a Black man is lynched in Mississippi because "he is poorer as a class than his white wage-slave brother of the North." Thus, following the classic socialist logic, racial violence would disappear once capitalism was overthrown. And the same went for women. In 1891 she published a series of articles on rape, divorce, and marriage for *Freedom: A Revolutionary Anarchist-Communist Monthly*, which argued that women's oppression was merely a function of capitalism. Parsons believed that sexism, like racism, would disappear with the construction of a socialist society.

I do not want to take anything away from Parsons, for she was one of the brightest lights in the history of revolutionary socialism, but she operated strictly within the confines of nineteenth-century Western socialist thought. Outside these left circles, however, there were radical Black women whose own analysis of America connected the dots between women's oppression and the color line. Ida B. Wells-Barnett was not a socialist, but she linked lynching, rape, and the maintenance of the color line to the oppression of all women. A year after Parsons wrote her series in *Freedom*, Wells-Barnett published a major study of lynching that exposed how the myth of the Black rapist allowed Southern white males to demand subordination and deference from white women in exchange for their "protection." So-called chivalry, in other words, was about the protection of white women as property in order to maintain the purity of the race. According to the ideology of white supremacy, a white woman desiring a nonwhite man was inconceivable, so any such encounter was presumed to be rape. On the flip side, all sexual encounters between white men and Black women were not only presumed to be consensual but initiated by the Black woman. The virginal white woman and Black rapist dialectic also produced the myth of the promiscuous Black woman. By defending the racial integrity of Black manhood (i.e., destroying the Black-man-as-rapist myth), Wells-Barnett simultaneously affirmed the virtue of Black womanhood and the independence of white womanhood.

By the early part of the twentieth century, a few independent Black intellectuals began to gravitate toward the socialist movement and brought a distinctive radical analysis with them. The prodigious W. E. B. Du Bois spent a year (1911–12) in the Socialist Party of America (SPA) and had worked closely with white socialists who had joined him as founding members of the National Association for the Advancement of Colored People (NAACP) in 1910. Yet before his association with the SPA, Du Bois had helped found the radical, all-black Niagara Movement, and in that context began to analyze how race and class worked together to sustain capitalism, imperialism, and racism in the modern world. As early as 1906, Du Bois argued that the imposition of the color line on a world scale, whether in the form of Jim Crow or colonial rule, "transferred the reign of commercial privilege and extraordinary profit from the exploitation of the European working class to the exploitation of backward races under the political domination of Europe." The "colored" laborer, therefore, was the key to socialism's success, and even before joining the party Du Bois warned that Marx's vision could not be realized without the Black worker, and that the Black worker would not come unless the socialists launched a full assault on racism. The racism of white workers, he argued, blinded them to their class interests; rather than see workers of color as allies, they treated them as enemies to be fought, feared, and Jim Crowed. Dissatisfied with the Socialists' response and seeing some potential in Woodrow Wilson's presidential campaign, Du Bois left the party.

Harlem Socialist Hubert Harrison went even further than Du Bois in his criticisms of the SPA. He not only insisted that his party make antiracism and the organization of Black workers a top priority, but he also supported Black nationalism and the development of autonomous Black institutions. He formed the Colored Socialist Club in 1911 and remained a stalwart critic of the SPA's position (or lack thereof) on the Negro Question until his expulsion in 1914. With the outbreak of World War I, the implications of colonialism and the global color line for the working-class movement became all the more apparent to both Harrison and Du

Bois. As socialists outside the socialist movement, they watched in horror as the white working class in Europe and the United States embraced nationalism, militarism, and imperialism. In Du Bois's words, they were "practically invited to share in this new exploitation, and particularly were flattered by popular appeals to their inherent superiority to 'Dagoes,' 'Chinks,' 'Japs,' and 'Niggers.'" Nevertheless, Du Bois believed that the fight to save democracy was so important that he called on Black folk to "close ranks" in support of the war, despite its clear imperialist motives. Harrison was not interested in détente. Echoing Du Bois's characterization of World War I as a conflict over "the lands and destinies of the colored majority in Asia, Africa, and the islands of the sea," Harrison simultaneously opposed the war and promoted a worldwide rebellion against all the Western colonizing nations. By the war's end, rebellion was everywhere, even in Harlem.

> Don't mind being called "Bolsheviki" by the same people who called you "nigger."
>
> —Unsigned comment in *The Crusader*, June 1920

The dream of international working-class solidarity crumbled on the battlefield, where the proletarians of Europe and America traded in their red flags for the flags of their respective nations. The exception was some of the peasants and workers in Russia, who were simply too poor and frustrated to fight for their ruling classes. Instead, they launched a revolution and backed Lenin and the Bolshevik Party, which eventually seized power in 1917 and pulled out of the "war to end all wars." The Bolsheviks established a Third International and gave birth to the worldwide Communist movement. For Black folk looking for radical alternatives to American socialism, Lenin turned out to be something of a friend. Despite his distance from American soil, he took a special interest in Black people, in part because most Russian workers and peasants were also divided and oppressed by nationality and ethnicity.

If the Third International, or the Comintern, proved more sympathetic and sensitive to the racial nature of American class struggle, it is largely because Black folk made it so. The momentary crisis of "Western civilization" caused by the chaos of war, worker rebellions, anticolonial uprisings, postwar racial violence, and talk of "self-determination for oppressed nations" contributed to the dramatic explosion of the Garvey movement and a new generation of "New Negroes" advocating a radical fusion of socialism and "race politics." In 1917, Socialists A. Philip Randolph and Chandler Owen launched the *Messenger,* a new magazine dedicated to radical socialism and Black freedom. Its essays and poetry graphically portrayed racist violence and Black resistance. Randolph and Owen also published editorials supporting Irish nationalism, women's suffrage, and the Russian Revolution, which they initially called "the greatest achievement of the twentieth century."

A year later, a new organization arrived on the Left bloc calling themselves the African Blood Brotherhood (ABB). A secret underground organization founded by the Caribbean-born editor Cyril Briggs, the ABB published *The Crusader*—originally the organ of the nationalistic Hamitic League of the World. Its leaders might be best described as militant Black-nationalist Marxists; they advocated socialism but the heart of their agenda was armed self-defense against lynching, universal suffrage, equal rights for Blacks, and the immediate end to segregation. Some, like W. A. Domingo, worked for both the socialists and the Garvey movement. Although a few women such as Grace Campbell and Bertha de Basco held important posts, the ABB presented its membership as Black Bolsheviks and manly redeemers of the race willing to defend their communities to the death. *The Crusader* was imbued with a martial spirit, thus echoing the Garveyite *Negro World* and its constant appeals to militarism and manhood redemption. Moreover, they criticized President Woodrow Wilson for not applying the concept of self-determination to Africa, and during the "red summer" of 1919 when angry white mobs attacked Black communities in several cities, founder Cyril Briggs demanded "government of the Negro, by the Negro and for the Negro." The ABB was a unique experiment in Black Marxist organization; ABB leaders had secretly joined the Workers (Communist) Party very soon after the Brotherhood was founded.

These New Negro radicals challenged traditional socialist logic by insisting that struggles for Black rights were inherently revolutionary. But the newly formed (and sharply divided) American Communist movement wasn't down with the program. Like the Socialists before them, the Workers Party initially believed that "the interests of the Negro worker are identical with those of the white" and that Black nationalism was "a weapon of reaction for the defeat and further enslavement of both [blacks] and their white brother workers." Comintern officials, however, sided with the other "brothers." Even before the Bolshevik victory, Lenin had begun to think of a strategy for dealing with "national minorities" in the event of a successful socialist revolution in Russia—a multinational creation of czarist imperialism. He proposed a union of socialist republics that gave nations within this union the right to secede. No matter how this might have worked in practice, in theory Lenin was saying that all nations had a right to self-determination, and that the working class was not just a conglomeration of atomized proletarians but possessed national identities. After the war, Lenin expanded his theses to include the colonies, which he regarded as oppressed nations. In 1920, with the assistance of Indian Communist M. N. Roy, Lenin drafted his famous "Theses on the National and Colonial Questions," insisting that the "communist parties give direct support to the revolutionary movements among the dependent nations and those without equal rights (e.g., Ireland, and among American Negroes), and in the colonies."

Lenin's injunction shocked the U.S. Communist movement and invited America's Black Bolsheviks to speak with authority. After a half-century of being seen and not heard in national leadership circles, Black radicals found a podium and an audience in the new headquarters of international Communism. One of the most important figures to take advantage of the Soviet bully pulpit was Claude McKay, the Jamaican-born writer of the Harlem Renaissance whose poem "If We Must Die" became the unofficial anthem of the New Negro movement. Thanks to the groundbreaking scholarship of William Maxwell and Winston James, McKay's role in the formation of Comintern policy has been recognized as larger than previously thought. He made his way to the Soviet Union in 1922, just in time to be an unofficial delegate to the Fourth World Congress of the Comintern. The Soviets were so fascinated with Negroes that he and the Communists' official Black delegate, Otto Huiswoud, were treated like celebrities. When McKay addressed the Congress, he put the question of race front and center, criticizing the American Communist Party and the labor movement for their racism and warning that unless the Left challenged white supremacy, the ruling classes would continue to use disaffected Black workers as a foil against the revolutionary movement. In the end, McKay's point was clear: The Negro stood at the fulcrum of class struggle; there could be no successful working-class movement without Black workers at the center. Otto Huiswoud also addressed the Congress, emphasizing the incredible racism Black workers confronted back home in the South and the role that Garveyism played as a force against imperialism worldwide. The Comintern responded immediately, forming a Negro Commission and committing resources to recruiting Black cadres and supporting Black liberation on a global scale.

Comintern officials were so impressed with McKay's speech that they asked him to expand it into a small book, which was published in Russia under the title *Negry v Amerike* (1923) and eventually translated as *The Negroes in America*. This little book profoundly shaped Comintern policy on the Negro Question, offering a revisionist approach to Marxism, the implications of which we have yet to fully comprehend. Drawing on his observations as well as the writings of other Harlem radicals, such as Hubert Harrison and W. A. Domingo, McKay argued that race and slavery were the heart and soul of the nation, repeating his point that only a commitment to Black freedom could ensure socialism's success in the United States. For McKay, a commitment to Black freedom also meant support for self-organization and self-determination. Rather than attack Black nationalist movements for not being "class conscious," McKay called on the Left to support them. Why? Because the overwhelming racism made it difficult for Black folk to think like a class; instead, they saw the world through colored glasses. He wryly observed, "the Negro in America is not permitted for one minute to forget his color, his skin, his race."

Delving into the psychology of race, class, and sexuality, McKay's analysis went much further than even his new friends in the Comintern dared to go. In a chapter titled "Sex and Economics," he concluded that the viciousness of white racism, which cut across class lines, could be partially explained by the white proletariat's "unusual neurotic fascination with the naked body and sexual organs of Negroes." Although this idea was underdeveloped, McKay hit on something traditional Marxism was ill equipped to deal with: the role of sex in the racial economy of the nation. McKay even resuscitated Ida B. Wells-Barnett's analysis of lynching and chivalry, arguing that the myth of the Black rapist oppressed not only the entire Black community but white women as well: "The white man who parades his chivalrous views of a woman . . . says to a white woman, 'You are under my protection and I can not trust you not to have relations with a colored man.' Thus, the white man directly confesses the white woman to be weak, and immoral in sexual conduct in her relations with a Negro man." In the end, he placed much of the responsibility on feminism to challenge racism directly, to challenge the Black rapist myth and to defend women's virtue if they chose to have relations with Black men.

McKay turned out to be much too critical for the American Communists and they soon parted company. And no matter how many resolutions were passed in Moscow in 1922, American Communist leaders were reluctant to go along with the program and generally distrusted Marcus Garvey and his appeals to race pride.

They even foolishly attempted to take over the UNIA! When that didn't work, the Communists (now the CPUSA) founded their own Black organizations—first, the short-lived American Negro Labor Congress (ANLC) in 1925, and later the League of Struggle for Negro Rights in 1930, headed by none other than Langston Hughes. In 1928, once again as a result of Black initiatives, the Comintern adopted its most radical position to date on the Negro Question. Promoted by Harry Haywood (née Haywood Hall), the Nebraska-born Black Communist who had come through the ranks of the ABB, and South African Communist James LaGuma, the Comintern passed a resolution recognizing Negroes in the "black belt" counties of the American South as an oppressed nation. As a nation, like the Lithuanians or Georgians of the old Russian empire, they had a right to self-determination. They could secede if they wanted, perhaps even form a Negro Soviet Socialist Republic, but they were not encouraged to do so. The resolution, not surprisingly, met fierce opposition from white, and some Black, party leaders, but for several Black Communists it confirmed what they had long believed: African Americans had their own unique revolutionary tradition and their interests were not identical to those of white workers.

> The Negro is nationalist to his heart and is perfectly right to be so.
>
> —C. L. R. James, "Letter to Constance Webb," 1945

The new slogan did not persuade Black Communists to attempt to seize Mississippi and secede from the United States, nor did it bring Black folk to the Party in droves. Those who did join were attracted to the CPUSA's fight for the concrete economic needs of the unemployed and working poor, its militant opposition to racism, its vigorous courtroom battles on behalf of the "Scottsboro Boys" (nine young Black men falsely accused of raping two white women in Alabama), and its active support and promotion of Black arts and culture. Nevertheless, "self-determination" did create an opening for African Americans to promote race politics in spite of the Party's formal opposition to "Negro nationalism." In 1929 the Party launched the *Liberator* under the editorship of Cyril Briggs. Like the *Crusader* before it, the *Liberator* nurtured something of a Black nationalist literary movement. Ironically, Stalin's mechanical definition of a nation, which embraced a "community of culture" as a central concept, reinforced the modern nationalist idea that the basis of nationhood was a coherent culture. Independently of Stalin, however, the proponents of Negritude were also searching for that essential Negro or African culture that could lay the basis for Pan-African identity. Stalin's notion of a community of culture merely provided a Marxist justification for Black Communists to join the search for the roots of a national Negro culture. As William L. Patterson, the outstanding attorney and Harlem Renaissance supporter turned Communist, wrote in 1933, the African-American nation was bound by a common culture: "The 'spirituals,' the jazz, their religious practices, a growing literature, descriptive of their environment, all of these are forms of cultural expression. . . . Are these not the prerequisites for nationhood?"

The Central Committee of the CPUSA was not interested in Patterson's question, nor was it promoting nationhood for Black people, or for anyone for that matter. By 1935, the self-determination slogan was abandoned in order to build a "popular front" against fascism. Even the Comintern bracketed the Negro Question and pushed its American cadre to build alliances with liberals and mainstream labor leaders. Yet the power of the idea lingered precisely in the cultural realm Patterson was addressing. In 1937, Richard Wright, then the Communist Party's Black literary giant, published his infamous "Blueprint for Negro Writing," in which he observed that "the Negro has a folklore which embodies the memories and hopes of his struggle for freedom." Even before Wright's proclamations, Communists of all colors promoted Black folk culture as implicitly rebellious, if not the true expression of an oppressed nation.

During the Popular Front, the Party's view of Black culture shifted even further, embracing a broad range of Black art and artists as not only inherently progressive but also profoundly American. Leftist critics, for example, had long promoted the idea that jazz represented the most profoundly democratizing culture the nation possessed—an argument we now associate with ex-Communist Ralph Ellison. Jazz permeated Communist Party events during the 1930s, and some of the first serious jazz critics got their start writing for the *Daily Worker* and other Communist publications. The Communist press became one of the biggest promoters of Black theater, music, dance, and the plastic arts. As Black artists began working for the federally funded Works Progress Administration in the late 1930s, a dynamic Black woman named Louise Thompson became the Party's critical liaison linking Black popular culture and Harlem's literati with Communist Popular Front politics. In 1938, for example, she and Langston Hughes organized the Harlem Suitcase Theatre, sponsored by the International Workers Order, which produced works by Black playwrights. The Party's high visibility in antiracist causes attracted more than a few bigwigs in the Black entertainment world. Count Basie, W. C. Handy, Lena Horne, Andy Razaf, and Canada Lee performed at Communist-organized benefits, and the circle of Black writers orbiting the Communist Left included Ralph Ellison, Sterling Brown, Chester Himes, Countee Cullen, Margaret Walker, Owen Dodson, Arna Bontemps, Frank Marshall Davis, Robert Hayden, Melvin Tolson, Dorothy West, the pioneering cartoonist Ollie Harrington, as well as the usual suspects, Hughes, McKay, and Wright.

One can certainly argue that the Communists fetishized Black culture, but their reasons differed from the corporate entities who had taken Langston's "blues and gone." Black radicals forced the white Left to see and hear differently, and they and a few white rebels heard in the sounds and movements and writings the birth of a utopian future rising out of the abyss of racism and oppression. In this regard, no one played a more pivotal role in demonstrating the revolutionary potential of African-American expressive culture than Paul Robeson.

Son of a prominent minister, all-American athlete, honors graduate of Rutgers University, star of stage and screen, and a brilliant concert singer to boot, Paul Robeson was on the road to becoming the richest, most famous Negro of the century. But in 1927 he and his wife, Eslanda Goode, moved to London and during their twelve-year sojourn were radicalized by their face-to-face confrontation with European fascism as well as by their meetings with British socialists and future leaders of the African, Caribbean, and Asian anticolonial movements. Robeson performed benefit concerts for British trade unions and learned firsthand of the wretched conditions of the English working class. He and Eslanda also toured the Soviet Union, whose people and history he came to admire even if he harbored private doubts about Stalin and his policies. The fact that the Soviet Union offered material support to anticolonial movements and backed democratically elected republican Spain against General Franco's fascist-backed armies further endeared Robeson to the Soviet Union and the Left more broadly.

This is only part of the story, for Robeson's radicalization cannot be summed up as simply a leftward migration into the orbit of international communism. As historian Sterling Stuckey convincingly argues, Robeson was drawn simultaneously toward a radical Black cultural nationalism. A product of the American racial order, Robeson needed no political lessons about racism or the plight of his people back home. Nor did he need to be lectured on the resilient spirit of Black people and the culture they had created to survive slavery and Jim Crow. What he did come to terms with in Europe was the deep cultural bonds between Africa and its diaspora. He and Eslanda enrolled in Ph.D. programs at the London School of Oriental Studies to study African culture (only Eslanda would complete her doctorate in anthropology). Robeson studied several African languages and planned to undertake a thorough study of West African folk song and folklore. As he wrote in a 1934 article in the London *Spectator*, his goal was to introduce the world to the beauty, power, and dignity of African and African-descended art. "I hope to be able to interpret this original and unpolluted [African] folk song to the Western world and I am convinced that there lies a wealth of uncharted musical material in that source which I hope, one day, will evoke the response in English and American audiences which my Negro spirituals have done."

He even understood himself to be "African," both culturally and spiritually, and he saw in Black cultural values the foundation for a new vision of a new society, one that could emancipate not only Black people but the entire West. Indeed, Robeson's cultural analysis became the basis for a radical revision of the Communist Party's idea of self-determination.* Even as he became more deeply attached to the CPUSA, he supported an independent Black radical movement grounded in the cultures and beliefs of the folk. As he wrote in his classic book, *Here I Stand* (1958),

> The power of spirit that our people have is intangible, but it is a great force that must be unleashed in the struggles of today. A spirit of steadfast determination, exaltation in the face of trials — it is the very soul of our people that has been formed through all the long and weary years of our march toward freedom. . . . That spirit lives in our people's songs — in the sublime grandeur of "Deep River," in the driving power of "Jacob's Ladder," in the militancy of "Joshua Fit the Battle of Jericho," and in the poignant beauty of all our spirituals.

That spirit, he insisted, was the key to the freedom of all humanity, particularly in the United States. Historically, Black people had expanded democracy and rescued the United States from undemocratic forces, and Black people had served as something of the moral conscience of the nation.

During the 1940s and 1950s, as the FBI, Senator Joe McCarthy, and various anti-Communist "witch hunters" dogged Robeson's every step, he reminded his audiences of "the important role which my people can and must play in helping to save America

---

*The story of the Party's shifting positions is too complicated to go into here. It suffices to say that in 1946 and 1947, when the Party experienced its own internal crisis with the expulsion of General Secretary Earl Browder and his replacement with William Z. Foster, the "black belt" slogan was resurrected as a reassertion of the extreme left wing, but it was hardly promoted, and dropped out as quickly as it had been readopted.

and the peoples of the world from annihilation and enslavement." He told Black labor leaders in Chicago: "In the Civil War, hundreds of thousands of Negro soldiers who took up arms in the Union cause won, not only their own freedom—the freedom of the Negro people—but, by smashing the institution of slave labor, provided the basis for the development of trade unions of free working men in America." In other words, Black self-determination was not simply a matter of guaranteeing democratic rights or removing the barriers to Black political and economic power, nor was it a matter of creating a nation wherever Black people found themselves to be an oppressed majority. It was about promoting and supporting an independent Black radical movement that could lead the way to a revitalized international working-class assault on racial capitalism. Of course, Robeson was simply refining a version of an ongoing idea promoted by the ABB, Claude McKay, Richard Wright, and others we've met. It was an idea echoed, too, by Robeson's friend, the Trinidadian Marxist and radical Pan-Africanist C. L. R. James, despite the fact that he aligned himself with the Communist Party's arch enemies, followers of Leon Trotsky. In 1948, James wrote,

> This independent Negro movement is able to intervene with terrific force upon the general social and political life of the nation, despite the fact that it is waged under the banner of democratic rights, and is not led necessarily either by the organized labor movement or the Marxist party. We say . . . that it is able to exercise a powerful influence upon the revolutionary proletariat, that it has got a great contribution to make to the development of the proletariat in the United States, and that it is in itself a constituent part of the struggle for socialism. In this way we challenge directly any attempt to subordinate or to push to the rear the social and political significance of the independent Negro struggle for democratic rights.

Even within the orbit of the Communist Party, Robeson found a few like-minded comrades who believed that an independent Black movement was decisive for the success of a socialist revolution. Trinidadian-born Communist Claudia Jones took this idea further than everyone else, insisting that Black women were a decisive group because they experienced capitalist oppression as Negroes, women, and workers, and thus their emancipation would result in the emancipation of all women and men. In her 1946 article, "An End to the Neglect of the Problems of Negro Women," she argued, "The Negro question in the United States is *prior* to, and not equal to, the woman question; that only to the extent that we fight all chauvinist expressions and actions as regards the Negro people and fight for full equality of the Negro people, can women as a whole advance their struggle for equal rights." In other words, the overthrow of class and gender oppression depended on the abolition of racism. For the women's movement to be successful, she insisted, antiracism must be at the forefront of its agenda and Black women must play leadership roles.

Whereas for Claudia Jones the structural position of Black people—Black women in particular—in the political economy placed them in the vanguard of the revolution, for Paul Robeson it was their culture that gave the Black movement its special insight and character. In many ways, Robeson drew on a very old biblical tradition of "choseness" that stretched from nineteenth-century Black nationalists such as David Walker to W. E. B. Du Bois to his later contemporaries like Dr. Martin Luther King Jr. Black folk were the chosen people, the soul of the nation whose redemptive suffering would bring salvation. But Robeson's talk of Black spirit or even Negro spirituals was not necessarily rooted in the Bible. Rather, it came from his understanding of African culture, the peculiar history of enslavement in the modern world, and most importantly, a critique of Western civilization. In a 1936 article titled "Primitives," Robeson took the Enlightenment tradition to task in an implicit attempt to explain the rise of fascism, which he saw as proof of "civilization's" utter failure. "A blind groping after Rationality," he mused, "resulted in an incalculable loss in pure Spirituality. Mankind placed a sudden dependence on the part of his mind that was brain, intellect, to the discountenance of that part that was sheer evolved instinct and intuition; we grasped at the shadow and lost the substance . . . and now we are not altogether clear what the substance was." The answer, he believed, was to make art and spirituality primary to social life, as it had been in the ancient world and as it continued to be in the folk cultures of Africa. He was convinced that American Negroes were in a unique position to make this happen, not only because they embodied many of the core cultural values of their ancestral homeland but because they represented the most self-conscious force living in the belly of the beast. They knew the West and its culture; they knew modernity and its limitations; their dreams of freedom could overturn a market-driven, warmongering rationality and give birth to a new humanity.

Again, Robeson was not alone in his critical assessment of Western civilization, especially in the aftermath of World War II. The horrors of Nazi genocide forced all thinking people, including Black intellectuals all over the African diaspora, to take stock. As Cedric Robinson argued, a group of radical Black intellectuals including W. E. B. Du Bois, Aimé Césaire, C. L. R. James, George Padmore, Ralph Bunche, Oliver Cox, and others, understood fascism not as some aberration from the march of progress, an unexpected right-wing turn, but a logical development of Western civilization itself. They viewed fascism as a blood relative of slavery and imperialism, global systems rooted not only in capitalist political economy but in racist ideologies that were already in place at the dawn of modernity. Du Bois made some of the clearest statements to this effect: "I knew that Hitler and Mussolini were fighting communism, and using race prejudice to make some white people rich and all colored people poor. But it was not until later that I realized that the colonialism of Great Britain and France had exactly the same object and methods as the fascists and the Nazis were trying clearly to use." In *The World and Africa* (1947), he writes: "There was no Nazi atrocity—concentration camps, wholesale maiming and murder, defilement of women or ghastly blasphemy of childhood—which Christian civilization or Europe had not long been practicing against colored folk in all parts of the world in the name of and for the defense of a Superior Race born to rule the world."

In other words, the chickens had come home to roost. The Holocaust that resulted in the murder of six million Jews was merely the most vicious manifestation of Europe's colonial policy. Although Jews did not occupy the same position held by colonial subjects in Africa, Asia, and the Caribbean, Du Bois and Robeson recognized that this act of mass genocide was not a "white-on-white crime." They understood anti-Semitism as a racist ideology and knew that it was embedded deep in the fabric of Western culture. Unfortunately, neither Du Bois nor Robeson nor anyone else with a continuing commitment to the Left had anything to say about Stalin's atrocities — the political assassinations, the gulags, the Soviet state's hidden war against political dissidents and Russian Jews. Although it is not clear who knew what before Khruschev unveiled these crimes to the world in 1956, the silence that followed these revelations is one of the great tragedies in the history of the Communist movement.

The other great tragedy, for the Black freedom movement in particular, was the silencing of radical leadership. Robeson, Du Bois, and Claudia Jones were among the many victims of state-sponsored anticommunist witch hunts. Jones was imprisoned in 1951 under the Smith Act, which essentially outlawed membership in the Communist Party. After serving four years, she was deported to England, where she spent the remaining ten years of her life as a political activist. The federal government revoked Du Bois's and Robeson's passports and the FBI tapped their telephones and dogged every step they took. Du Bois was arrested in 1951 for his involvement in the Peace Information Center and charged with treason and conspiracy, though the charges were subsequently dropped. Dr. Du Bois was deemed such a significant threat to national security that federal marshals handcuffed him; he was just a few days shy of his eighty-third birthday. Established Black middle-class leadership also turned a cold shoulder to both men, criticizing Robeson in particular for suggesting that Black people ought to struggle for peace rather than wage war on the Soviet Union. In an effort to offset Robeson's criticisms of U.S. foreign policy and discredit him, the House Un-American

Activities Committee (HUAC) brought out Jackie Robinson, the first Black player in major league baseball, to testify against Robeson. Although Robeson spoke eloquently on behalf of civil liberties and African-American rights before HUAC, he was labeled a "Red" by the state, and the label stuck. This event marked the beginning of his downward descent; by the end of the 1950s, Robeson's career had been pretty much destroyed. He had trouble securing bookings (especially during the period when his passport was revoked), fell into a deep depression, and eventually suffered a nervous breakdown.

Cold War repression did not stop the movement, however. Inside the belly of the beast, Black radical leaders began working actively in support of anticolonial movements. Robeson, Du Bois, Alphaeus Hunton, Shirley Graham (soon to be Du Bois's wife), William L. Patterson and Louise Thompson Patterson, writer-playwright Lorraine Hansberry, and others began actively backing anticolonial movements in Africa and the Caribbean. Du Bois and Robeson headed the Council on African Affairs to promote and support the African nationalist movement. They appealed to the UN to demand independence for the colonies, including South-West Africa, which had been placed under South Africa's "trusteeship." And they brought the international struggle home. In 1951, they submitted a petition to the UN, with support from the Civil Rights Congress—a left-leaning national civil-rights organization akin to the old International Labor Defense and led by William L. Patterson—charging the United States with genocide and violation of human rights. They cited, among other things, the continuation of racist terror in the South, segregation, joblessness, poverty, police violence, and disfranchisement. The petition did not get very far, however; American representatives used their influence to block the Human Rights Commission from even discussing it.*

*This was not the first such petition submitted to the UN. In 1946, as soon as the UN established its Commission on Human Rights, W. E. B. Du Bois, on behalf of the National Negro Congress, presented a petition on behalf of the entire Black world seeking "relief from oppression." It emphasized issues like poverty, schooling, housing conditions, high Black mortality rates, and segregation, and it linked the conditions

But the efforts of the Civil Rights Congress were just the beginning. After 1954, the Southern freedom movement rose with
such force that it shocked white supremacists and liberals alike.
The streets of Montgomery, Birmingham, New Orleans, and
even Jackson, Mississippi, began to look like Johannesburg and
Durban, South Africa. Nothing could stop these movements, not
even the jailing and deportation of suspected Communists, the
outlawing of the NAACP, or the general suspension of civil liberties. Nevertheless, it was clear to all that the next wave of Black
radicalism would not be the same. Decolonization and the Chinese Revolution meant that there were new kids on the historical
bloc, new sources for political imagination, and new prospects
for freedom.

---

of African Americans with that of the colonized world. Less than a year later, the
NAACP submitted its own petition. Du Bois was also central to this effort: submit-
ted on behalf of fourteen million Black people, the petition was endorsed by Black
organizations and leaders from around the world. The 155-page document, titled "An
Appeal to the World: A Statement on the Denial of Human Rights to Minorities in the
Case of Citizens of Negro Descent in the United States of America and an Appeal to
the United States for Redress," was a detailed list of grievances against the U.S. state.
See Azza Salama Layton, *International Politics and Civil Rights Policies in the United
States, 1941–1960* (Cambridge: Cambridge University Press, 2000), 48–58. See also
William L. Patterson, *The Man Who Cried Genocide: An Autobiography* (New York:
International Publishers, 1971); Penny Von Eschen, *Race Against Empire* (Ithaca,
N.Y.: Cornell University Press, 1997); Brenda Gayle Plummer, *Rising Wind: Black
Americans and United States Foreign Affairs, 1935–1960* (Chapel Hill, N.C.: University
of North Carolina Press, 1996), 167–297; Hollis R. Lynch, *Black American Radicals
and the Liberation of Africa: The Council on African Affairs, 1937–1955* (Ithaca, N.Y.:
Center for Research in Africana Studies, 1978); and Gerald Horne, *Communist Front?
The Civil Rights Congress, 1946–1956* (London and Toronto: Fairleigh Dickinson University Press, 1988).

"ROARING FROM THE EAST":
THIRD WORLD DREAMING

The specter of a storm is haunting the Western world. . . . The Great Storm, the coming Black Revolution, is rolling like a tornado; roaring from the East; shaking the moorings of the earth as it passes through countries ruled by oppressive regimes; toppling the walls of mighty institutions; filling the well paved, colonial streets with crimson rivers of blood. Yes, all over this sullen planet, the multi-colored "hordes" of undernourished millions are on the move like never before in human history. They are moving to the rhythms of a New Song, a New Sound; dancing in the streets to a Universal Dream that haunts their wretched nights: they dream of Freedom! Their minds are fueled and refueled by the fires of that dream.

—Rolland Snellings (Askia Muhammad Toure),
"Afro-American Youth and the Bandung World," 1965

The story of the shift from civil rights to "Black Power" has been told so many times, in books, documentary films, in African-American history courses all across the United States, that it has become a kind of common sense. It usually begins with the murder of Emmett Till, quickly followed by *Brown v. Board of Education*

Portions of this chapter were cowritten with Betsy Esch.

in 1954—both events spurring an already hopeful, if not angry, Black community into action. Black anger and hopefulness are traced to Black support for the Good War against fascism abroad a decade earlier; Blacks were, after all, loyal to America, and now it was time for the state to grant Black folk democracy and citizenship. Then Montgomery showed the world what Black protest could accomplish, thus giving birth to the modern civil rights movement. Local and national campaigns waged by the Southern Christian Leadership Conference (SCLC), the Congress on Racial Equality (CORE), the Student Non-Violent Coordinating Committee (SNCC), to name only the big three, fought for citizenship, the right to vote, and desegregation, and succeeded in getting the federal government to pass the Civil Rights Act (1964) and the Voting Rights Act (1965).

These were Pyrrhic victories, to say the least. Activists were killed and the FBI did nothing about it. The Democratic Party rejected the only hope for real democracy in Mississippi—the Mississippi Freedom Democratic Party led by Fannie Lou Hamer, who tried but failed to represent disfranchised Black voters at the 1964 Democratic convention. In 1965, civil rights marchers in Selma were "turned back" by Alabama state troopers and local police, and Dr. King apparently relented, striking a mighty blow to the morale of the movement. Meanwhile, the emergence of Malcolm X and his subsequent assassination, events exacerbated by the wave of urban rebellions between 1964 and 68, served as catalysts for rising Black nationalist sentiment. SNCC members start to carry guns to protect themselves; SNCC's Black leaders, particularly folks like Stokely Carmichael and Willie Ricks, began to question the movement's integrationist agenda. Then, during the summer of 1966, the slogan "Black Power" emerged full blown among Black SNCC and CORE militants. They were tired of and impatient with the slow pace of the civil rights establishment, and a new attitude overtook the movement: no more compromise, no more "deals" with white liberals, no more subordinating the struggle to the needs of the Democratic Party. Out of bitter disappointment rose a new Black revolution.

In other words, high expectations begot the civil rights movement; the movement's failure to achieve all its goals and to deal with urban poverty begot Black Power. The flowering of Black nationalism in the mid- to late 1960s is usually presented as an evolutionary process, a stage in the development of postwar Black politics. It's a neat typology, to be sure, but one that obscures more than it reveals. First, it is a tale too often limited to the domestic sphere, to the U.S. nation-state. Even Black nationalism tends to be cast in terms of riots and "buy Black" campaigns rather than Black activists' support for anticolonial movements and Third World solidarity. Second, given historians' South-to-North trajectory, the Northern urban political landscape of the late 1950s was overshadowed by the Southern struggle; after all, the South was where the TV cameras were before the riots. The third reason, of course, has to do with a general conspiracy of silence against the most radical elements of the Black freedom movement, the movements and activists that spoke of revolution, socialism, and self-determination, and looked to the Third World for models of Black liberation in the United States. These movements, while often small and sometimes isolated, confound our narrative of the Black freedom movement, for they were independent of both the white Left and the mainstream civil rights movement. Directing much of their attention to working-class struggles, urban poverty and racism, and police brutality, little-known groups such as the Revolutionary Action Movement (RAM) were also influenced by uprisings and revolutions in Africa, Asia, and Latin America. Following the lead of Malcolm X, Vicki Garvin, Robert Williams, Harold Cruse, and others, RAM militants sought to understand the African-American condition through an analysis of global capitalism, imperialism, and Third World liberation well before the riots of the mid-1960s. In other words, a vision of global class revolution led by oppressed people of color was not an outgrowth of the civil rights movement's failure but existed alongside, sometimes in tension with, the movement's main ideas. To paraphrase Malcolm X, Black radicals were not interested in integrating into a burning house; they wanted revolutionary transformation and recognized that such a revolution was inextricably linked to the struggles of colonized people around the world.

The Specter of a Storm

As we learned in the previous chapter, Black radicals viewed the emerging freedom movement in the United States as part of a global assault on empire. Inspired in part by the historic 1955 meeting of nonaligned nations in Bandung, Indonesia—mostly former colonies that set out on a path independent of American or Soviet influence—African-American radicals were genuinely excited by the possibility of allies in the Third World who might support their own local movements. Some heard the idea of a Black American alliance with the nonaligned world in young Malcolm X, who gave a speech as early as 1954 comparing the situation in Vietnam with that of the Mau Mau rebellion in colonial Kenya. The Mau Mau rebellion was an uprising of the predominantly Kikuyu Land and Freedom Army, which waged an armed movement during the early 1950s to force the British colonists off the Kikuyus' land. In Malcolm's view, both these movements were uprisings of the "darker races" and thus part of a "tidal wave" against U.S. and European imperialism. In fact, Africa remained his primary political focus outside Black America. He toured Egypt, Sudan, Nigeria, and Ghana in 1959, well before his famous trip to Africa and the Middle East in 1964. And when Fidel Castro, the new Cuban president and leader of the revolution there, visited the UN for the first time in 1960 and decided to relocate from a downtown hotel to Harlem's Hotel Theresa, Malcolm was among the first to greet him.

Well over a year before the 1963 march on Washington, critic, activist, and ex-Communist Harold Cruse seemed to have his finger on the pulse when he suggested that the Cuban, Chinese, and African revolutions influenced radical thought among Black Americans. In a provocative essay published in the *New Leader*,

Cruse wrote that the new generation looked to the former colonial world for leadership:

> Already they have a pantheon of modern heroes—Lumumba, Kwame Nkrumah, Sekou Toure in Africa; Fidel Castro in Latin America; Malcolm X, the Muslim leader, in New York; Robert Williams in the South; and Mao Tse-tung in China. These men seem heroic to the Afro-Americans not because of their political philosophy, but because they were either former colonials who achieved complete independence, or because, like Malcolm X, they dared to look the white community in the face and say: "We don't think your civilization is worth the effort of any black man to try to integrate into." This to many Afro-Americans is an act of defiance that is truly revolutionary.

Revolutions in Cuba, Africa, and China had a similar effect on poet, playwright, and critic Amiri Baraka. As Baraka explained it, "Ghana's Kwame Nkrumah had hoisted the black star over the statehouse in Accra, and Nkrumah's pronouncements and word of his deeds were glowing encouragement to colored people all over the world. When the Chinese exploded their first A-bomb I wrote a poem saying, in effect, that *time* for the colored peoples had rebegun." Baraka, along with Cruse and several other Black intellectuals, visited Cuba in 1960 and returned home transformed. "I carried so much back with me," he recalled in his autobiography, "that I was never the same again. The dynamic of the revolution had touched me." Upon his return he published an important essay, "Cuba Libre," in *Evergreen Review* that challenged his generation of artists to become involved in radical movements.

The Ghana-China matrix is perhaps best embodied in the career of Vickie Garvin, a stalwart radical who traveled in Harlem's Black leftist circles during the postwar period. Raised in a Black working-class family in New York, Garvin spent her summers working in the garment industry to supplement her family's income. As early as her high school days, she became active in Black protest politics, supporting efforts by Adam Clayton Powell Jr. to obtain better-paying jobs for African Americans in Harlem

and creating Black history clubs dedicated to building library resources. After earning her B.A. in political science from Hunter
College and an M.A. in economics from Smith College, she
spent the war years working for the National War Labor Board
and continued on as an organizer for the United Office and
Professional Workers of America–Congress of Industrial Organizations (UOPWA-CIO) and as national research director and
co-chair of the Fair Employment Practices Committee. During
the postwar purges of the Left in the CIO, Garvin was a strong
voice of protest and a sharp critic of the CIO's failure to organize
in the South. As executive secretary of the New York chapter of
the National Negro Labor Council and vice-president of the national organization, Garvin established close ties to Malcolm X
and helped him arrange part of his tour of Africa.

Garvin joined the Black intellectual exodus to Nkrumah's
Ghana, where she initially roomed with poet Maya Angelou
and eventually moved into a house next to Du Bois. She spent
two years in Accra, surrounded by several key Black intellectuals
and artists, including Julian Mayfield, artist Tom Feelings, and
cartoonist Ollie Harrington. As a radical who taught conversa-
tional English to the Cuban, Algerian, and Chinese diplomatic
core in Ghana, she found it hard *not* to develop a deeply internationalist outlook. Conversations with Du Bois during his last
days in Ghana only reinforced her internationalism and kindled
her interest in the Chinese Revolution. Indeed, through Du Bois
Garvin got a job as a "polisher" for the English translations of the
Peking Review and a teaching position at the Shanghai Foreign
Language Institute. She remained in China from 1964 to 1970,
building bridges between the Black freedom struggle, African independence movements, and the Chinese Revolution.

Poet and veteran radical Ramon Durem learned his first lessons in international solidarity on the battlefields of Spain more
than two decades before the Cuban Revolution. Like many of his
Black comrades, he believed that fighting in defense of republican Spain against Franco's fascists (1936–39) was a way of aveng-
ing Ethiopia for Mussolini's bloody invasion in 1935. Durem had

hoped that after World War II the Left would devote its energies to the Black freedom movement, but he was disappointed. "At the end of World War Two," he wrote, "I discovered that even the white radicals were not interested in a radical solution to the Negro Question." Although Durem embraced Black nationalism, his commitment to internationalism did not seem to waiver. As early as 1962, he shared Cruse's insight that the rise of urban Black nationalism was "part of the general world colonial revolution." His poem, "Hipping the Hip" is even more telling. A critique of the Beat generation and its false claim to radicalism, he suggested looking to Africa and China for possible alternatives:

> Juice
> is no use
> and H
> don't pay
> I guess revolution
> is the only way
> Blues—is a tear
> Bop—a fear
> of reality.
> There's no place to hide
> in a horn
> Chinese may be lame
> but they ain't tame
> Mau Mau only got a five-tone scale
> but when it comes to Freedom, Jim—
> they wail!
> dig?

Like Africa, China was on the move and there was a general sense that the Chinese supported the liberation movements throughout the Black world, including in the United States. In 1957, two years after the historic meeting of nonaligned nations in Bandung, China formed the Afro-Asian People's Solidarity Organization. Mao not only invited W. E. B. Du Bois to spend his ninetieth birthday in China, but three weeks before the great march on Washington in 1963, Mao issued a statement criticizing American racism and casting the African-American freedom movement as part of the worldwide struggle against imperialism. "The evil system of colonialism and imperialism," Mao stated, "arose and throve with the enslavement of Negroes and the trade in Negroes, and it will surely come to its end with the complete emancipation of the black people." A decade later, novelist John Oliver Killens was impressed by the fact that several of his own books, as well as works by other Black writers, had been translated into Chinese and were widely read by students. Everywhere he went, it seemed, he met young intellectuals and workers "tremendously interested in the Black movement and in how the art and literature of Black folks reflected that movement."

The status of the Chinese as people of color served as a powerful political tool in mobilizing support from Africans and African-descended people. In 1963, for example, Chinese delegates in Moshi, Tanzania, proclaimed that the Russians had no business in Africa because they were white. The Chinese, on the other hand, were not only part of the colored world but unlike Europeans they never took part in the slave trade. Of course, most of these claims serve to facilitate alliance building. The fact was that African slaves could be found in Guangzhou during the twelfth century, and African students in Communist China occasionally complained of racism. (Indeed, after Mao's death, racial clashes on college campuses occurred more frequently, notably in Shanghai in 1979, Nanjing in 1980, and Tianjin in 1986.) Furthermore, Chinese foreign policy toward the Black world was often driven more by strategic considerations than by a commitment to Third World revolutionary movements, especially after the Sino-Soviet split. China's anti-Soviet position resulted in foreign policy decisions that ultimately undermined China's standing with certain African liberation movements. In southern Africa, for example, the Chinese backed movements that also received support from the apartheid regime of South Africa!

Despite China's dismal foreign policy toward Africa, countless Black radicals of that era regarded China, not unlike Cuba or

Ghana or even Paris, as the land where true freedom might be had. It wasn't perfect, but it was much better than living in the belly of the beast. When Black Panther leader Elaine Brown visited Beijing in the fall of 1970, she was pleasantly surprised by what the Chinese revolution had achieved in terms of improving people's lives. "Old and young would spontaneously give emotional testimonies, like Baptist converts, to the glories of socialism." A year later she returned with Black Panther founder Huey Newton, who described his experience in China as a "sensation of freedom—as if a great weight had been lifted from my soul and I was able to be myself, without defense or pretense or the need for explanation. I felt absolutely free for the first time in my life—completely free among my fellow men."

More than a decade before Brown and Newton set foot on Chinese soil, W. E. B. Du Bois had regarded China, along with Africa, as a "sleeping giant" poised to lead the colored races in the worldwide struggle against imperialism. He had first traveled there in 1936—before the war and the revolution—during an extended visit to the Soviet Union. Returning in 1959 when it was illegal to travel to China, Du Bois discovered a new country. He was struck by the transformation of the Chinese, in particular what he perceived as the emancipation of women, and left convinced that China would lead the underdeveloped nations on the road toward socialism. "China after long centuries," he told an audience of Chinese Communists attending his ninety-first birthday celebration, "has arisen to her feet and leapt forward. Africa arise, and stand straight, speak and think! Act! Turn from the West and your slavery and humiliation for the last five hundred years and face the rising sun."

In short, China offered Black radicals a "colored" or Third World Marxist model that enabled them to challenge a white and Western vision of class struggle—a model they shaped and reshaped to suit their own cultural and political realities. Although China's role was contradictory and problematic in many respects, the fact that Chinese peasants, as opposed to the European proletariat, had made a socialist revolution and carved out a position in world politics distinct from the Soviet and U.S. camps endowed Black radicals with a deeper sense of revolutionary importance and power. Finally, Mao not only proved to Black folks the world over that they need not wait for "objective conditions" to make revolution, but his elevation of the cultural struggle also profoundly shaped debates surrounding Black arts and politics.

"The Coming Black Revolution"

For future Black Panther Party (BPP) leader Huey Newton, the African revolution seemed even less crucial than events in Cuba and China. As a student at Merritt College in the early 1960s, he read a little existentialism, began attending meetings sponsored by the Progressive Labor Party, and supported the Cuban Revolution. Not surprisingly, Newton began to read Marxist literature voraciously. Mao, in particular, left a lasting impression: "My conversion was complete when I read the four volumes of Mao Tse-tung to learn more about the Chinese Revolution." Thus well before the founding of the BPP, Newton was steeped in Mao's thought as well as the writings of Che Guevara, the Cuban revolutionary and theorist of guerrilla movements, and Frantz Fanon, the Martinican-born psychiatrist who moved to Algeria and participated in the revolution there. Fanon was well known for two books, *Black Skin, White Masks* and *The Wretched of the Earth*, both reflections on the social, cultural, economic, and psychological impact of colonialism. "Mao and Fanon and Guevara all saw clearly that the people had been stripped of their birthright and their dignity, not by a philosophy or mere words, but at gunpoint. They had suffered a holdup by gangsters, and rape; for them, the only way to win freedom was to meet force with force."

The Chinese and Cubans' willingness "to meet force with force" also made these revolutions attractive to Black radicals in the age of nonviolent passive resistance. Of course, the Southern movement had its share of armed activists, with groups like the Deacons for Defense and Justice and Gloria Richardson's Cambridge movement, which defended nonviolent protesters when necessary. But the figure who best embodied Black traditions of armed self-defense was Robert Williams, a hero to the new wave of Black internationalists, whose importance almost rivaled that of Malcolm X. A former U.S. Marine with extensive military training, Williams earned notoriety in 1957 for forming armed self-defense groups in Monroe, North Carolina, to fight the Ku Klux Klan. At the time, Williams, the local NAACP president, and Dr. Albert Perry, head of the Union County Council on Human Relations, were engaged in a nonviolent campaign to desegregate the city's swimming pools. The Klan attempted to intimidate movement activists by firebombing and shooting into Black homes, which then prompted Williams to organize armed self-defense groups. Apparently, their efforts were effective. When a Klan caravan attempted to shoot into Dr. Perry's home, the men stationed to protect Dr. Perry returned fire, forcing the Klansmen to retreat. The attacks suddenly stopped and the presence of armed self-defense groups in Monroe's Black community brought a dramatic drop in incidents of violence. Two years later, Williams's statement that Black people must "meet violence with violence" as the only way to end injustice in an uncivilized South led to his suspension as president of the Monroe chapter of the NAACP.

Williams's break with the NAACP and his open advocacy of armed self-defense pushed him further left, into the orbit of the Socialist Workers Party, the Workers World Party, and some members of the old CPUSA. However, Williams had had contact with Communists since his days as a Detroit autoworker in the 1940s. He not only read the *Daily Worker* but published a story in its pages called "Some Day I Am Going Back South." Williams was also something of an intellectual dabbler and autodidact, having studied at West Virginia State College, North Carolina College, and Johnson C. Smith College. Nevertheless, his more recent leftist associations led him to Cuba and the Fair Play for Cuba Committee. Upon returning from his first trip in 1960, he hoisted the Cuban flag in his backyard and ran a series of articles in his mimeographed publication, the *Crusader*, about the transformation of working peoples' lives in Cuba as a result of the revolution. In one of his editorials published in August 1960, Williams insisted that African Americans' fight for freedom "is related to the Africans', the Cubans', all of Latin Americans' and the Asians' struggles for self-determination." His support of the Chinese Revolution was also evident in the pages of the *Crusader*; he emphasized the importance of China as a beacon of strength for social justice movements the world over. Like Baraka, Williams took note of China's detonation of an atomic bomb in 1960 as a historic occasion for the oppressed. "With the bomb," he wrote, "China will be respected and will add a powerful voice to those who already plead for justice for black as well as white."

By 1961, as a result of trumped-up kidnapping charges and a federal warrant for his arrest, Williams, his wife Mabel, and their children were forced to flee the country and seek political asylum in Cuba. During the next four years, Cuba became Williams's base for promoting Black world revolution and elaborating an internationalist ideology that embraced Black nationalism and Third World solidarity. With support from Fidel Castro, Williams hosted a radio show called *Radio Free Dixie* that was directed at African Americans, continued to edit the *Crusader* (which by now had progressed from a mimeograph to a full-blown magazine), and completed his book *Negroes with Guns* (1962). He did not, however, identify himself as a Marxist. At the same time, he rejected the "nationalist" label, calling himself an "internationalist" instead: "That is, I'm interested in the problems of Africa, of Asia, and of Latin America. I believe that we all have the same struggle; a struggle for liberation."

Williams recalls having had good relations with Castro, but political differences over race led to a rift between him and the Cuban Communists. "The Party," Williams remembered, "maintained that it was strictly a class issue and that once the class problem had been solved through a socialist administration, racism would be abolished." Williams not only disagreed but had moved much closer to Che Guevara, who embodied much of what Williams had been advocating all along: Third World solidarity, the use of armed struggle, and a deep and unwavering interest in the African revolution. Che's formal breach with the Soviet Communist Party came when, addressing the Organization for Afro-Asian Solidarity at Algiers in February 1965, he charged the USSR with being a "tacit accomplice of imperialism" by not trading exclusively with the Communist bloc and by not giving underdeveloped socialist countries aid without any thought of return. He also attacked the Soviet government for its policy of peaceful coexistence. Although Fidel and Che disagreed, they continued to work together, and Guevara focused his attention on internationalizing the revolutionary socialist movement with Castro's blessing. In 1965 he led a small army to the Congo in a failed effort to back a dissident movement there, and two years later he and his men joined guerrilla forces in Bolivia, where he was captured and executed. It seems clear that Che's commitment to internationalism as well as his leanings toward China influenced Robert and Mabel Williams's decision to leave Cuba for Beijing in 1966.

As an exiled revolutionary in China during its most tumultuous era, Williams nevertheless predicted that urban rebellions in America's ghettos would transform the country. Although one might argue that by publishing the *Crusader* from Cuba and then China, Williams had very limited contact with the Black freedom movement in the United States, his magazine reached a new generation of young Black militants by mail and promoted the vision of Black world revolution articulated by critics such as Harold Cruse. The fact is, the *Crusader* and Williams's own example compelled a small group of Black radical intellectuals and activists to form what might loosely be called the first Black Maoist-influenced organization in history: the Revolutionary Action Movement (RAM).

Robert Williams's flight to Cuba turned out to be a major catalyst for the creation of RAM. In Ohio around 1961, Black members of the campus-based Students for a Democratic Society (SDS) as well as Civil Rights activists in SNCC and CORE, met in a small group to discuss the significance of Williams's work in

Monroe and his subsequent exile. Led by Donald Freeman, a Black student at Case Western Reserve University in Cleveland, the group's main core consisted of a newly formed organization made up of Central State College at Wilberforce students calling themselves Challenge. Members of Challenge were especially taken with Harold Cruse's 1962 essay "Revolutionary National-ism and the Afro-American," which was circulated widely among young Black militants. In it he argued that Black people in the United States were living under domestic colonialism and that their struggles must be seen as part of the worldwide anticolonial movement. "The failure of American Marxists," he wrote, "to un-derstand the bond between the Negro and the colonial peoples of the world has led to their failure to develop theories that would be of value to Negroes in the United States." He reversed the tra-ditional argument that the success of socialism in the developed West was key to the emancipation of colonial subjects and the development of socialism in the Third World. Instead, he saw the former colonies as the vanguard of the revolution; at the fore-front of this new socialist revolution were Cuba and China. "The revolutionary initiative has passed to the colonial world, and in the United States is passing to the Negro, while Western Marxists theorize, temporize and debate."

Inspired by Cruse's interpretation of domestic colonialism and the global importance of the Black freedom struggle, Freeman hoped to turn Challenge into a revolutionary nationalist move-ment possessed of the discipline, organization, and pro-Black ide-ology of the Nation of Islam, but one that would engage in sit-ins, marches, and various acts of civil disobedience. After a lengthy debate, Challenge members decided to dissolve the organization in spring 1962 and form the Revolutionary Action Movement (RAM) led primarily by Freeman, Max Stanford, and Wanda Marshall. Initially, the group called themselves the *Reform* Ac-tion Movement so as not to alarm the administration, but once they decided to maintain RAM as a semiunderground organiza-tion, they changed the name and decided to become a small, select vanguard of the Black liberation movement.

Freeman and RAM members in Cleveland continued to work publicly through the Afro-American Institute, an activist policy-oriented think tank formed in fall 1962. Under Freeman's directorship, its board—dubbed the Soul Circle—consisted of a small group of Black men with ties to community organizations, labor, and civil rights and student groups. Board members such as Henry Glover, Arthur Evans, Nate Bryant, and Hanif Wahab gave lectures on African history and politics and organized forums to debate the future of the civil rights movement, Black participation in Cleveland politics, and the economic conditions of urban Blacks. The institute even recruited the great drummer Max Roach to help organize a panel on "The Role of the Black Artist in the Struggle for Freedom." Institute members also used leaflets and pamphlets to influence Black community thinking on a number of local and international issues. Addressed "To Whom It May Concern," these short broadsides were intended to stimulate discussion and offer the Black community positions on pressing topics such as "elections, urban renewal, Black economic subservience, the 'arms race,' and the struggle in the South." Within a year, the institute graduated from leafleting to a full-blown newsletter titled *Afropinion*. Through the Afro-American Institute, RAM members in Cleveland worked with CORE activists and other community organizers to demand improvements in hospital care for Black patients and to protest the exclusion of African and Afro-American history from the public school curriculum. Their most important campaign of 1963 was the defense of Mae Mallory, a Black woman who was being held in the county jail in Cleveland for her association with Robert Williams in Monroe, North Carolina. Soon after Williams's flight to Cuba, Mallory was arrested in Ohio and awaited extradition charges. The institute and its allies, including the Nation of Islam in Cleveland, petitioned the governor of Ohio to revoke the warrant of extradition and organized a mass demonstration in front of the county jail demanding Mallory's immediate release.

In northern California, RAM grew primarily out of the Afro-American Association. Founded by Donald Warden in 1962, the

Afro-American Association consisted of students from the University of California at Berkeley and Merritt College—many of whom, such as Leslie and Jim Lacy, Cedric Robinson, Ernest Allen, and Huey Newton, would go on to play important roles as radical activists and intellectuals. In Los Angeles, the president of the Afro-American Association was a young man named Ron Everett, who later changed his name to Ron Karenga and went on to found US Organization. The Afro-American Association quickly developed a reputation as a group of militant intellectuals willing to debate anyone. By challenging professors, debating groups such as the Young Socialist Alliance, and giving public lectures on Black history and culture, these young men left a deep impression on fellow students as well as on the Black community. In the East Bay, where the tradition of soapbox speakers had died in the 1930s, save individual campaigns guided by the Communist-led Civil Rights Congress during the early 1950s, the Afro-American Association was walking and talking proof that a vibrant, highly visible militant intellectual culture could exist.

Meanwhile, the Progressive Labor Movement (PL) had begun sponsoring trips to Cuba and recruited several radical Black students in the East Bay to go along. Among them was Ernest Allen, a University of California at Berkeley transfer student from Merritt College who had been active in the Afro-American Association. A working-class kid from Oakland, Allen was part of a generation of Black radicals whose dissatisfaction with the civil rights movement's strategy of nonviolent passive resistance drew them closer to Malcolm X and Third World liberation movements. Not surprisingly, through his trip to Cuba in 1964 he discovered RAM. Allen's travel companions included a contingent of Black militants from Detroit: Luke Tripp, Charles ("Mao") Johnson, Charles Simmons, and General Baker. All were members of the student group Uhuru, and all went on to play key roles in the formation of the League of Revolutionary Black Workers, a radical workers' group formed out of a series of wildcat strikes in Detroit's auto industry. Incredibly, RAM leader Max Stanford was already on the island visiting Robert Williams. When it was time to go back to the states, Allen and the Detroit group were committed to building RAM. Allen stopped in Cleveland to meet with RAM members on his cross-country bus trip back to Oakland. Armed with copies of Robert Williams's *Crusader* magazine and related RAM material, Allen returned to Oakland intent on establishing RAM's presence in the East Bay. Never more than a handful of people, folks such as Isaac Moore, Kenn Freeman (Mamadou Lumumba), Bobby Seale (future founder of the BPP) and Doug Allen (Ernie's brother) established a base at Merritt College through the Soul Students Advisory Council. The group's intellectual and cultural presence, however, was broadly felt. Allen, Freeman, and others founded a journal called *Soulbook: The Revolutionary Journal of the Black World*, which published prose and poetry that was best described as leftist Black-nationalist in orientation. Freeman, in particular, was highly respected among RAM activists and widely read. He constantly pushed his members to think about Black struggle in a global context. The editors of *Soulbook* also developed ties with Old Left Black radicals, most notably former Communist Harry Haywood, whose work they published in an early issue.

Although RAM had established itself in northern California and Cleveland, Ohio, by 1964 Philadelphia appeared to be RAM's home base. It was in Philadelphia, after all, that RAM maintained an open existence, operating under its own name rather than a variety of front organizations. The strength of the Philadelphia chapter has much to do with the fact that it was also the home of Max Stanford, RAM's national field chairman. From Philadelphia RAM published a bimonthly paper called *Black America* and a one-page newsletter called *RAM Speaks*; made plans to build a national movement oriented toward revolutionary nationalism, youth organizing, and armed self-defense; and recruited several Philadelphia activists to the group, including Ethel Johnson (who had also worked with Robert Williams in Monroe), Stan Daniels, and Playthell Benjamin. Subsequently, RAM recruited a group of young Philadelphia militants who would go on to play key roles in radical organizations, including Michael Simmons—one of the authors of SNCC's famous "Black Consciousness Paper"—whose resistance to the draft resulted in his serving a two-and-a-half-year prison sentence, and Tony Monteiro, who went on to become a leading national figure in the CPUSA during the 1970s and 1980s.

At the outset, it seemed as though RAM leaders were not all in agreement on the usefulness of Marxism for Black liberation. Indeed, circumstantial evidence suggests that the Philadelphia leadership was to the left of people like Warden in California and Freeman in Ohio. Freeman did call for collectively owned Black enterprises "in order to eliminate total subjugation to white capitalism" but he insisted that white "socialists and Marxists do not possess the solutions to the ills of Black America." Warden was even less ambivalent about Black capitalism: "We must develop our own planned businesses where efficiency, thrift and sacrifice are stressed. . . . The capital for such industries also is available from our own community, if it could be diverted from the consumption of alcohol, bleaching creams and preachers' Cadillacs." On the other hand, we cannot assume that Warden's position was representative of the entire California Association, for as Ernie Allen reminds us and the pages of *Soulbook* indicate, Warden's ideas were constantly challenged from the left.

By the middle of 1964 and early 1965, the left wing of RAM had clearly won out. Under Max Stanford's leadership, RAM proclaimed its adherence to "Marxism-Leninism Mao Tse-tung thought" as it applied to the conditions of Black people. They also claimed to be the first organization to advance "the theory that the Black liberation movement in the United States was part of the vanguard of the world socialist revolution." RAM's greater leftward turn can be attributed in part to its ideological mentors, who in some respects bridged 1930s and 1940s radicalism and the Black New Left. Besides Robert Williams, young RAM militants sought political guidance from a number of former Black Communists who had either been expelled for "ultraleftism" or "bourgeois nationalism," or had bolted the Party because of its "revisionism." Among this group of elders were Harold Cruse, Harry Haywood, Abner Berry, and "Queen Mother" Audley Moore.

Indeed, Moore would go on to become one of RAM's most important mentors on the East Coast, offering members training in Black nationalist thought and Marxism. The Queen Mother's Philadelphia home, which she affectionately called Mount Addis Ababa, practically served as a school for a new generation of young Black radicals. She founded the African-American Party of National Liberation in 1963, which formed a provisional government and elected Robert Williams as premier in exile. RAM also turned to Detroit's legendary ex-Trotskyists James and Grace Lee Boggs, former comrades of C. L. R. James, whose Marxist and Pan-Africanist writings greatly influenced RAM members as well as other New Left activists.

Another source of RAM's attraction to revolutionary Marxism was the urban uprisings that had just started to occur during summer 1964. Although inadequate housing, unemployment, poor city services, poor schools, and a lack of Black-owned businesses exacerbated conditions in urban ghettos, the catalyst for most of these rebellions was an act of police misconduct. Between 1964 and 1972, riots erupted in some 300 cities, involving close to a half-million African Americans and resulting in 250 deaths, about 10,000 serious injuries, and millions of dollars in property damage. Police and the National Guard turned Black neighborhoods into war zones, arresting at least 60,000 people and employing tanks, machine guns, and tear gas to pacify the community. Even before the riot wave, RAM militants had read Robert Williams's prophetic essay in the *Crusader* titled "USA: The Potential of a Minority Revolution." His words were portentous: "This year, 1964, is going to be a violent one, the storm will reach hurricane proportions by 1965 and the eye of the hurricane will hover over America by 1966. America is a house on fire—FREEDOM NOW!—or let it burn, let it burn. Praise the Lord and pass the ammunition!!" He described in detail what sorts of weapons Black urban guerrillas should use, how to make homemade bombs and flamethrowers, and how to knock out communications systems. In a later installment of the same essay published almost three years later, Williams's directions for launching a ghetto rebellion were even more explicit. At times he sounded like the protagonist Freeman in Sam Greenlee's *The Spook Who Sat by the Door*, a novel (and later film) about a Black former CIA agent who used his training to turn gang members into a revolutionary army. He informed his readers how to squeeze a trigger, called for selective fires "set over a wide area," and even suggested that brothers be sent to Africa for "specialized training in the manufacture and use of the poisonous dart."

Williams's ideas could be easily dismissed as the puerile rantings of an armchair adventurer, especially given his status as an expatriate living half a world away from the movement. But we must consider the context for advocating such strident acts of violence. African Americans had been victims of violence ever since their descendants arrived on these shores as property. Generations lived under mob rule, and even as Williams wrote these articles Black activists, and even some whites, were being brutally murdered for their efforts to bring about social justice and equality in the South. By 1964, the number of casualties in the Southern freedom movement was mounting—a growing list that included four girls ages eleven to fourteen. Addie Mae Collins, Denise McNair, Carole Robertson, and Cynthia Wesley were killed on September 15, 1963, by a bomb planted by white terrorists underneath Birmingham's Sixteenth Street Baptist Church. In the summer of 1964 alone, during SNCC's Mississippi campaign to register voters, white terrorists bombed thirty Black homes, burned thirty-five churches, beat at least eighty people, and murdered six. No one was convicted. And, of course, Williams's own experience with the Klan in North Carolina directly informed his ideas about the need to "meet violence with violence." While even the most liberal white sympathizers suffered from historical amnesia when it came to the history of racist violence, African Americans of Williams's generation had heard stories of the mob attacks on Black communities, from the Wilmington, North Carolina, "massacre" in 1898 to the bombing of the Tulsa, Oklahoma, Black business district in 1921. In July 1917 in East St. Louis, Illinois, for example, white mobs (including police and local militias) slaughtered

Black residents who they believed were taking white jobs. They drove through the Black community shooting indiscriminately from their cars. When the smoke cleared, at least 150 Black residents had been shot, burned, hanged, or maimed for life, and about six thousand were driven from their homes. Thirty-nine Black people lost their lives, including small children whose skulls were crushed or who were tossed into bonfires. As was characteristic of nearly all white mob violence before the civil rights era, no one was punished for these crimes. The same can be said for state-sanctioned violence in the form of homicides and beatings at the hands of police. As incidents of lynching and mob violence declined, police brutality cases involving Black victims rose dramatically. A study conducted by the Department of Justice found that in the eighteen-month period from January 1958 to June 1960, 34 percent of all reported victims of police brutality were Black.

Given the history and current reality of racist violence in America, we should not be surprised that RAM leaders echoed Williams's calls for armed insurrection and drew inspiration and ideas directly from his theory of guerrilla warfare in the urban United States, even if they never tried to carry them out. It should be clear that RAM members never attempted to implement Williams's military strategies, and they never engaged police or anyone else in an armed confrontation. They only wrote about it. In print, at least, RAM's official position was that a guerrilla war was not only possible but could be won in ninety days. The combination of mass chaos and revolutionary discipline was the key to victory. The fall 1964 issue of *Black America* predicted Armageddon:

> Black men and women in the Armed Forces will defect and come over to join the Black Liberation forces. Whites who claim they want to help the revolution will be sent into the white communities to divide them, fight the fascists and frustrate the efforts of the counter-revolutionary forces. Chaos will be everywhere and with the breakdown of mass communications, mutiny will occur in great numbers in all facets of the oppressors' government. The

stock market will fall; Wall Street will stop functioning; Washington, D.C. will be torn apart by riots. Officials everywhere will run—run for their lives. The George Lincoln Rockwellers, Kennedys, Vanderbilts, Hunts, Johnsons, Wallaces, Barnetts, etc., will be the first to go. The revolution will "strike by night and spare none." . . . The Black Revolution will use sabotage in the cities, knocking out the electrical power first, then transportation and guerrilla warfare in the countryside in the South. With the cities powerless, the oppressor will be helpless.

RAM not only prepared for war, it prepared for the coming society. Its twelve-point program called for the development of freedom schools, national Black student organizations, rifle clubs, Black farmer cooperatives (not just for economic development but to keep "community and guerrilla forces going for a while"), and a liberation guerrilla army made up of youth and unemployed. They also placed special emphasis on internationalism, pledging support for national liberation movements in Africa, Asia, and Latin America as well as the adoption of "Pan-African socialism." In line with Cruse's seminal essay, RAM members saw themselves as colonial subjects fighting a "colonial war at home." As colonial subjects with a right to self-determination, RAM saw Afro-America as a de facto member of the nonaligned nations. They even identified themselves as part of the "Bandung world," going so far as to hold a conference in November 1964 in Nashville on "The Black Revolution's Relationship to the Bandung World." In a 1965 article published in RAM's journal *Black America*, they started to develop a theory of "Bandung humanism" or "revolutionary black internationalism," which argued that the battle between Western imperialism and the Third World— more than the battle between labor and capital—represented the most fundamental contradiction in our time. They linked the African-American freedom struggle with what was happening in China, Zanzibar, Cuba, Vietnam, Indonesia, and Algeria, and they characterized their work as part of Mao's international strategy of encircling Western capitalist countries and challenging imperialism. This position was echoed in a particularly moving, eloquent essay by Rolland Snellings (better known as Askia Muhammad Toure, the extraordinary poet and leader in the Black Arts Movement) titled "Afro American Youth and the Bandung World." The urban rebellions in the United States were cast in terms of an international rebellion against imperialism, one where "Black America became one with the students and people of Panama, Venezuela, Japan, South Vietnam, the Congo, and all colonial peoples rioting in protest against injustice and exploitation by puppet regimes stemming from or allied with White America, colossus of the West." These rebellions were not tragedies but celebrations, temporarily freed spaces akin to liberated zones in which the oppressed are "Dancing in the Streets!"

After 1966, the term "Bandung humanism" was dropped entirely and replaced with "black internationalism." Precisely what "black internationalism" meant was laid out in an incredibly bold thirty-six-page pamphlet published by RAM in 1966 titled "The World Black Revolution." Echoing the *Communist Manifesto* (its opening line was "All over Africa, Asia, South, Afro and Central America a revolution is haunting and sweeping. . . .") the pamphlet identified strongly with China against both the capitalist West and the Soviet empire. The "emergence of Revolutionary China began to polarize caste and class contradictions within the world, in both the bourgeoisie [*sic*] imperialist camp and also in the European bourgeois communist-socialist camp." In other words, China was the wedge that sharpened contradictions between colonial peoples and the West. Rejecting the idea that socialist revolution would arise in the developed countries of the West, RAM insisted that the only true revolutionary solution was the "dictatorship of the world by the Black Underclass through World Black Revolution." Of course, RAM wasn't working from today's definitions; it used "underclass" to encompass all peoples of color in Asia, Latin America, Africa, and elsewhere; the "Black Underclass" was merely a synonym for the colonial world. To coordinate this revolution, RAM called for the creation of a Black International as well as a "People's Liberation Army on a world scale."

Although Mao's thought loomed large in "The World Black Revolution," much of the document reflects original thinking on the part of RAM members; they also drew from a wellspring of Black radical thought. W. E. B. Du Bois's pronouncement that the problem of the twentieth century was the problem of the color line undergirded much of their argument. And just as Du Bois argued in his magisterial book *Black Reconstruction in America*, RAM maintained the position that the problem of the color line lay at the heart of class struggle on a world scale. Furthermore, the pamphlet gave a nod to Indian Communist leader M. N. Roy, who debated Lenin at the Second Communist International Congress in 1920 over the "national-colonial question." Roy, they argued, not only recognized nationalist and anticolonial movements as a revolutionary force but also insisted that class distinctions in the colonies placed the peasantry in a more pivotal position than the colonial petite bourgeoisie for waging a revolutionary movement. By resurrecting Roy, who had remained relatively obscure among the panoply of Communist theoreticians, they revealed, once again, a stream of radical thought from the Third World critical of Western Marxism and capable of offering insights where European radicals had failed.

For all its strident nationalism, "The World Black Revolution" concludes that Black nationalism "is really internationalism." Only by demolishing white nationalism and white power could liberation be achieved for everyone. Not only would national boundaries be eliminated with the "dictatorship of the Black Underclass," but "the need for nationalism in its aggressive form will be eliminated." This is a pretty remarkable statement given RAM's social and ideological roots. But rather than representing a unified position, the statement reflects various tensions that persisted throughout RAM's history. On one side were nationalists who felt that revolutionaries should fight for the Black nation first and build socialism separately from the rest of the United States. On the other side were socialists like James and Grace Boggs who wanted to know who would rule the white nation and what such a presence would mean for Black freedom. They also rejected

efforts to resurrect the "black nation" thesis—the old Communist line that people in Black majority counties of the South (the
"black belt") had a right to secede from the union. The Boggses
contended that the real source of power lay in the cities, not the
rural Black belt. In January 1965, James Boggs resigned from his
post as ideological chairman.

"Moving to the Rhythms of a New Song"

As members of an organization made up primarily of college-
educated intellectuals (though many did not matriculate in order to participate in the movement full-time), RAM activists
thought long and hard about the role of students and the petite
bourgeoisie in the coming revolution. Askia Muhammad Toure
charted the history and limits of Black bourgeois reformism
(e.g., the NAACP, the Urban League, the "so-called responsible Negro Leaders") and Black bourgeois nationalism ("'Back
to Africa' which is still struggling within the bonds of Western
neo-colonialism, or asking for 'separate states' while White America sneers with scorn"). He then suggested that the conditions
that had produced this generation of revolutionary youth had also
given birth to a radical petite bourgeoisie that "identif[ies] strongly
with the desires and aspirations of the black masses." This group
was uniquely situated historically to "create a new synthesis from
the militant, mass-oriented, universality of [Marcus] Garvey and
the scientific, analytical scholarship of Du Bois"—a synthesis that
would remain uncompromisingly anti-imperialist and anticapitalist. Max Stanford also recognized the revolutionary potential
within certain segments of the Black petite bourgeoisie, particularly among students. In an article, "Revolutionary Nationalism
and the Afroamerican Student," published in January 1965, Max
Stanford argued that Black students of the "war baby" generation
embodied several contradictions at once—contradictions that
could lead them to embrace capitalism and white values, check
out altogether, or join the revolutionary movement. The fact that

racism still kept these well-educated and assimilated Negroes from fulfilling their aspirations could be either a wake-up call for the younger generation or an incentive to work harder within the system, or it could propel some into what Stanford called the "hip society." In other words, there was no guarantee that students would take the path of revolution, but the contradictions of racial capitalism and bourgeois democracy had led to the formation of a "revolutionary intelligentsia capable of leading black America to true liberation."

At the same time, Stanford suggested that the most alienated segment of Black working-class youth, the young men who co-alesced in gangs, offered yet another rich reservoir for the revolution. "Gangs are the most dynamic force in the black community. Instead of fighting their brothers and sisters, they can be trained to fight 'Charlie.' They can be developed into a blood brotherhood (black youth army) that will serve as a liberation force in the Black revolution." Like Robert Williams's musings on urban guerrilla warfare, Stanford anticipated the central themes in Greenlee's *The Spook Who Sat by the Door*. Stanford's piece appeared around the same time as the *Autobiography of Malcolm X*, which convinced unknown numbers of kids that even second-rate gangsters could become political radicals. Besides, the BPP in Los Angeles, founded less than two years after Stanford's article, recruited several ex-gang members into its ranks. Los Angeles Panther leaders Bunchy Carter and John Huggins were former members of a street gang called the Slausons, and their fellow gang banger, Brother Crook (a.k.a. Ron Wilkins), founded the Community Alert Patrol to challenge police brutality in the late 1960s.

RAM itself had more success with those petit bourgeois youth willing, as African revolutionary Amilcar Cabral once put it, to commit "class suicide." These were the folks Stanford labeled "the Outlaws," the "Revolutionary black Nationalists" committed to world revolution. In May 1964, dozens of these "outlaws" came together at the first Afro-American Student Conference on Black Nationalism on Fisk University's campus. The conference was significant, in part because it occurred before Malcolm X's address to civil rights activists in Selma—an event often regarded a turning point in winning many young Southerners over to Black nationalism. Conference participants boldly called for the development of a radical nationalist movement in the South and elsewhere, criticized civil rights leaders for "bourgeois reformism," and echoed W. E. B. Du Bois's sentiment that "capitalism cannot reform itself, a system that enslaves you cannot free you." A handful of Africans were also in attendance, including one young scholar who presented a paper on Pan-Africanism and called on Black Americans to support the overthrow of "neo-colonialist puppet regimes" and "the development of a socialist Africa."

RAM activists wrote quite a bit about class, culture, and internationalism, but like many of their nationalist and left-wing counterparts, they had little to say about women. The revolution was seen as a man's job; women barely figured in the equation. Indeed, one of the striking facts about the history of the antirevisionist left is how male dominated it remained. Although Wanda Marshall had been one of the founding members of RAM, she did not hold a national leadership post in 1964. Besides promoting the creation of "women's leagues" whose purpose would be "to organize black women who work in white homes," RAM remained relatively silent on women's liberation.

RAM's masculinist orientation should not be surprising given the male orientation of Black nationalist—not to mention white New Left—organizations in the 1960s, whether they were advocating civil rights or some incipient version of Black Power. The masculinism of RAM, however, was heightened by the fact that its leaders saw themselves as urban guerrillas, members of an all-Black version of Mao's Red Army. Not all RAM members viewed themselves this way, but those who did were deeply committed to a set of revolutionary ethics Mao had laid down for his own Party cadre and members of the People's Army. We see this very clearly in RAM's "Code of Cadres," a set of highly didactic rules of conduct that members were expected to live by. Here are some examples:

> A Revolutionary nationalist maintains the highest respect for all authority within the party. . . .

> A Revolutionary nationalist cannot be corrupted by money, honors or any other personal gains. . . .

> A Revolutionary nationalist will unhesitatingly subordinate his personal interest to those of the vanguard [without] hesitation. . . .

> A Revolutionary nationalist will maintain the highest level of morality and will never take as much as a needle or single piece of thread, from the masses—Brothers and Sisters will maintain the utmost respect for one another and will never misuse or take advantage of one another for personal gain— and will never misinterpret, the doctrine of revolutionary nationalism for any reason. . . .

The similarities with *Quotations from Chairman Mao Tse-tung* are striking. The last example comes straight out of Mao's "Three Main Rules of Discipline," which urges cadres to "not take a single needle or piece of thread from the masses." Selflessness and total commitment to the masses is another theme that dominates *Quotations*. Again, the comparisons are noteworthy: "At no time and in no circumstances," says Mao, "should a Communist place his personal interests first; he should subordinate them to the interests of the nation and of the masses. Hence, selfishness, slacking, corruption, seeking the limelight, and so on are most contemptible, while selflessness, working with all one's energy, whole-hearted devotion to public duty, and quiet hard work will command respect."

RAM's emphasis on revolutionary ethics and moral transformation, in theory at least, resonated with Black religious traditions, and like the Nation of Islam, they preached self-restraint, order, and discipline. It's quite possible that, in the midst of a counter-culture that embodied elements of hedonism and drug use, a new wave of student and working-class radicals found Maoist ethics attractive. Max Stanford offered a withering critique of what he called the "hip society," Black youth caught between ghetto reali-ties and white aspirations. Although these contradictions in Black youth culture were produced by frustration and alienation, he characterized their world as "hedonistic" and "built on extreme pleasure seeking." He noted somewhat disdainfully that "adher-ents of the hip society release themselves by being 'hard,' digging jams (listening to jazz records), 'getting off' (releasing frustration through dancing to rock n' roll), smoking pot, tasting (heavy drinking), 'doing the thing or taking care of business' (loose sex morals, sometimes sex orgies)."

For many Black revolutionaries, including those not directly linked to RAM, the moral and ethical dimension of Mao's thought centered on the notion of personal transformation. Upon his return from China in 1969, Robert Williams insisted that all young Black activists "undergo personal and moral trans-formation. There is a need for a stringent revolutionary code of moral ethics. Revolutionaries are instruments of righteousness." It was a familiar lesson embodied in the lives of Malcolm X and (later) George Jackson—the idea that one possesses the revolu-tionary will to transform *himself*. (These narratives were almost exclusively male despite the growing number of memoirs by rad-ical Black women.) Whether or not RAM members lived by the "Code of Cadres," Maoist ethics ultimately served to reinforce Malcolm's status as a revolutionary role model.

Self-transformation through some kind of cultural revolution was a central tenet in RAM's ideology. As early as 1964, during the nationalist student conference at Fisk University, activists in RAM agreed that "a fundamental cultural revolution or re-Africanization of black people in America was a prerequisite for a genuine black Revolution." They spoke of "re-Africanization" in terms of a re-jection of Western materialism in favor of an essential African communalism, humanism, and spiritualism that, many insisted, was intrinsic to traditional African society. Of course, the effort to "re-Africanize," at least in the post–World War II period, predates RAM. Black women singers such as Abbey Lincoln, Odetta, and Nina Simone not only began wearing short "Afros" or "naturals" during the early 1960s but also identified with the African liberation movement and the African-American cultural interest in Africa through the formation of groups such as the American Society of African Culture (AMSAC). Even *Ebony*, *Jet*, and *Sepia* magazines were covering Africa, and African publications such as *Drum* were being read by Black people in the States who could get their hands on them. Indeed, as early as 1962, Harold Cruse predicted that in the coming years "Afro-Americans . . . will undoubtedly make a lot of noise in militant demonstrations, cultivate beards and sport their hair in various degrees of la mode au naturel, and tend to be cultish with African- and Arab-style dress."

Yet, while RAM's call for "re-Africanization" reflected a growing trend within elements of Black youth culture, particularly among nationalist-minded intellectuals and artists, the very idea that culture was one of the most important terrains upon which to make revolution was given a boost when China declared its own Great Proletarian Cultural Revolution in 1966. Of course, Mao meant something different when he launched the Cultural Revolution in China—he was proposing a vision of society where divisions between the powerful and powerless were blurred, where status and privilege didn't necessarily distinguish leaders from the led. Thus while Mao's call for a Cultural Revolution meant getting rid of the vestiges (cultural and otherwise) of the old order, Black radicals like Robert Williams (now publishing the *Crusader* from China) was talking about purging Black culture of a "slave mentality." Less than a year into the Cultural Revolution, Robert Williams published an article in the *Crusader* titled "Reconstitute Afro-American Art to Remold Black Souls," which was widely circulated among RAM members. Williams's essay sought to build on the idea rather than the ideology of the Cultural Revolution.

He called on Black artists to cast off the shackles of the old traditions and make art only in the service of revolution. Likewise, an
internal RAM document circulated in 1967, titled "Some Questions concerning the Present Period," called for a full-scale Black
cultural revolution in the United States whose purpose would
be to "destroy the conditioned white oppressive mores, attitudes,
ways, customs, philosophies, habits, etc., which the oppressor has
taught and trained us to have. This means on a mass scale a new
revolutionary culture." It also meant an end to processed hair, skin
lighteners, and other symbols of parroting the dominant culture.
Indeed, the revolution targeted not only assimilated bourgeois Negroes but also their accomplices—barbers and beauticians!

"A Universal Dream That Haunts Their Wretched Nights"

After RAM had spent years as an underground organization, the
mainstream press published a series of "exposés," including a
particularly inflammatory piece in *Life* magazine that identified
RAM as one of the leading extremist groups "Plotting a War on
'Whitey.'" The "Peking-backed" group was not only considered
armed and dangerous, but also "impressively well read in revolutionary literature—from Marat and Lenin to Mao, Che Guevara
and Frantz Fanon." (The Harlem Branch of the Progressive Labor Party responded to the articles with a pamphlet titled "The
Plot against Black America," which argued that China was not fi-
nancing revolution, but only setting a revolutionary example by its
staunch anti-imperialism. The real causes of Black rebellion, they
insisted, could be found in the conditions of ghetto life.) Not surprisingly, these highly publicized articles were followed by a series
of police raids on the homes of RAM members in Philadelphia
and New York City. In June 1967, RAM members were rounded
up and charged with an alleged conspiracy to instigate a riot, poison police officers with potassium cyanide, and assassinate Roy
Wilkins, secretary of the NAACP and Whitney Young, head of the
National Urban League. The charges had no basis and were subsequently dropped. A year later, under the repressive atmosphere of

the FBI's Counterintelligence Program (COINTELPRO), RAM transformed itself into the Black Liberation Party, or the African American Party of National Liberation. By 1969, RAM had pretty much dissolved itself, though its members opted to "melt back into the community and infiltrate existing Black organizations," continue to push the twelve-point program, and develop study groups that focused on the "Science of Black Internationalism, and the thought of Chairman Rob [Robert Williams]."

"On the Move Like Never Before in Human History"

It is ironic that RAM's demise coincided with the Cultural Revolution in China. In 1966, when Mao initiated the Cultural Revolution, police repression had driven most RAM members even further underground. And yet it was the Cultural Revolution that seemed to have the most direct impact on Black radical movements in the United States.

We know with hindsight that millions of people were jailed, beaten, and killed in the name of the Cultural Revolution; inside China itself, it hardly constituted a bright moment in socialist history. But to the outside world at the time, among radicals at least, it projected a vision of society where divisions between those with power and those without no longer exist, where society can truly be called egalitarian. Hierarchies in the party and in the Red Army were ostensibly eliminated. Criticism and self-criticism were encouraged—as long as they coincided with Mao Tse-tung's thought. Communists suspected of supporting a capitalist road were brought to trial. Bourgeois intellectuals in the academy and government were expected to perform manual labor, to work among the people as a way of breaking down social hierarchies. And all vestiges of the old order were to be eliminated. The youth, now the vanguard, attacked tradition with a vengeance and sought to create new cultural forms to promote the revolution. The people of China were now called on to educate themselves. The Cultural Revolution intensified the constituent elements of Maoism: the idea of constant rebellion and conflict, the concept of the centrality of people over economic laws or productive forces, the notion of revolutionary morality.

Socialists Paul Sweezey and Leo Huberman, editors of the U.S. independent socialist journal *Monthly Review,* recognized the huge implications such a revolution had for the urban poor in the United States: "Just imagine what would happen in the United States if a President were to invite the poor in this country, with special emphasis on the blacks in the urban ghettos, to win the war on poverty for themselves, promising them the protection of the army against reprisals!" Of course, the United States is not a socialist country and never pretended to be, and despite a somewhat sympathetic President Lyndon Johnson, Black people in this country were not regarded by the state as "the people." Their problems were a drain on society and their ungrateful riots and the proliferation of revolutionary organizations did not elicit much sympathy for the Black poor.

For many in the New Left, African Americans were not only *"the* people" but the most revolutionary sector of the working class. The Cultural Revolution's emphasis on eliminating hierarchies and empowering the oppressed reinforced the idea that Black liberation lay at the heart of the new American Revolution. Mao Tse-tung himself gave credence to this view in his widely circulated April 1968 statement "in Support of the Afro-American Struggle Against Violent Repression." The statement was delivered during a massive demonstration in China protesting the assassination of Dr. Martin Luther King Jr., at which Robert Williams and Vicki Garvin were among the featured speakers. According to Garvin, at least, "millions of Chinese demonstrators" marched in the pouring rain to denounce American racism. Responding to the rebellions touched off by King's assassination, Mao characterized these urban uprisings as "a new clarion call to all the exploited and oppressed people of the United States to fight against the barbarous rule of the monopoly capitalist class." Even more than the 1963 statement, Mao's words endowed the urban riots with historic importance in the world of revolutionary upheaval. His statement, as well as the general logic of Lin Biao's "theory of the new democratic revolution" justified support for Black nationalist movements and their right of self-determination.

It was in the context of the urban rebellions that several streams of Black radicalism, including RAM, converged and gave birth to the Black Panther Party for Self-Defense in Oakland, California. Although it was perhaps the most visible Black organization promoting Mao's thought, by some accounts its members were probably the least serious about reading Marxist, Leninist, or Maoist writings and developing a revolutionary ideology. Founded by Huey Newton and Bobby Seale, a former RAM member, the Panthers went well beyond the boundaries of Merritt College and recruited the "lumpenproletariat." Much of the rank-and-file engaged more in sloganeering than anything else, and their bible was the "Little Red Book."

That the Panthers were Marxist, at least in rhetoric and program, was one of the sources of their dispute with Ron Karenga's US Organization and other groups they derisively dismissed as cultural nationalists. Of course, not only did the Panthers have their own cultural nationalist agenda, but the so-called cultural nationalists were not a monolith or uniformly procapitalist. And the divisions between these groups were exacerbated by COINTELPRO. Still, there was a fundamental difference between the Panthers' evolving ideology of socialism and class struggle and that of Black nationalist groups, even on the Left. As Bobby Seale explained in a March 1969 interview,

> We're talking about socialism. The cultural nationalists say that socialism won't do anything for us. There's the contradiction between the old and the new. Black people have no time to practice black racism and the masses of black people do not hate white people just because of the color of their skin. . . . We're not going to go out foolishly and say there is no possibility of aligning with some righteous white revolutionaries, or other poor and oppressed peoples in this country who might come to see the light about the fact that it's the capitalist system they must get rid of.

How the Panthers arrived at this position and the divisions within the party over their stance is a long and complicated story that we cannot address here. For our purposes, we want to make a few brief points about the party's embrace of Mao's thought and its position vis-à-vis Black self-determination. For Huey Newton, whose contribution to the party's ideology rivals that of Eldridge Cleaver and George Jackson, the source of the Panthers' Marxism was the Chinese and Cuban revolutions. The Chinese and Cubans developed an analysis directly out of their respective histories rather than from the pages of *Capital*. The Chinese and Cuban examples, according to Newton, empowered the Panthers to develop their own unique program and to discard theoretical insights from Marx and Lenin that had little or no application to Black reality. Indeed, a quick perusal of the Panthers' "Ten-Point Program" reveals quite clearly that Malcolm X continued to be one of their biggest ideological influences.

Eldridge Cleaver was a little more explicit about the role of Maoism and the thought of Korean Communist leader Kim Il Sung in reshaping Marxism-Leninism for the benefit of national liberation struggles of Third World peoples. In a 1968 pamphlet titled "On the Ideology of the BPP (Part 1)," Cleaver made clear that the Panthers were a Marxist-Leninist party but added that Marx, Engels, Lenin, and their contemporary followers did not offer much insight with regard to understanding and fighting racism. The lesson was to adopt and alter what was useful and reject what was not. Cleaver wrote,

> With the founding of the Democratic People's Republic of Korea in 1948 and the People's Republic of China in 1949, something new was interjected into Marxism-Leninism, and it ceased to be just a narrow, exclusively European phenomenon. Comrade Kim Il Sung and Comrade Mao Tse-tung applied the classical principles of Marxism-Leninism to the conditions of their own countries and thereby made the ideology into something useful for their people. But they rejected that part of the analysis that was not beneficial to them and had only to do with the welfare of Europe.

In Cleaver's view, the sharpest critique of Western Marxism's blindness with regard to race came from Frantz Fanon.

By seeing themselves as part of a global national-liberation movement, the Panthers also spoke of the Black community as a colony with an inherent right to self-determination. Yet, unlike many other Black or interracial Maoist groups, they never advocated secession or the creation of a separate state. Rather, describing Black people as colonial subjects was a way of characterizing the materialist nature of racism; it was more a metaphor than an analytical concept. Self-determination was understood to mean community control within the urban environment, not necessarily the establishment of a Black nation. In a paper delivered at the Peace and Freedom Party's founding convention in March 1968, Cleaver tried to clarify the relationship between interracial unity in the U.S. revolution and "national liberation in the black colony." On one hand, he essentially called for a dual approach in which Black and white radicals worked together to create coalitions of revolutionary organizations and develop a political and military machinery that could overthrow capitalism and imperialism. On the other hand, he called for a UN-sponsored plebiscite that would allow Black people to determine whether they wished to integrate or separate. Such a plebiscite, he argued, would bring clarity to Black people on the question of self-determination, just as first-wave independence movements in Africa had to decide whether they wanted to maintain some altered dominion status or achieve complete independence.

Cleaver represented a wing of the party more interested in guerrilla warfare than in rebuilding society or doing the hard work of grassroots organizing. The attraction to Mao, Kim Il Sung, Giap, Che, and for that matter Fanon, were these thinkers' writings on revolutionary violence and people's wars. Many self-styled Panther theoreticians focused so much on developing tactics to sustain the imminent revolution that they skipped over a good deal of Mao's writings. Recognizing the problem, Newton sought to move the party away from an emphasis on guerrilla warfare and violence to a deeper, richer discussion of what the party's vision for the future might entail. Shortly after his release from prison in August 1970, he proposed the creation of an "ideological institute" where participants actually read and taught what he regarded as the "classics"—Marx, Mao, and Lenin, as well as Aristotle, Plato, Rousseau, Kant, Kierkegaard, and Nietzsche. Unfortunately, the ideological institute did not amount to much; few party members saw the use of abstract theorizing or the relevance of some of these writings to revolution. Besides, the fact that *Quotations from Chairman Mao* read more or less like a handbook for guerrillas didn't help matters much. Even Fanon was read pretty selectively, his chapter "Concerning Violence" being a perpetual favorite among militants. George Jackson contributed to the Panthers' theoretical emphasis on war since much of his own writings, from *Soledad Brother* to *Blood in My Eye*, drew on Mao primarily to discuss armed resistance under fascism. Efforts to read the works of Marx, Lenin, or Mao beyond issues related to armed rebellion did not always find a willing audience among the Panthers. Sid Lemelle, then a radical activist at California State University at Los Angeles, recalls being in contact with a few Panthers who had joined a study group sponsored by the California Communist League. The reading, which included Mao's *Four Essays on Philosophy* and lengthy passages from Lenin's selected works, turned out to be too much and they eventually left the group amid a stormy debate.

Perhaps the least read section of *Quotations from Chairman Mao*, at least by men, was the five-page chapter on women. In an age when the metaphors for Black liberation were increasingly masculinized and Black movement leaders not only ignored but perpetuated gender oppression, even the most Marxist of the Black nationalist movements belittled the "Woman Question." The BPP was certainly no exception. Indeed, it was during the same historic meeting of the SDS in 1969, where the Panthers invoked Marx, Lenin, and Mao to expel the Progressive Labor Party (PLP) for its position on the national question, that Panther Minister of Information Rufus Walls gave his infamous speech about the need to have women in the movement because they possessed "pussy power." Clearly a vernacular takeoff on Mao's line that "China's women are a vast reserve of labour power [that] . . . should be tapped in the struggle to build a great socialist country," Walls's statement turned out to be a profoundly antifeminist defense of women's participation.

While China's own history on the Woman Question is pretty dismal, Mao's dictum that "women hold up half the sky" as well as his brief writings on women's equality and participation in the revolutionary process endowed women's liberation with some revolutionary legitimacy on the Left. Of course, Maoism didn't make the movement: The fact is, women's struggles within the New Left played the most important role in reorienting leftist movements toward a feminist agenda or at least putting feminism on the table. But for Black women in the Panthers suspicious of "white feminism," Mao's language on women's equality provided space within the party to develop an incipient Black feminist agenda. As the newly appointed minister of information, Panther Elaine Brown announced to a press conference soon after returning from China in 1971 that "the BPP acknowledges the progressive leadership of our Chinese comrades in all areas of revolution. Specifically, we embrace China's correct recognition of the proper status of women as equal to that of men." Even beyond the rhetoric, Black women Panthers such as Lynn French, Kathleen Cleaver, Erica Huggins, Akua Njere, and Assata Shakur (formerly Joanne Chesimard) sustained the tradition of carving out free spaces within existing male-dominated organizations in order to challenge the multiple forms of exploitation that Black working-class women faced daily. Through the Panthers' free breakfast and educational programs, for example, Black women devised strategies that, in varying degrees, challenged capitalism, racism, and patriarchy. And in some instances, African-American women radicals rose to positions of prominence and, sometimes by sheer example, contributed to developing a militant, class-conscious, Black feminist perspective. In some instances, the growing strength of a Black leftist feminist perspective, buttressed by certain Maoist slogans on the Woman Question, shaped future Black Maoist formations. One obvious example is the Black Vanguard Party, another Bay Area Maoist group active in the mid- to late 1970s whose publication *Juche!* maintained a consistent socialist-feminist perspective. Michelle Gibbs (also known as Michelle Russell, her married name at the time) promoted a Black feminist ideology as a Detroit supporter of the League of Revolutionary Black Workers and a member of the Black Workers Congress. A "red diaper baby" whose father, Ted Gibbs, fought in the Spanish Civil War and who grew up in a household where Paul Robeson and artist Elizabeth Catlett were occasional guests, Gibbs's Black socialist-feminist perspective flowed from her political experience, from the writings of Black feminist writers, and from a panoply of radical thinkers ranging from Malcolm, Fanon, and Amilcar Cabral to Marx, Lenin, and Mao. Conversely, the predominantly white radical feminist organization Redstockings was not only influenced by Mao's writings but modeled itself somewhat on the Black Power movement, particularly on the movement's separatist strategies and identification with the Third World.

Ironically, the BPP's greatest identification with China occurred at the very moment when China's status among the Left began to decline worldwide. Mao's willingness to host President Nixon and China's support of the repressive governments of Pakistan and Sri Lanka left many Maoists in the United States and elsewhere disillusioned. Nevertheless, Newton and Elaine Brown not only visited China on the eve of Nixon's trip, but also announced that their entry into electoral politics was inspired by China's entry into the UN. Newton argued that the Black Panthers' shift toward reformist, electoral politics did not contradict "China's goal of toppling U.S. imperialism nor [was it] an abnegation of revolutionary principles. It was a tactic of socialist revolution." Even more incredible was Newton's complete abandonment of Black self-determination, which he explained in terms of developments in the world economy. In 1971, he concluded quite presciently that the globalization of the economy rendered the idea of national sovereignty obsolete, even among the socialist countries. Thus Black demands for self-determination were no longer relevant; the only viable strategy was global revolution. "Blacks in the U.S. have a special duty to give up any claim to nationhood now more than ever. The U.S. has never been our country; and realistically there's no territory for us to claim. Of all the oppressed people in the world, we are in the best position to inspire global revolution."

In many respects, Newton's position on the national question was closer to Mao's than those of many self-proclaimed Maoist organizations that popped up in the 1970s. Despite his own statements in support of national liberation movements and Lin Biao's "theory of democratic revolutions," Mao did not support independent organizations along nationalist lines. To him, Black nationalism looked like ethnic or racial particularism. He was, after all, a Chinese nationalist attempting to unify peasants and proletarians and eliminate ethnic divisions within his own country. We might recall his 1957 statement in which he demanded that progressives in China "help unite the people of our various nationalities . . . not divide them." Thus while recognizing that racism was a product of colonialism and imperialism, his 1968 statement insisted that the "contradiction between the black masses in the United States and U.S. ruling circles is a class contradiction. . . . The black masses and the masses of white working people in the United States share common interests and have common objectives to struggle for." In other words, the Black struggle was bound to merge with the working-class movement and overthrow capitalism.

On the issue of Black liberation, however, most American Maoist organizations founded in the early to mid-1970s took their lead from Stalin, not Mao. Black people in the United States were not simply proletarians in Black skin but a nation, or as Stalin put it, "a historically evolved, stable community of language, territory, economic life, and psychological make-up manifested in a community of culture." Marxist groups that embraced Stalin's definition of a nation, such as the Communist Labor Party (CLP) and the October League, also resurrected the old Communist Party's position that African Americans in the Black belt counties of the South constituted a nation and had a right to secede if they wished. Conversely, groups like the PLP—once an advocate of "revolutionary nationalism"—moved to a position repudiating all forms of nationalism by the start of the Cultural Revolution.

The CLP was perhaps the most consistent advocate of Black self-determination among the Marxist-Leninist movements. Founded in 1968 largely by African Americans and Latinos, the CLP's roots can be traced to the old Provisional Organizing Committee (POC)—itself an outgrowth of the 1956 split in the CPUSA which led to the creation of two separate groups called Hammer and Steel and the Progressive Labor Movement. Ravaged by a decade of internal splits, the POC had become a predominantly Black and Puerto Rican organization divided between New York and Los Angeles. In 1968, the New York leadership expelled its Los Angeles comrades for, among other things, refusing to denounce Stalin and Mao. In turn, the Los Angeles group, largely under the guidance of veteran Black Marxist Nelson Peery, founded the California Communist League that same year and began recruiting young Black and Chicano radical workers and intellectuals. Peery's home in South Central Los Angeles had already become something of a hangout for young Black radicals after the Watts uprising; he organized informal groups to study history, political economy, and classic works in Marxist-Leninist-Maoist thought and entertained all sorts of activists, from Black Panthers to student activists from California State University at Los Angeles to Los Angeles Community College. The California Communist League subsequently merged with a group of SDS militants calling themselves the Marxist-Leninist Workers Association and formed the Communist League in 1970. Two years later they changed their name again to the Communist Labor Party.

Except for perhaps Harry Haywood's long essay, *Toward a Revolutionary Position on the Negro Question* (first published in 1957 but kept in circulation throughout the 1960s and 1970s), Nelson Peery's short book *The Negro National Colonial Question* (1972) was probably the most widely read defense of Black self-determination in Marxist-Leninist-Maoist circles at the time. Peery was sharply criticized for his defense of the term *Negro*, a difficult position to maintain in the midst of the Black Power movement. But Peery had a point: National identity was not about color. The Negro nation was a historically evolved, stable community with its own unique culture, language (or rather dialect), and territory — the Black belt counties and their surrounding areas, or essentially the thirteen states of the Old Confederacy. Because Southern whites shared with African Americans a common territory, and by his account a common language and culture, they were also considered part of the "Negro nation." More precisely, Southern whites composed the "Anglo-American minority" within the Negro nation. As evidenced in soul music, spirituals, and rock and roll, Peery insisted, what had emerged in the South was a hybrid culture with strong African roots manifest in the form of slave folk tales and female head wraps. Jimi Hendrix and Sly and the Family Stone as well as white imitators Al Jolson, Elvis Presley, and Tom Jones were all cited as examples of a shared culture. He even saw "soul" culture embedded in dietary habits: "The custom of eating pigs' feet, neck bones, black-eyed peas, greens, yams, and chitterlings are all associated with the region of the South, particularly the Negro Nation."

Peery's positioning of Southern whites as part of the Negro Nation was a stroke of genius, particularly since one of his intentions was to destabilize racial categories. However, at times his commitment to Stalin's definition of a nation weakened his argument. At the very moment when mass migration and urbanization were depleting the rural South of its Black population, Peery insisted that the Black belt was the natural homeland of Negroes. He even attempted to prove that a Black peasantry and stable rural proletariat still existed in the Black belt. Because the land question was the foundation upon which his understanding of self-determination was built, he ended up saying very little about the nationalization of industry or socialized production. Thus he could write in 1972, "The Negro national colonial question can only be solved by a return of the land to the people who have toiled over it for centuries. In the Negro Nation this land redistribution will demand a combination of state farms and cooperative enterprises in order to best meet the needs of the people under the conditions of modern mechanized agriculture."

The movement with perhaps the deepest roots in the Black cultural politics of the 1960s that developed a Marxist-Leninist-Maoist position somewhat akin to that of RAM was the Revolutionary Communist League (RCL)—founded and led by none other than the poet, critic, and activist Amiri Baraka. To understand the RCL's ideological history, we need to go back to 1966 when Baraka founded Spirit House in Newark, New Jersey, with the help of local activists as well as people he had worked with in Harlem's Black Arts Repertory Theater. Although Spirit House artists were involved in local political organizing from the beginning, the police beating of Baraka and several other activists during the Newark uprising in 1967 politicized them even further. After the uprising they helped organize a Black Power conference in Newark, which attracted several national Black leaders, including SNCC's Stokely Carmichael and H. Rap Brown, Huey Newton of the BPP, and Imari Obadele of the newly formed Republic of New Africa (partly an outgrowth of RAM). Shortly thereafter, Spirit House became the base for the Committee for a Unified Newark (CFUN), a new organization made up of United Brothers, Black Community Defense and Development, and Sisters of Black Culture. In addition to attracting Black nationalists, Muslims, and even a few Marxist-Leninist-Maoists, CFUN bore the mark of Ron Karenga's US Organization. CFUN adopted Karenga's version of cultural nationalism and worked closely with him. Although tensions arose between Karenga and some of the Newark activists over his treatment of women and the overly centralized leadership structure CFUN had imported from US Organization, the movement continued to grow. In 1970, Baraka

renamed CFUN the Congress of African Peoples (CAP), transformed it into a national organization, and at its founding convention broke with Karenga. CAP leaders sharply criticized Karenga's
cultural nationalism and passed resolutions that reflected a turn
to the Left—including a proposal to raise funds to help build the
Tanzania-Zambia railroad.

There are several sources for Baraka's left turn during this period. One has to do with the painful lesson he learned about the
limitations of Black "petty bourgeois" politicians. After playing a
pivotal role in the 1970 election of Kenneth Gibson, Newark's first
Black mayor, Baraka witnessed an increase in police repression
(including attacks on CAP demonstrators) and Gibson's failure to
deliver what he had promised the African-American community.
Feeling betrayed and disillusioned, Baraka broke with Gibson in
1974, though he did not give up entirely on the electoral process.
His role in organizing the first National Black Political Assembly
in 1972 reinforced in his mind the power of Black independent
politics and the potential strength of a Black united front.

One source of Baraka's left turn was CLP East Coast regional
coordinator William Watkins. Harlem-born and raised, Watkins
was among a group of radical Black students at California State
University at Los Angeles who helped found the Communist
League. In 1974 he got to know Baraka, who was trying to find
someone to advance his understanding of Marxism-Leninism.
"We'd spend hours in his office," Watkins recalled, "discussing
the basics—like surplus value." For about three months, Baraka
met with Watkins regularly; Watkins taught him the fundamen-
tals of political economy and tried to expose the limitations of cultural nationalism. These meetings certainly influenced Baraka's
leftward turn, but when Watkins and Nelson Peery asked Baraka
to join the CLP, he refused. Although he had come to appreciate
Marxism-Leninism-Maoism, he wasn't ready to join a multiracial
organization. The Black struggle was first and foremost.

It is fitting that the most important source of Baraka's radicalization came out of Africa. Just as Baraka's first left turn after 1960

was spurred on by the Cuban Revolution, the struggle in southern Africa prompted his post-1970 turn to the left. The key event
was the creation of the African Liberation Support Committee
(ALSC) in 1971. It originated with a group of Black nationalists led by Owusu Sadaukai, director of Malcolm X Liberation
University in Greensboro, North Carolina, who traveled to Mozambique under the aegis of FRELIMO (The Front for the Liberation of Mozambique). FRELIMO's president Samora Machel
(who, coincidentally, was in China at the same time as Huey
Newton) and other militants persuaded Sadaukai and his colleagues that the most useful role African Americans could play in
support of anticolonialism was to challenge American capitalism
from within and let the world know the truth about FRELIMO's
just war against Portuguese domination. A year later, during his
last visit to the United States, Amilcar Cabral, the leader of the
anticolonial movement in Guinea-Bissau and the Cape Verde
Islands, said essentially the same thing. Moreover, Cabral and
Machel represented explicitly Marxist movements; they rejected
the idea that precolonial African societies were inherently democratic and practiced a form of "primitive communism" that could
lay the groundwork for modern socialism. Rather, they asserted
that African societies were not immune from class struggle, and
that capitalism was not the only road to development.

The ALSC reflected the radical orientation of the liberation
movements in Portuguese Africa. On May 27, 1972 (the anniversary of the founding of the Organization of African Unity), the
ALSC held the first African Liberation Day (ALD) demonstration, drawing approximately 30,000 protesters in Washington,
D.C., alone, and an estimated 30,000 more across the country.
The ALD Coordinating Committee consisted of representatives
from several nationalist and Black leftist organizations, including
the Youth Organization for Black Unity (YOBU); the All-African
People's Revolutionary Party (AAPRP) headed by Stokely Carmichael (Kwame Ture); the Pan-African People's Organization;
and the Maoist-influenced Black Workers Congress (BWC). Because the ALSC brought together such a broad range of Black

activists, it became an arena for debate over the creation of a Black radical agenda. While most ALSC organizers were actively anti-imperialist, the number of Black Marxists in leadership positions turned out to be a point of contention. Aside from Sadaukai, who would go on to play a major role in the Maoist-oriented Revolutionary Workers League (RWL), the ALSC's main leaders included Nelson Johnson (future leader in the Communist Workers Party) and Abdul Alkalimat (a brilliant writer and founding member of the RWL). As early as 1973, splits occurred within the ALSC over the role of Marxists, though when the dust settled a year later, Marxists from the RWL, the BWC, the Revolutionary Workers Congress (an offshoot of the BWC), CAP, and the Workers Viewpoint Organization (precursor to the Communist Workers Party) remained in the organization. Unfortunately, internal squabbling and sectarianism proved too much for the ALSC to handle. Chinese foreign policy struck the final blow; its support for the National Union for the Total Independence of Angola (UNITA) during the 1975 Angolan civil war and Vice-Premier Li Xiannian's suggestion that dialogue with white South Africa was better than armed insurrection, placed Black Maoists in the ALSC in a difficult position. Within three years the ALSC had utterly collapsed, bringing to an inauspicious close perhaps the most dynamic anti-imperialist organization of the decade.

Nevertheless, Baraka's experience in the ALSC profoundly altered his thinking. As he recalls in his autobiography, by the time of the first African Liberation Day demonstration in 1972, he was "going left, I was reading Nkrumah and Cabral and Mao." Within two years he was calling on CAP members to examine "the international revolutionary experience (namely the Russian and Chinese Revolutions) and integrate it with the practice of the Afrikan revolution." Their study lists expanded to include works such as Mao's *Four Essays on Philosophy*, Stalin's *Foundations of Leninism*, and *History of the Communist Party Soviet Union (Short Course)*. By 1976, CAP had dispensed with all vestiges of nationalism, changed its name to the Revolutionary Communist League (RCL), and sought to remake itself into a multiracial

Marxist-Leninist-Maoist movement. Perhaps as a way to establish its ideological moorings as an antirevisionist movement, the RCL followed in the noble tradition of resurrecting the Black belt thesis. In 1977, the RCL (most likely Baraka) published a paper titled "The Black Nation," which analyzed Black liberation movements from a Marxist-Leninist-Maoist perspective and concluded that Black people in the South and in large cities constituted a nation with an inherent right to self-determination. While rejecting "bourgeois integration," the essay argued that the struggle for Black political power was central to the fight for self-determination.

The RCL attempted to put its vision of self-determination in practice through efforts to build a Black united front. It organized coalitions against police brutality, mobilized support for striking cafeteria workers and maintenance workers, created a People's Committee on Education to challenge budget cuts and shape educational policy, and protested the *Bakke* decision. The RCL's grassroots organizing and coalition building brought its members into contact with the League of Revolutionary Struggle (LRS), a California-based movement formed from a merger between I Wor Kuen, the Chinese-American Maoist organization, and the predominantly Chicano August Twenty-ninth Movement (Marxist-Leninist). In 1979, the RCL and the LRS decide to unite, one of the foundations of their joint program being their support of the Black nation thesis. As a result of the merger and the debates that preceded it, the RCL's position changed slightly: Southern Black people and Chicanos in the Southwest constituted oppressed nations with the right to self-determination. By contrast, for Black people locked in Northern ghettos the struggle for equal rights took precedence over the land question.

Invariably, the merger was short-lived, in part because of disagreements over the issue of self-determination and the continuing presence of what LRS cadres regarded as "narrow nationalism" in the RCL. LRS Chairperson Carmen Chang was never comfortable with the Black nation thesis but accepted it for the sake of unity. Baraka's group, by contrast, never abandoned Black unity for multiracial class struggle. And as a dyed-in-the-wool artist with deep roots in the Black Arts Movement, Baraka persistently focused his cultural and political interests on the contradictions of Black life under capitalism, imperialism, and racism. For Baraka, as with many of the characters discussed in this essay, this was not a simple matter of narrow nationalism. On the contrary, understanding the place of racist oppression and Black revolution within the context of capitalism and imperialism was fundamental to the future of humanity. In the tradition of Du Bois, Fanon, and Harold Cruse, Baraka insisted that the Black (hence colonial) proletariat was the vanguard of world revolution "not because of some mystic chauvinism but because of our place in objective history. . . . We are the vanguard because we are at the bottom, and when we raise to stand up straight everything stacked upon us topples."

Moreover, despite his immersion in Marxist-Leninist-Maoist literature, his own cultural work suggests that he knew, as did most Black radicals, that the question of whether Black people constituted a nation was not going to be settled through reading Lenin or Stalin. If it ever could be settled, the battles would take place, for better or for worse, on the terrain of culture. Although the Black Arts Movement was the primary vehicle for Black cultural revolution in the United States, it is hard to imagine what that revolution would have looked like without China. Black radicals seized the Great Proletarian Cultural Revolution by the horns and reshaped it in their own image.

COINTELPRO operations only partly explain the dissolution of RAM and the various movements that followed. We can point to a number of strategic errors as well, the most glaring being the movements' eagerness to confront the state head-on and boldly attack anyone they deemed misleaders or reformists. Consequently, groups like RAM were unable to build a strong base in Black urban communities. Part of the problem lay in the movement's emphasis on the liberatory potential of revolutionary violence. It would be unfair to indict RAM alone for this because practically all its contemporaries in revolutionary movements, especially by the mid- to late 1960s, understood violence as inevitable. They suffered extreme terror from groups like state police agencies, local red squads, and the FBI, and were often pushed to armed self-defense by the circumstances at hand. At the same time, they read Fanon, paid attention to guerilla warfare in the Third World, and knew of the many armed self-defense groups that played a key role in the protection of civil rights marchers. But because Fanon had argued that violence was, for the Algerian peasantry at least, a necessary step in the creation of a new revolutionary man, the young Black men who accepted the enormous task of over-throwing U.S. imperialism might have placed too much stock in warfare. Indeed, I think RAM activists were so concerned with self-defense and on how to win militarily that they devoted little time and energy to the most fundamental question of all: what kind of world they wanted to build if they did win. Perhaps it was a matter of a lack of political imagination, for as I pointed out earlier RAM militants never really engaged in violence—they just wrote and talked about it. Some of its early members did go on to help form organizations that did participate in armed self-defense campaigns—notably the BPP, the Black Liberation Army, and the Republic of New Afrika. Nevertheless, the ques-tion of violence and warfare remained at the core of RAM's po-litical strategy.

On the other hand, RAM was hardly a failure. While it never re-ceived the glory or publicity bestowed on groups like the BPP, its influence far exceeded its numbers—not unlike the ABB four de-cades earlier. RAM's success ought to be measured in terms of its theoretical contributions and its "agitprop" work. Its publications and forums consistently placed the Black freedom movement in an international context, drew powerful analogies between the Black condition in the United States and those of colonized peo-ple throughout the world, offered incisive critiques of capitalism and bourgeois democracy aimed at Black urban communities, and elevated revolutionary Black nationalism to a position of crit-ical theoretical importance for the Left in general. By placing a critique of neocolonialism and imperialism at the center of their theory, RAM militants never agonized over whether to support reactionary Black regimes in Africa or the Caribbean. They flatly rejected unconditional racial unity and developed a nationalism built on a broader concept of revolutionary Third World solidarity.

Most of all, RAM contributed to a nearly forgotten tradition in Black radicalism: This tiny group of young, mostly male intellectuals were internationalists before they were nationalists. They fought for the ghettos of North America but saw their struggle in terms of the entire globe. Their Goliath was the entire Western world, not just Kennedy and Johnson, or even the Rockefellers. And they entered battle with a sense that victory was inevitable, for not even the ruling class could control the weather. Listen again to Askia Muhammad Toure: "How long does the white 'Free World' have before the Gong of History announces the Storm? Who knows in terms of days, months, in terms of years? One thing is certain: it is coming as surely as the Great Sun rises in the East and lights up the planet, dispelling the foggy mists and murky darkness of the long, cold, miserable Night."

But one question remained unanswered: What would the coming dawn bring and what would we build after the storm?

"A DAY OF RECKONING": DREAMS OF REPARATIONS

I'm not bitter, neither am I cruel
But ain't nobody paid for slavery yet
I may be crazy, but I ain't no fool.
About my forty acres and my mule. . . .
One hundred years of debt at ten percent
Per year, per forty acres and per mule
Now add that up. . . .

—Oscar Brown Jr., "Forty Acres and a Mule," 1964

You hear these white people talk about they've pulled themselves
up by their own bootstraps. Well they took our boots, no less our
straps, and then after they made us a citizen, honey, what did they
turn around and do? They passed black codes in order to take from
us all the benefits of citizenship.

—"Queen Mother" Audley Moore, 1978

The Civil War had barely been settled when Colonel P. H. Anderson of Big Spring, Tennessee, dispatched a letter to his former slave, Jourdon, inviting him to return to the Anderson plantation as a paid laborer. Despite promises of freedom, good treatment, and fair wages, Jourdon was more than a little suspicious of the offer. With the help of Lydia Maria Child, a prolific writer, abolitionist, and schoolteacher, he dictated a very powerful letter to his old master. He began by expressing concern that he and his wife, Mandy, were

> afraid to go back without proof that you were disposed to treat us justly and kindly; and we have concluded to test your sincerity by asking you to send us our wages for the time we served you. This will make us forget and forgive old scores, and rely on your justice and friendship in the future. I served you faithfully for thirty-two years, and Mandy twenty years. At twenty-five dollars a month for me, and two dollars a week for Mandy, our earnings would amount to eleven thousand six hundred and eighty dollars. Add to this the interest for the time our wages have been kept back, and deduct what you paid for our clothing, and three doctor's visits to me, and pulling a tooth for Mandy, and the balance will show what we are in justice entitled to. Please send the money by Adam's Express, in care of V. Winters, Esq., Dayton, Ohio. If you fail to pay us for faithful labors in the past, we can have little faith in your promises in the future. We trust the good Maker has opened your eyes to the wrongs which you and your fathers have done to me and my fathers, in making us toil for you for generations without recompense. Here I draw my wages every Saturday night; but in Tennessee there was never any pay-day for the Negroes any more than for the horses and cows. Surely there will be a day of reckoning for those who defraud the laborer of his hire.
>
> In answering this letter, please state if there would be any safety for my Milly and Jane, who are now grown up, and both good-looking girls. You know how it was with poor Matilda and Catherine. I would rather stay here and starve — and die, if it come to that — than have my girls brought to shame by the violence and wickedness of their young masters. . . .
>
> Say howdy to George Carter, and thank him for taking the pistol from you when you were shooting at me.

By even the most elementary principles of liberal capitalism, Jourdon Anderson presents a sound, reasonable case for receiving compensation for years of unpaid labor. He was the colonel's property, to be sure, but the fact that he could write such a letter and make such a brilliant case distinguishes him from "the horses and cows" that also served the needs of the plantation without pay. Indeed, by today's standards Jourdon is being charitable by asking only for back wages and interest. He does not make a case for damages despite the physical and psychological abuse visited upon his whole family—the rape, the violence, the horrible living conditions, the mere fact of bondage.

My guess is that most of you laughed out loud after reading Jourdon's letter and some might have found it incredible. The colonel probably laughed, too, dismissing his former slave's request as absurd. One hundred and thirty-seven years have passed since the enactment of the Thirteenth Amendment ending slavery in the United States, and most of America is still dismissing demands for reparations, claiming that the very idea violates the basic principles of U.S. democracy and laissez-faire capitalism. As I wrote these words, the U.S. delegation to the historic World Conference against Racism in Durban, South Africa, walked out, in part because the delegation refused even to discuss the question of reparations. Slavery is behind us, we are told, and any payments to Black people would be divisive or an act of discrimination *against white people*. Others argue that Black people have already received billions of dollars of aid through welfare and poverty programs and therefore if there was a debt owed us, it has been paid many times over. Right-wing critics like Dinesh D'Souza go one step further, arguing that the only people deserving of reparations are the slave masters, and presumably their descendants, since the government "freed" their property without compensation! Besides denying the basic humanity of the enslaved and not accounting for the tremendous wealth the master class acquired by exploiting unpaid labor, D'Souza's twisted logic conveniently ignores the fact that the vast majority of slaveholders committed treason against the United States and were never punished. Jourdon's letter exposes this irony as well: "I thought the Yankees would have hung you long before this, for harboring Rebs they found at your house. I suppose they never heard about your going to Colonel Martin's to kill the Union soldier that was left by his company in their stable."

For African Americans in search of freedom, the question of reparations was never a laughing matter. And as Jourdon Anderson's letter makes clear, it is a very old issue. Indeed, as early as 1854, a convention of Black emigrationists called on the federal government to provide a "national indemnity" as a "redress of our grievances for the unparalleled wrongs . . . which we suffered at the hands of this American people." Immediately after the war, Sojourner Truth organized a petition seeking free public land for former slaves. "America owes to my people some of the dividends," she argued. "I shall make them understand that there is a debt to the Negro people which they can never repay. At least, then, they must make amends." Bishop Henry McNeil Turner calculated the debt at some forty billion dollars. For the next century and a half, there have been numerous movements intent on making "amends."

Today there are countless proposals for reparations as partial compensation for slavery and/or postslavery racial discrimination. The growing support for reparations is partly linked to the passage of the Civil Liberties Act of 1988 authorizing reparations payments to Japanese Americans interned during World War II, and to Congressman John Conyers's bill, which has been in committee since it was first introduced in 1989, to create a commission to study the issue of reparations for Black people. And, of course, there are many precedents. Besides interned Japanese and Jewish Holocaust victims, the latter having received payments both from the German state and private corporations, we can point to the Alaska Claims Settlement of 1971, in which the United States awarded indigenous Alaskans one billion dollars and more than forty-four million acres. An even more immediate and perhaps more relevant example is the Rosewood, Florida, settlement. In 1995, nine former residents of Rosewood, once an all-Black town, were awarded $150,000 each as restitution for property destroyed by white mobs during the 1923 pogrom. Given the overwhelming destruction and loss of life, these sums were hardly adequate. Nevertheless, the settlement set a precedent for all victims of racist violence and exploitation, especially when they were indirectly sanctioned by the state through legalized segregation or, in other instances, legalized slavery.

Partly as a result of these precedents and the organizing efforts of various movements, we have seen a proliferation of books, articles, and public debates on the issue of reparations based on all manner of economic calculations, legal loopholes, and a wide range of political and moral arguments. My purpose is not to weigh the pros and cons of one proposal against another, or to come up with my own calculations of what slavery and racial discrimination cost us. Much outstanding work along these lines has been done by writers such as Robert Allen, Kimberle Crenshaw, William Darity Jr., David Swinton, Robert K. Fullinwinder, Clarence Munford, Melvin Oliver and Thomas Shapiro, Randall Robinson, and a battery of law professors too numerous to list here. While I do make a case for reparations, I'm more interested in the historical vision and imagination that has animated the movement since the days of slavery. Except for among groups like the National Coalition of Blacks for Reparations in America (N'COBRA) and the Black Radical Congress (BRC), such a vision of the future is sorely lacking in most contemporary arguments for reparations. By looking at the reparations campaign in the United States as a social movement, we discover that it was never entirely, or even primarily, about money. The demand for reparations was about social justice, reconciliation, reconstructing the internal life of Black America, and eliminating institutional racism. This is why reparations proposals from Black radical movements focus less on individual payments than on securing funds to build autonomous Black institutions, improving community life, and in some cases establishing a homeland that will enable African Americans to develop a political economy geared more toward collective needs than toward accumulation.

"Forty Acres and a Mule"

African-American troops who survived the Civil War had it right: They were the liberators, their ex-masters the rebels. They believed that the rebels' land should be divided up among the folks who toiled for so many generations without pay. And some of the ex-slaves did just that, parceling out their former masters' property, staking claims to abandoned plantation lands, preparing to inherit the earth they had turned into wealth for idle white people. There were a few precedents for their expectations. In January 1865, Union General William T. Sherman had issued Special Field Order 15, designating land along the South Carolina coast and on the Sea Islands to be distributed among freed people. Each family was to receive forty acres, and General Sherman made some army mules and confiscated animals available for cultivation. The idea, of course, was to make the ex-slaves self-sufficient. Altogether, Sherman was able to settle some 40,000 freed people on seized lands. Congress followed up two months later with the first Freedmen's Bureau Bill, which promised to provide "every male citizen, whether refugee or freedman," with "not more than forty acres of land." President Andrew Johnson wasn't having it: He promptly vetoed Congress's bill and reversed General Sherman's order. In 1867, radical Republican leader Thaddeus Stevens tried again, introducing a resolution in Congress calling for the enforcement of the Confiscation Act of 1861 to seize some four hundred million acres of land from the ex-Confederate states. One million families of former slaves would have received forty-acre plots and fifty dollars in cash as start-up money. Stevens believed that the South should pay an indemnity for the war, and the seizure of land was part of that payment. It would have also broken the back of the plantation economy, because the power and wealth of the planter class depended on the availability of cheap Black labor. But Congress did not support land seizure. Eventually, under President Johnson, nearly all the land confiscated from the Confederate plantation owners was restored in exchange for oaths of loyalty. Although the Freedmen's Bureau was created to administer to the needs of Black people, it legally controlled only 0.2 percent of the land in the South, and not all of it was arable.

African Americans began the period of Reconstruction landless and frustrated, though many remained hopeful that the federal government would fulfill its promise of land. At mass meetings, in churches, in the privacy of their own homes, they spoke of their anticipated forty acres not as some kind of gift or handout but as back payment for slavery. A few Radical Republicans continued to press for a redistribution of land that could make Southern Black people self-sufficient and neutralize the power of the landlord class. Meanwhile, proplanter forces pressured the federal government to compensate the former slave owners for their losses. Believe it or not, they succeeded in Washington, D.C. In 1862, Congress passed laws compensating slave owners for freeing their slaves. The payments were rendered through the Board of Commissioners for the Emancipation in the District of Columbia. Nine years later, Congress established the Southern Claims Commission so that Southerners loyal to the Union during the war might be compensated for their own loss of property.

In the late nineteenth century, the movement to secure some kind of restitution for Black people was given new life when William R. Vaughan, a white Democrat from Alabama, launched a national movement to grant pensions to ex-slaves. Vaughan believed that such a pension plan not only was just but could also relieve Southern taxpayers from the burden of supporting this rapidly aging Black population. (Of course, under Jim Crow Southern Blacks were hardly a tax burden; in many cases, the African-American taxpaying and laboring population carried more than its share of the burden, to the point of subsidizing public services for white people.) Vaughan proposed that ex-slaves age seventy and older receive an initial payment of $500 and then $15 a month. Those between sixty and seventy years old would receive $300 and $12 a month, and ex-slaves fifty to sixty years old would receive $100 and $8 a month. Any freed people younger than fifty would not receive an initial payment, but a monthly pension of $4. Between 1890 and 1903, Vaughan succeeded in getting nine bills to this effect introduced into the Congress, but none became law—indeed, none of these bills got past committee.

Vaughan tried to drum up grassroots support for the pension campaign, publishing a newspaper and launching chapters of Vaughan's Ex-Slave Pension Club throughout the country. As historian Walter B. Hill points out, by 1897 several other organizations came on the scene, challenging Vaughan's hegemony over the ex-slave pension movement. A few of these groups proved to be frauds, intent on stealing from unsuspecting Black people. Individuals would falsely represent themselves as club organizers or as officers of the U.S. government, and collect fees and issue certificates that the newly recruited members were told they needed in order to verify their former status as slaves. The Black people who bought into these phony clubs mailed their bogus certificates to the Pension Bureau for payment only to be told that the certificates were worthless. Although Vaughan himself was never indicted for fraud, it is worth noting that by the time his movement collapsed around 1903, he had earned over one hundred thousand dollars from fees collected.

One of the organizations challenging Vaughan's clubs was the Ex-Slave Mutual Relief, Bounty & Pension Association, founded in 1897 by two African Americans, Reverend Isaiah H. Dickerson and Mrs. Callie D. House. Their purpose was to petition Congress to pass the Mason Bill—the legislation introduced by Nebraska Congressman W. J. Connell at Vaughan's behest—and build a broad movement that could provide mutual assistance to its members. Indeed, it seems as though some of the clubs functioned like mutual benefit associations, reinforcing strong community bonds and a deep sense of mission. The association chartered several chapters throughout the South, holding annual conventions and mobilizing community support for the pension bill. The federal government launched an investigation of Dickerson and House almost as soon as they started recruiting members. In March 1901 Dickerson was imprisoned for "obtaining money under false pretense" and thirteen years later Callie D. House, who now headed the association, was indicted on mail fraud charges. She ended up pleading guilty, claiming that she thought the pensions bill had passed and had been sincerely working to help ex-slaves file claims. House's defense is entirely plausible, especially considering the fact that neither she nor Dickerson made any money. Nevertheless, by 1917 the Ex-Slave Mutual Relief, Bounty & Pension Association, the last organization fighting for pension legislation, and the only one led by Black people, had been thoroughly destroyed.

Free the Land, Reparations Now!

During the first half of the twentieth century, few African-American movements took up the demand for reparations, though by then "forty acres and a mule" had become shorthand for broken promises. The Garvey movement condemned Europe's seizure of Africa and its wealth, including its people, as an act of theft, all of which the UNIA vowed to "reclaim," but it made no direct request for reparations. However, explicit demands for some kind of indemnity picked up steam after World War II, inspired in part by the creation of the state of Israel and Germany's reparations to Holocaust victims, which began in earnest in 1952. All told, Germany paid more than $58 billion. Not surprisingly, territory once again became a critical issue for some radical Black nationalist groups. Organizations such as the Forty-ninth State Movement and the African Nationalist (Alajo) Independence-Partition Party of North America, advocated reparations in the form of land on which to create a Black state. The Alajo Party's "Declaration of Self-Determination of the African-American Captive Nation," issued in January 1963, argued for restitution based on the fact that the United States "was built with the unrequited slave labor of our African ancestors." As restitution, the declaration demanded that "all land south of the Mason Dixon line where our people constitute the majority, be partitioned to establish a territory for Self-Government for the African Nation in the United States."

One of the pioneers of the post–World War II Black reparations movement was "Queen Mother" Audley Moore. A major figure in the history of Black radicalism, she started out as a devoted member of the Garvey movement before joining the CPUSA in the 1930s, although she had never abandoned Black nationalism. In 1950 she left the CP and founded, among other things, the Universal Association of Ethiopian Women, which focused attention on welfare, prisoners rights, antilynching, and interracial rape. She also launched the African-American Party of National Liberation in 1963, and as we saw in chapter 3, played a major role mentoring young activists in RAM. By her recollections, she came to the issue of reparations in 1962 after discovering a clause in the *Methodist Encyclopedia* that "considers an enslaved people satisfied with their condition if the people do not demand recompense before 100 years have passed." As it was the centennial of the Emancipation Proclamation, she promptly formed the Reparations Committee of Descendants of U.S. Slaves, Inc., and issued a demand for federal reparations as partial compensation for slavery and Jim Crow. Her organization came up with a figure of five hundred trillion dollars to be spread over the next four generations, and it made an effort to present its case to President Kennedy—though Moore got only as far as his secretary.

The crucial point that Moore emphasized in making the demand was that a thoroughly democratic structure needed to be in place so that ordinary people could decide what to do with the money. The money was not to be controlled by a "little clique," nor was it intended to line the pockets of individuals. It had to be both substantial and community controlled to enable African Americans "to put up some steel mills, some industry with the reparation, to benefit the whole people." She also wanted to accommodate those who "wanted to take their reparation and go to Africa." What she did not want, however, was a "poverty program." She insisted that had the government focused on reparations rather than on a War on Poverty, Black people would have been much better off. Besides being a pittance of what was owed Black people, she complained that the War on Poverty gave the government and a handful of Black elites control over our destiny. And the very idea that Black people were damaged

goods in need of help had dire psychological consequences: "We
don't realize how detrimental it is for us to be under a poverty
program. We, who gave the world civilization, we the wealthiest
people on earth who have been robbed of all of our birthright,
our inheritance."

By the mid- to late 1960s, most Black radical movements had
either adopted some form of reparations claim or at least debated
the issue. The Nation of Islam added a demand to its plan for
a separate state that "our former slave masters"—in the form of
the U.S. government—provide "fertile and minerally rich" land
and fund the territory for the first twenty to twenty-five years, or
until the residents were self-sufficient. The Black Panther Party
for Self-Defense, founded in 1966, included a demand for reparations in its platform. Point 3 stated: "We believe that this racist government has robbed us and now we are demanding the
overdue debt of forty acres and two mules. Forty acres and two
mules were promised 100 years ago as restitution for slave labor
and mass murder of Black people. We will accept payment in
currency which will be distributed to our many communities." It
went on to argue that German reparations for the Holocaust set
a precedent, especially since the "American racist has taken part
in the slaughter of over fifty million Black people." The Panthers
never came up with a figure or a plan, just the principle that
Black people deserved reparations.

The "Black Manifesto," issued in spring 1969, was the first sys-
tematic, fully elaborated plan for reparations to emerge from the
Black freedom movement. The document came about when
James Forman, a leader and radical voice in SNCC, was asked
to speak at the national Black Economic Development Conference (BEDC) in Detroit organized by the Interreligious Foundation for Community Organization (IFCO). Forman and activists
he had met in the Detroit-based League of Revolutionary Black
Workers, notably Mike Hamlin, Ken Cockrel, and John Watson,
decided to take over what would have been a liberal community development conference. They succeeded, positioning six

league members on the BEDC steering committee and creating what was essentially a Black socialist agenda. The key document, however, was the "Black Manifesto," which demanded five hundred million dollars in reparations to be paid by *white Christian churches* (later they included Jewish synagogues). That IFCO was a major Protestant institution only partly explains why Forman targeted churches. His primary reason was that white religious institutions participated in and benefited from racist and capitalist exploitation of Black people.

Half a billion dollars is a paltry sum (by their estimate, it amounted to fifteen dollars a head), but Forman and fellow drafters of the "Black Manifesto" considered their request seed money to build a new revolutionary movement and to strengthen Black political and economic institutions. Topping the list was the need for land. Given the long history of African Americans' struggle for land, it is not surprising that two hundred million dollars was set aside for a Southern Land Bank (a poignant demand today given the recent one-billion-dollar settlement for Black farmers discriminated against by the U.S. Department of Agriculture). Because of the explicit anticapitalist vision of the drafters of the manifesto, the land bank was intended especially for "people who want to establish cooperative farms but who have no funds."

Some of the other demands turned out to be even more imaginative. To protect Black workers and their families "fighting racist working conditions" at work as well as within their unions, the manifesto designated twenty million dollars for a National Black Labor Strike Fund. And to help welfare recipients organize more effectively, the BEDC planned to give the National Welfare Rights Organization a subsidy of ten million dollars. The "Black Manifesto" also recognized the racist war being waged on Black people's image, here and abroad. Forman and other BEDC drafters of the document wanted Black people to exercise more control over the media. They insisted that the media and the educational system brainwashed Black youth, in particular, teaching "us to believe in the U.S.A. and salute the flag and go off to Santo Domingo, the Congo, or Vietnam fighting for this white 'Christian' nation." And so they earmarked forty million dollars to launch publishing houses in Detroit, Atlanta, Los Angeles, and New York; another forty million was to be used to establish four television networks. They wanted thirty million dollars to build a research skills center to facilitate the study of "the problems of black people," and designated ten million for a skills training center to teach community organization, photography, movie making, television and radio manufacturing and repair, and other communications-related skills. Another twenty million dollars would be used to support a United Black Appeal responsible for raising money for the BEDC. Besides funding "a Black Anti-Defamation League which will protect our African image," the appeal would promote the development of cooperatives in African countries and provide material support to African liberation movements. The remaining one hundred and thirty million dollars were to be used to establish a Black university in the South, acknowledging that the majority of historically Black colleges and universities in the region at the time were largely funded and administered by liberal whites.

It was a tall order, to be sure, but still monetarily less than what most reparations movements were asking for. In order to realize the demands of the "Black Manifesto," BEDC proposed massive civil disobedience directed at churches. The planned sit-ins and mass disruptions were not simply tactics to win reparations but deliberate attacks on the institutionalized Church itself. Forman, in particular, felt that Christianity had been a source of oppression; by teaching passivity and acceptance of the dominant order, he argued, Christianity had kept Black people from embracing revolution. Nevertheless, despite Forman's unrelenting frontal attack on white churches, a few religious leaders were moved enough by the manifesto's arguments to contribute money. Altogether, the movement raised about one million dollars, though most of it went to IFCO, which eventually withdrew its support for the "Black Manifesto." The BEDC received only about three hundred thousand dollars, and most of that was parceled out to other movements. The little bit it did keep was used to launch Black Star Publications, a publishing house for radical Black writers.

For Forman and the radical leadership of the BEDC, the "Black Manifesto" was not an end in itself. They wanted to revolutionize society and they knew that even if their campaign succeeded, money alone would not lead to the kind of society they hoped to build. As Forman explained,

> Reparations did not represent any kind of long-range goal in our minds, but an intermediate step on the path to liberation. We saw it as a politically correct step, for the concept of reparation reflected the need to adjust past wrongs—to compensate for the enslavement of black people by Christians and their subsequent exploitation by Christians and Jews in the United States. Our demands . . . would not merely involve money but would be a call for revolutionary action, a Manifesto that spoke of the human misery of black people under capitalism and imperialism, and pointed the way to ending those conditions.

In 1971, Forman and his comrades in the BEDC founded the Black Workers Congress (BWC) in an effort to realize their radical anticapitalist vision. The BWC advocated workers' control of industry, the economy, and the state, to be brought about through cooperatives, united front groups, neighborhood centers, student organizations, and ultimately a revolutionary party. Within three years, the BWC transformed itself into a multiracial Marxist-Leninist party, purging Forman in the process.

If bringing the issue of reparations to a national audience was one of the goals of the "Black Manifesto," it proved to be a stunning success. During the early 1970s, articles and books on reparations were everywhere. The *Review of Black Political Economy* ran several substantive articles using regression analysis and a variety of databases to calculate the cost of slavery and Jim Crow. In 1973, a white law professor named Boris Bitker published *The Case for Black Reparations*, which argued for redress not for slavery but for segregation, arguing that Jim Crow violated the equal protection clause of the Fourteenth Amendment. He found language in what was basically an anti-Klan statute passed during Reconstruction that provided for redress to any injured party deprived of Constitutional rights. While the flurry of publications and debates advanced the economic and juridical case for reparations, they were less concerned with the larger question of how to reconstruct society.

In contrast to the professors, other social movements picked up where the "Black Manifesto" left off. The Republic of New Africa (RNA), another organization with roots in Detroit, advocated reparations but with the intention of building an independent Black nation in the continental United States. Founded in 1968 by brothers Gaidi and Imari Obadele (Milton and Richard Henry), the RNA reformulated the old Black belt thesis, arguing that the states of South Carolina, Georgia, Alabama, Mississippi, and Louisiana constituted "subjugated territory" with the right to self-determination. They demanded that the U.S. government hand over the territory to African Americans and establish the RNA as a government in exile. In addition to the transfer of land, the RNA initially called for reparations from the U.S. government in the amount of four hundred billion dollars to sustain the new nation during its first few years.

The plan, authored by Imari Obadele in 1972, was called the "Anti-Depression Program of the Republic of New Africa." In it he portrayed the new nation as a beautiful, free space for Black people, somewhat reminiscent of the way Black people have imagined Africa. It stood in stark contrast to the overcrowded, rat-infested ghettoes many urban African Americans knew as home. But the promise of a Republic of New Africa also meant transforming the ghettos of North America. "We shall bring about a new dimension in breathing and growing space for those who remain where they are; We shall immensely relieve pressure on the crowded northern and western ghettoes and spatially and materially restructure and abolish the growing black slums of the South." The new nation would not follow in the path of American capitalism. Rather, its economy would be based on Tanzania's model of African socialism, *Ujamaa*—roughly translated, "cooperative economics." Like Forman and the BEDC, the RNA concluded that New Africans need a system "for need, not for profit." "The means of production in New Africa," Obadele declared, "will be in the trust of the state to best accomplish this end, and the further ends of rapidly ending want and creating surpluses."

Many critics, even those sympathetic to territorial nationalist organizations, are quick to dismiss the land question as impractical or even impossible. But if we treat the land issue literally in terms of controlling territory with national borders and moving people back and forth across those borders, then we miss key elements of the RNA's vision and its implications for a broader Black radical conception of freedom. First, land is wealth, pure and simple. Historically, it has been fundamental for economic independence and sustainability, not to mention a central source of heritable wealth in the United States. Indeed, even if we limited our scope to homeownership, the miracle of the postwar (white) middle class can be explained by rising property values. The return on their investment enabled suburban white homeowners to pass on wealth as well as educational opportunities to their children. Fewer African Americans owned property, in part because they started out with no capital, were paid less for the same work, tended to have higher rates of unemployment, and confronted a system of Jim Crow that denied them access to much of the housing market. And those who did own homes suffered from discriminatory policies and practices from lending institutions, real estate firms, and the Federal Housing Administration. As a result, substantially lower Black home values not only reduces gross equity but makes it difficult for African Americans to use their residences as collateral for obtaining loans for other investments, such as college or business.

Second, and perhaps more importantly, land is space, territory on which people can begin to reconstruct their lives. The dream, after all, is to create a new society free of the overseer's watchful eye. How can any group of people govern itself without land? How can the RNA establish communal villages on the Tanzanian model without territory on which to do so? When MOVE, a Black nationalist group in Philadelphia, tried to create an alternative society in the middle of the city, confrontations with neighbors and the police ultimately led to its violent destruction: 11 MOVE members died and 250 people were left homeless as a result of a military campaign against them. Besides, as I tried to suggest in chapter 1, proponents of a new state or repatriation to another place are really just looking for a new beginning, a place where they can be free and develop their own culture without interference. The impulse for territory, then, is not just a matter of land; it is a matter of finding free space. And this desire for free space cannot be suppressed or dismissed.

So, if new land is not available, is it possible to persuade the people of the "old land" to support the same things the movement wants? Can groups like the RNA win over the multiracial masses to their program and turn the United States into the kind of society they imagine for the Republic of New Africa? On the surface, the question may seem absurd, but when we examine the RNA's broad aims its general commitment to the liberation of humanity is crystal clear. Despite its nationalist rubric, the aims of the "Anti-Depression Program" are deeply internationalist and humanist in that they call for the overthrow all forms of oppression around the globe and propose to make new subjects who are self-reliant, intelligent, self-possessed, and committed to social change. The RNA made it perfectly clear, in the "Anti-Depression Program" and in other statements and actions, that these larger goals cannot be accomplished by simply receiving land and money from the state:

> Ours is a revolution against oppression—our own oppression and that of all people in the world. And it is a revolution for a better life, a better station for mankind, a surer harmony with the forces of life in the universe. We therefore see these as the aims of our revolution:
>
> —*to assure all people in the New Society maximum opportunity and equal access to that maximum;*

—*to promote industriousness, responsibility, scholarship, and service;*

—*to protect and promote the personal dignity and integrity of the individual and his natural rights;*

—*to encourage and reward the individual for hard work and initiative and insight and devotion to the Revolution. . . .*

The RNA experienced more than its share of state repression during the late 1960s and 1970s; several of its members, including Imari Obadele, were jailed on charges ranging from assault to conspiracy and sedition. But the RNA survived, reconstituted itself as the New Afrikan Movement, and continued to press for reparations through N'COBRA. Imari Obadele, founder of N'COBRA, drafted a plan for reparations that went far beyond the RNA's "Anti-Depression Program." Presented to the U.S. Congress in 1987, the document was called "An Act to Stimulate Economic Growth in the United States and Compensate, in part, for the Grievous Wrongs of Slavery and the Unjust Enrichment which Accrued to the United States Therefrom." In this plan, Congress would be obliged to pay out not less than three billion dollars annually to African Americans. One-third of this sum was to be paid directly to families; another one-third would go to the duly elected government of the Republic of New Afrika. (Elections would be monitored by the UN or some comparable international body.) The remaining one-third would support a National Congress of Organizations composed of churches, Black civic organizations, and community-based movements committed to ending "the scourge of drugs and crime in New Afrikan communities and [advancing] the social, economic, educational, or cultural progress and enrichment of New Afrikan people." Participating groups would have had to been in operation for a minimum of two years before the passage of legislation.

Knowing that the United States would not simply hand over the Southern states, Obadele proposed a plebiscite to determine the will of the Black community for a separate state. Employing carefully worded, legalistic language, the plan required that at least 10 percent of the Black population older than sixteen years of age sign petitions before such a plebiscite could be held. The petition process would be overseen by judges appointed by the president of the United States, the UN, and the RNA. The sovereign status of each state in question, then, would be determined by a majority of voters. If the majority of voters elected to become part of the Republic of New Afrika, residents of these states could leave and maintain U.S. citizenship, stay and become citizens of the RNA, or enjoy dual citizenship irrespective of where they lived. What is not clear from the document, however, is whether or not white people can choose New Afrikan citizenship or residency in the South. Judging from the carefully worded and extremely democratic tone of the document, it seems quite possible that non-Black people fully committed to Black liberation and a "New Afrikan" way of life could join the republic, though it is not encouraged.

On May 19, 1999 (Malcolm X's birthday), N'COBRA did hold a plebiscite on reparations, though the purpose was to raise community awareness and mobilize African Americans to elect "economic development commissioners" (EDCs) who would serve as local organizers for the reparations campaign. Preparation for the plebiscite gave N'COBRA an opportunity to circulate its latest "main and immediate demands." These included: twenty-five thousand dollars in cash for Black families and individuals; the immediate release of all political prisoners as well as nonviolent Black prisoners with cash reparations and, for those who needed it, "medical care/substance abuse treatment"; "10 billion dollars to create 10 schools" to retrain African (American) youth, the unemployed, and recently released prisoners; and a billion dollars to create an economic development fund that would be run by the EDCs. The "Act" also registered N'COBRA's support of Black farmers' billion-dollar lawsuit against the federal government, and reiterated its commitment to self-determination and the right to form an independent Black state.

In short, N'COBRA continues to uphold a radical concept of reparations as more than a paycheck and an apology. It regards the campaign as part of a many-pronged attack on race and class oppression, an analysis of the root cause of inequality, and a means to mobilize African Americans to struggle for social change, self-transformation, and self-reliance. Indeed, self-reliance is a key phrase: N'COBRA and the New Afrikan Movement consistently advocate educational programs with the intention of reducing crime, drug addiction, and self-hatred, and promoting communal values, self-worth, and a commitment to community. Grassroots community involvement in the campaign not only builds support but also has the potential to transform participants through study groups, forums, and relationships forged in the context of a social movement—perhaps not unlike the Black ex-slave pension movement at the beginning of the last century. Finally, like so many other reparations campaigns coming out of Black radical movements, N'COBRA continues to view the struggle in global terms. Among other things, it maintains links to the Africa Reparations Movement (ARM). An outgrowth of the First Pan-African Conference on Reparations in Abuja, Nigeria, held in 1993, ARM focuses on issues relating to the continent, notably the cancellation of African nations' debt, the return of stolen art objects, and recognition of the Atlantic slave trade as a crime against humanity.

A Case for Reparations . . . and Transformation

If we think of reparations as part of a broad strategy to radically transform society—redistributing wealth, creating a democratic and caring public culture, exposing the ways capitalism and slavery produced massive inequality—then the ongoing struggle for reparations holds enormous promise for revitalizing movements for social justice. Consider the context: For at least the last quarter century we have witnessed a general backlash against the Black community. As I argued in Yo' Mama's Disfunktional! (1997), Republican and Democratic administrations dismantled most state protections for poor people of color, expanded the urban police state, virtually eliminated affirmative action and welfare as we knew it, and significantly weakened institutions and laws created to protect civil rights. All these cutbacks were justified by a discourse that blamed Black behavior for contemporary urban poverty and turned what were once called "rights" (i.e., welfare) into "privileges." The argument for reparations not only recasts these measures as rights but as payback. It shows how more than two centuries of U.S. policy facilitated accumulation among white property owners while further impoverishing African Americans. Thus federal assistance to Black people in any form is not a gift but a down payment for centuries of unpaid labor, violence, and exploitation.

We need not go all the way back to slavery to make the case. We can point to more than a century of discrimination to explain the myriad ways U.S. policies have enriched upper- and middle-class whites at the expense of Black people and other people of color (and we've already looked at housing policies). Let us take just one example: education. During Reconstruction, African Americans led the fight for free universal public education in the United States, not just for themselves but for everyone. After being barred from reading and writing while in bondage, newly freed people regarded education as one of the most basic rights and privileges of citizenship. Education was so important, in fact, that they were willing to pay for public schools or start their own. In South Carolina, for example, freed people contributed nearly thirteen thousand dollars to keep twenty-three schools running, schools that had been established by the Freedmen's Bureau. Indeed, between 1866 and 1870, newly freed people contributed more than three-quarters of a million dollars in cash to sustain their own schools. Once African Americans won the franchise, they made it possible for universal compulsory education to be written into state constitutions throughout the South. They also elected Black legislators who succeeded in establishing boards of education and requiring compulsory education with "no distinction to be made in favor of any class of persons." In South Carolina in 1868, Black and progressive white legislators made sure textbooks were provided free of charge, and within two years close to sixteen thousand Black children and eleven thousand white children attended public schools.

As soon as the federal government withdrew its support for Reconstruction and the Southern planter class and New South industrialists imposed formal segregation, Black students were relegated to inferior schools and denied full attendance. Rural schools for Blacks, for example, often operated only a few weeks out of the year. And yet Black wage earners continued to pay taxes to support public education. In the Jim Crow South it was not unusual for African Americans to contribute 40 percent of the school budget but attend schools that received 10 percent of the expenditures. One study conducted by researchers at Atlanta University in 1901 concluded that Black taxpayers were actually subsidizing white schools. More recently, two years after the Supreme Court ordered desegregation of schools in 1954, the state of Virginia introduced publicly funded school vouchers to help white families send their children to private schools rather than endure integration. The vouchers were eventually deemed unconstitutional, but during that short period of time African American taxes were being used to help pay for white children's private-school tuition. In light of how our separate and unequal education has benefited whites and cost African Americans, claims that affirmative action is "reverse discrimination" or a "special privilege" ring hollow at best.

The reparations movement exposes the history of white privilege and helps us all understand how wealth and poverty are made under capitalism—particularly a capitalism shaped immeasurably by slavery and racism. It stresses the fact that labor—not CEOs, not scientists and technicians, not the magic of the so-called free market—creates wealth. The reparations movement provides an analysis of our situation that challenges victim-blaming explanations, explaining that exploitation and regressive policies create poverty, not bad behavior. It ought to compel us to pay attention to the centrality of racism in the U.S. political economy, because one of the consequences of racial differentials in income and economic opportunity is downward pressure on wages for *all* working people, irrespective of color. It should also make us look at gender, because men and women did not experience exploitation in the same manner. We need to consider things like women's unpaid labor (see chapter 5), reproduction, sexual abuse, and ways to make restitution for these distinctive forms of exploitation. At the very least, the reparations movement ought to clarify issues like what constitutes a "family" if payments are to be made to such units, or how we might imagine remaking relationships between men and women, boys and girls, adults and children. If radical transformation of society is one of the goals of the reparations movement, then these questions cannot be ignored. Unfortunately, most arguments in support of reparations scarcely mention gender.

In the end, a successful reparations campaign has the potential to benefit the entire nation, not just the Black community. Since most plans emphasize investments in institutions rather than individual payments, the result would bring a massive infusion of capital for infrastructure, housing, schools, and related institutions in communities with large Black populations. Monies would also be made available to support civic organizations and help establish a strong civil society among people of African descent, which in turn would strengthen civil society as a whole. Presumably, social ills such as crime, drug use, and violence would be reduced considerably and thus alter the world's image of Black people. Furthermore, the historically Black ghetto communities to which substantial investments would be made also house other poor people of color: Latinos, Afro-Caribbeans, Native Americans, Asian Americans (namely Filipinos, Samoans, South Asians, Koreans, etc.). They, too, would benefit from improved schools, homes, public life, and a politically strengthened Black community. Given the relationship of slavery and racism to the global economy, this outcome makes perfect sense. Many of these poor immigrant groups are themselves products of centuries of imperialism—slavery's handmaiden, if you will—or descendants of slaves, as in the case of many Caribbean and Latin American immigrants. Finally, it should be stressed that reparations for one group will not harm working-class whites. As Robert Westley argued in a recent *Boston College Law Review* article on reparations:

Racist exploitation has contributed to the persistence of poverty among Blacks and the unjust privilege of whites. Redressing these harms through Black reparations would help to alleviate part of the problem of persistent poverty. To the extent that poverty remains a problem among nonBlacks and Blacks alike, it is both just and consistent with the equality principle to demand adequate social welfare, equal educational opportunity and access to jobs. Other national goals, like space exploration or defense, may need to be downsized in order to fulfill the moral obligation of social justice.

Of course, we do not yet live in a society where social justice takes precedence over national defense. This is why the reparations campaign, despite its potential contribution to eliminating racism and remaking the world, can never be an end in itself. Movement leaders have known this all along. The hard work of changing our values and reorganizing social life requires political engagement, community involvement, education, debate and discussion, and dreaming. Money and resources are always important, but a new vision and new values cannot be bought. And without at least a rudimentary critique of the capitalist culture that consumes us, even reparations can have disastrous consequences. Imagine if reparations were treated as start-up capital for Black entrepreneurs who merely want to mirror the dominant society. What would really change?

Again, we have to return to Detroit, this time to veteran radical Grace Lee Boggs. For decades she has been making this very point, insisting that we stop begging for inclusion in a corrupt system, take responsibility for transforming our culture, and remake ourselves as human beings. I hope that all of us who believe freedom is worth pursuing will heed her words and recognize the power we already possess:

> What we need to do . . . is encourage groups of all kinds and all ages to participate in creating a vision of the future that will enlarge the humanity of all of us and then, in devising concrete programs on which they can work together, if only in a small

way, to move toward their vision. In this unique interim time between historical epochs, this is how we can elicit the hope that is essential to the building of a movement and unleash the energies that in the absence of hope are turned against other people or even against oneself. . . . When people come together voluntarily to create their own vision, they begin wishing it to come into being with such passion that they begin creating an active path leading to it from the present. The spirit and the way to make the spirit live coalesce. Instead of seeing ourselves only as victims, we begin to see ourselves as part of a continuing struggle of human beings, not only to survive but to evolve into more human human beings.

"THIS BATTLEFIELD CALLED LIFE": BLACK FEMINIST DREAMS

I say, come, sister, brother to the battlefield
Come into the rain forests
Come into the hood
Come into the barrio
Come into the schools
Come into the abortion clinics
Come into the prisons
Come and caress our spines

I say come, wrap your feet around justice
I say come, wrap your tongues around truth
I say come, wrap your hands with deeds and prayer
You brown ones
You yellow ones
You black ones
You gay ones
You white ones
You lesbian ones

Comecomecomecomecome to this battlefield
Called life, called life, called life. . . .

I'm gonna stay on the battlefield
I'm gonna stay on the battlefield
I'm gonna stay on the battlefield til I die. . . .

—Sonia Sanchez, "For Sweet Honey in the Rock"

*I want the same thing that I did thirty years ago when I joined
the Civil Rights movement and twenty years ago when I joined
the women's movement, came out, and felt more alive than I ever
dreamed possible: freedom.*

—Barbara Smith, *The Truth That Never Hurts*

What is the position of women in Black radical visions of freedom? Prone . . . to disappear, that is. The dream of African
redemption comes to us largely as a male dream of armies liberating the motherland from their imperialist adversaries. Women
do have a place in a postredemption Africa, but rarely do they de-
viate from their traditional roles as nurturers and caretakers. The
position of women has been debated in socialist and communist
circles, but even there it is usually left as a question. And Black
women specifically? They have never been a primary subject of
the American Left, always falling somewhere in the cracks between the Negro Question and the Woman Question. As we've
seen, key interventions by the likes of Ida B. Wells or Claudia
Jones attempted to disrupt color- and class-struggle-as-usual,
but few leftists paid attention. Nearly half a century ago, Black
playwright and critic Lorraine Hansberry took the Communists
to task for failing to recognize that the Woman Question stood
alongside class, race, colonialism, and the struggle for peace as
"the greatest social question existent." Third World–identified
revolutionaries had much to say about class, culture, and internationalism, but very little to say about women. When women
appeared in the radical imagination of the 1960s and 1970s, it was
often as the iconic gun-slinging, baby-toting, Afro-coifed Amazon
warrior. Even the radical architects of reparations completely collapsed Black women within an undifferentiated mass called the
Black community.

Here lay the crux of the problem: The relative invisibility of
Black women in these radical freedom dreams is less a matter
of deliberate exclusion than *conception,* or the way in which the
interests and experiences of Black people are treated. The Black

community is too often conceived as an undifferentiated group with common interests. The men and even many of the women who lead these movements see the yoke of race and class oppression and accordingly create strategies to liberate the race, or Black working people in particular. This ostensibly gender-neutral conception of the Black community (nothing is really gender neutral), presumes that freedom for Black people as a whole will result in freedom for Black women. Oppressions of sex and gender went unacknowledged or were considered the secondary residue of racial capitalism that would eventually wither away. A long list of Black women challenged these ideas—running the gamut from Sojourner Truth, who challenged white feminists and male abolitionists to acknowledge the oppression and potential of Black women, to turn-of-the-century intellectual Anna Julia Cooper, whose writings offered a withering analysis of how race and gender worked to oppress white women and all communities of color. Indeed, these women flipped the script on the Black freedom movement, arguing that freedom for Black women would result in freedom for Black people as a whole—better yet, all people. But it was not until the formation of an autonomous radical Black feminist movement in the late 1960s and early 1970s that we find the most thorough, sustained interrogation of sex and gender as part of a general challenge to conceptions of Black liberation.

Radical Black feminists have never confined their vision to just the emancipation of Black women or women in general, or all Black people for that matter. Rather, they are the theorists and proponents of a radical humanism committed to liberating humanity and reconstructing social relations across the board. When bell hooks says "Feminism is for everybody," she is echoing what has always been a basic assumption of Black feminists. We are not talking about identity politics but a constantly developing, often contested, revolutionary conversation about how all of us might envision and remake the world. Of course, one might argue that we should be talking about feminism writ large, and that identifying something called "black feminism" is itself essentialist, if not divisive. But I am using *Black* in order to be historically precise, because the ideas and visions I discuss in this chapter grew primarily out of the Black freedom movement and Black women's experience, not interracial sisterhood solidarity. Radical Black feminists not only struggled against race, class, and gender oppression, but also critically analyzed the racial ideologies underlying patriarchy and challenged mainstream feminist conceptions of woman as a universal category.

It would also be a mistake to read radical Black feminism as a negative response to Black male sexism within the movement. Instead, as Paula Giddings, Evelyn Brooks-Higginbotham, Deborah Gray White, Beverly Guy-Sheftall, Rosalyn Terborg-Penn, Elsa Barkely Brown, Patricia Hill-Collins, and countless historians of the movement attest, Black feminism's core vision grows out of a very long history of Black women attempting to solve the general problems of the race but doing so by analyzing and speaking from both "public" and "private" realms. To be more precise, their work exposes the false wall erected between public and private, especially given the importance of Black women's labor in the maintenance of white households as well as the critical role of sexual violence and lynching in upholding race and gender hierarchies here and abroad.

In the end, perhaps we *are* talking about feminism writ large; or better yet, freedom writ large, for these women profoundly deepened the Black radical imagination, producing a vision of liberation expansive enough for all.

Smashers of Myths . . . Destroyers of Illusion

Black women don't usually appear in histories of "second wave" radical feminism, except as frustrated critics of white women. But a few were there at the very beginning. Florynce "Flo" Kennedy and Pauli Murray, both attorneys with a long history of civil rights and feminist activism, were founding members of the National Organization for Women (NOW) in 1966. Murray, in fact, served on President Kennedy's Commission on the Status of Women. Flo Kennedy earned a reputation as independent and outspoken;

among other things, she formed the Feminist Party in support of Black Congresswoman Shirley Chisholm's presidential bid in 1972 and went on to become a founding member of the National Black Feminist Organization in 1973. Both Murray and Kennedy felt that NOW and other mainstream feminist organizations ignored Black women and tended to see the experiences of middle-class white women as representative of the experiences of all women. Kennedy was drawn to the radical feminist movement, which began to take off around 1968–69. She participated in demonstrations with New York Radical Women partly because they engaged in civil disobedience and advocated a revolution in gender relations, not just reforms that would give women more access to the power structure.

Yet even the radical feminist vision of revolution paid little attention to race or the unique position of women of color. New York Radical Women's "Principles," distributed in 1968, made no mention of differences between women by race or class and presumed the existence of a universal women's culture. On the other hand, one line in the "Principles" could potentially have opened the door for an analysis of how race, gender, and class worked together: "We define the best interests of women as the best interests of the poorest, most insulted, most despised, most abused woman on earth." And who might that woman be? Most likely a Black woman or a woman of color. It is an observation central to Black feminist thought, going back at least to Anna Julia Cooper, whose book *A Voice from the South* (1893) made the case that the condition of Black women could be a barometer for the condition of all women as well as for that of the Black community. Cooper wrote, "Not till the universal title of humanity to life, liberty, and the pursuit of happiness is conceded to be inalienable to all; not till then is woman's lesson taught and woman's cause won—not the white woman's nor the black woman's, not the red woman's but the cause of every man and every woman who has writhed silently under a mighty wrong."

Shortly after its founding in 1968, New York Radical Women began to splinter into other organizations. One group calling itself

Redstockings was launched in 1969 and produced its own "Manifesto" promoting the idea that women constituted an oppressed class by virtue of their exploitation as unpaid and underpaid labor, child bearers, and sex objects. Although the "Manifesto" acknowledged differences between women, it treated these differences as impediments to overcome rather than as demonstrations of unequal power relationships. It repeats New York Radical Women's injunction that women's best interests are that "of the poorest, most brutally exploited woman," but also vows to "repudiate all economic, racial, educational or status privileges that divide us from other women. We are determined to recognize and eliminate any prejudices we may hold against other women."

Thus radical feminist groups such as Redstockings, WITCH (Women's International Terrorist Conspiracy from Hell), and The Feminists made antiracism an important part of their agendas, even if their analyses of race and the position of women of color was lacking. Socialist feminist groups during the same period, most notably the Women's Liberation Union (WLU), paid more attention to racism, arguing that capitalism, racism, and patriarchy worked together to oppress women. WLU activists organized working-class women and directed their attention to basic needs of the poor, such as health care, child care, and labor organizing. And a few white feminists made significant sacrifices for the Black freedom movement: Sylvia Baraldini, Marilyn Buck, and Susan Rosenberg, for example, were imprisoned for their role in assisting Assata Shakur escape from Clinton Correctional Facility in New Jersey. However, radical, socialist, and liberal feminist organizations did not attract substantial numbers of Black women.

Historians explain the absence of Black women in the radical feminist movement by citing Black women's distrust of white women and their commitment to autonomous Black organizations. Black women also resented the way some white feminists drew analogies between white women's plight and that of the Black community. The argument that the sexism experienced by middle-class white women was analogous to the racism experienced by Black people struck many Black women as absurd, particularly in light of the police and mob violence meted out to African Americans at the time. Moreover, the analogy rendered Black women invisible. In 1967, a group of women within SDS issued a statement, "To Women on the Left," warning women to "not make the same mistake the blacks did at first of allowing others (whites in their case, men in ours) to define our issues, methods, goals." So Blacks versus whites equaled women versus men; and in both cases Black women's interests were still being defined for them. Furthermore, when white women appealed to sisterhood, women of color not only cited the history of racism within the women's rights movement but made the point that the labor of Black domestics often made it possible for middle-class white women to organize. White women and women of color have often related to each other as employers and employees rather than as "sisters."

However, it would be a mistake to accept the too common claim that Black women activists rejected feminism out of hand. They simply did not separate the fight for women's rights from issues affecting the entire Black community, nor did they believe that men were necessarily the enemy. But they did confront and criticize sexism within the Black freedom movement to which they were committed. Margaret Wright, an activist in the Los Angeles–based group Women Against Repression, was frequently told by male leaders in the Black Power movement that Black women oppressed Black men, that Black women were domineering, that successful Black women stripped Black men of their manhood. "Black women aren't oppressing them," she announced in a 1970 interview. "We're helping them get their liberation. It's the white man who's oppressing, not us. All we ever did was scrub floors so they could get their little selves together!" The very idea that Black women kept Black men down made her even more angry when she thought about the role most Black women had to play in the civil rights and Black liberation movements. "We run errands, lick stamps, mail letters and do the door-to-door. But when it comes to the speaker's platform, it's all men up there blowing their souls, you dig." Indeed, Black women who spoke publicly and led protests instead of running mimeograph machines were sometimes accused of doing "men's work" or undermining Black manhood. Some women, like Gloria Richardson—leader of the Cambridge Non-Violent Action Movement who organized armed self-defense groups in her hometown of Cambridge, Maryland—were called "castrators" by their fellow male activists. Black women in the movement did not accept sexism without a fight, but an aggressive patriarchal culture became increasingly visible during the mid- to late 1960s.

In some respects, assertions that Black women's activism "emasculated" Black men were even more virulent in the mid- to late 1960s than in previous generations, prompted in part by the publication of Daniel Patrick Moynihan's widely circulated report *The Negro Family: The Case for National Action* (1965). Moynihan attributed the alleged "disorganization" and "pathology" of Black families to the rise of a matriarchal culture originating on the slave plantation. The report blamed the persistence of Black matriarchy, most evident in homes led by single mothers, for sexual promiscuity, crime, and poverty because it contributed to the demoralization of Black men. The best way to eliminate this "crushing burden on the Negro male" is to remove young Black men to "an utterly masculine world . . . away from women." (Moynihan conveniently suggested that a tour of duty in Vietnam might do the trick.) Although the report drew fire from many Black activists, some Black men agreed with the fundamental premise that assertive, strong Black women undermined Black men's authority.

The Moynihan report only fueled existing patriarchal impulses within male-led movements of the day. Black nationalists—like virtually all nationalists—tended to embrace patriarchal values, and some promoted the idea that women should contribute to the revolution by making babies and supporting their menfolk on the front lines. Undoubtedly, not all Black nationalist men were hopelessly sexist. On the contrary, some openly challenged sexist statements, rejected talk of polygamy and mothering for the nation, and fought for real gender equality. Let us not forget that Robert L. Allen's *Black Awakening in Capitalist America*, which contained a blistering critique of sexism in Black nationalist movements, was published in 1969. Besides, we need to understand the problem of patriarchy and male domination as a problem for the entire New Left movement in the 1960s. White New Left male leaders were often unwilling to share leadership, adopted many of the same patriarchal attitudes as their Black nationalist comrades, and frequently scoffed at the idea of women's liberation. In a word, the masculinist posturing of both the New Left and Black Power movements, the failure of many white feminist groups to grapple with racism, and the growing presence of a Third World feminist critique set the context for radical Black feminism.

Rather than mourn, radical Black women organized. Between 1966 and 1970, Black women formed several autonomous organizations, including the Black Women's Liberation Committee of SNCC and its offspring, the Third World Women's Alliance; the Harlem-based Black Women Enraged; and the Oakland-based Black Women Organizing for Action, among others. Some of the critical discussions and debates about Black women's liberation took place inside organizations one might not consider "feminist," such as the Black Panther Party and the National Welfare Rights Organization, both founded in 1966, as well the National Domestic Workers Union, formed in 1968. Representatives from local movements around the country came together to launch the National Black Feminist Organization (NBFO). Founded in 1973, the NBFO attracted some four hundred women to its founding convention, making it the largest independent Black feminist group at that time.

They organized and they analyzed. In 1970, a brilliant young writer and English professor at New Jersey's Livingston College named Toni Cade (later Toni Cade Bambara) edited a landmark collection of essays called *The Black Woman*. It was a kind of manifesto for Black feminism, a critique of both the women's movement and male-led Black politics, and a complex analysis of how gender, race, and class worked together to oppress everyone. Contributors ranged widely, from singer, composer, and activist Abbey Lincoln to a young novelist and editor by the name of Toni Morrison. The book critiqued the culture's degradation of Black women and exposed how traditional ideas of masculinity not only undermined gender relations within Black communities but also served as a fetter to the liberation of men and women. In other words, a politics wedded to the idea that men needed to rule women would not result in liberation for anyone. Frances Beal, a founding member of SNCC's Black Women's Liberation Committee and the Third World Women's Alliance, made the point eloquently in her contribution, "Double Jeopardy." She reminded readers that the liberation of Black women was not mere identity politics but a struggle to eliminate all manifestations of oppression. Echoing earlier generations of Black feminists, she insisted that "the exploitation of black people and women works to everyone's disadvantage. . . . The liberation of these two groups is a stepping-stone to the liberation of all oppressed people in this country and around the world." She did not call for the liberation of Black women only, but for the liberation of humanity in its totality—a liberation that did not subordinate women's issues. "Unless women in any enslaved nation are completely liberated, the change cannot really be called a revolution." To achieve such a revolution meant fighting racism, capitalism, and imperialism and "changing the traditional routines that we have established as a result of living in a totally corrupting society. It means changing how you relate to your wife, your husband, your parents, and your coworkers."

Black feminist writings, in both *The Black Woman* and elsewhere (i.e., Angela Davis's pioneering 1971 essay "Reflections on the Black Woman's Role in the Community of Slaves") extended the discussion of revolution from public institutions and the workplace to the home, the family, even the body. The exploitation of women's labor within families, sexual assault, and birth control were among the more highly debated topics. For example, whereas many "second wave" feminists understood motherhood as inherently oppressive because it doomed (white middle-class) women to a lonely life as suburban housewives, Black women were forced by economic circumstance into low-wage labor and never had the luxury of spending a lot of time with their families. Most Black working women wanted more choices, more time, and more resources rather than an outright rejection of motherhood itself. Besides, Black women had had a very different experience with birth control. While white women demanded greater access to contraceptives and abortion as a road to sexual freedom, Black women were fighting forced sterilization and family planning policies that sought to limit Black births. After World War I, the birth control movement, led by none other than the militant women's rights activist Margaret Sanger, formed an alliance with the eugenicist movement. Together they advocated limiting fertility among the "unfit," which included poor Black people. Sanger viewed birth control as "the very pivot of civilization" and "the most constructive and necessary of the means to racial health." Sanger, along with Dr. Clarence Gamble (the mastermind behind the massive sterilization of women in Puerto Rico in the 1950s), launched the notorious Negro Project in 1938 to promote birth control among Southern African Americans. Birth control centers were established in Black communities all over the South during the 1930s; the number of Black women sterilized involuntarily rose exponentially and continued to rise through the 1970s. As Dorothy Roberts writes in *Killing the Black Body*, "It was a common belief in the South that Black women were routinely sterilized without their informed consent and for no valid medical reason. Teaching hospitals performed unnecessary hysterectomies on poor Black women as practice for their medical residents. This sort of abuse was so widespread in the South that these operations came to be known as 'Mississippi appendectomies.'"

Given the historical links between the early birth control movement and eugenics, Fran Beal was not off track when she described family planning policies under racism as a potential road to "outright surgical genocide." Indeed, Black feminists criticized the National Abortion Rights League's support for abortion on demand and immediate access to voluntary sterilization. The Committee to End Sterilization Abuse, an organization made up primarily of women of color, wanted guidelines that would prevent the practice of obtaining consent for sterilization during labor or immediately after childbirth, or for an abortion under the threat of losing welfare benefits. They argued that abortion or sterilization on demand did not acknowledge the class and race biases in reproductive policy, the life circumstances that compelled poor women to abort, or the long history of forced sterilization imposed on women of color.

Battling forced sterilization and racist reproductive policies was not the same as rejecting birth control. In fact, Black feminists found themselves fighting on another front, this time against Black male leaders who proclaimed birth control "genocide." Some Black nationalist organizations denounced contraception as a white plot to eliminate the Black community, going so far as to shut down local birth control clinics. At one point, members of the Nation of Islam invaded birth control clinics and published articles in *Muhammad Speaks* accompanied by depictions of bottles of birth control pills marked with skull and crossbones, or graves of unborn Black infants. A radical group of Black welfare mothers from Mount Vernon, New York, led by Pat Robinson, responded to these kinds of attacks, issuing a powerful statement in 1968 accusing nationalists of ignoring the condition of poor Black people. A radical social worker and former volunteer worker for Planned Parenthood, Robinson had had firsthand experience with the issue of birth control and poor Black women. Their statement rejected claims that contraception was a form of genocide, arguing instead that "birth control is freedom to fight genocide of black women and children." Unless wealth was more evenly distributed, they observed, poor women having more babies for the "race" only exacerbated their poverty. They closed with a prophetic critique of class differences within the movement: "But we don't think you are going to understand us because you are a bunch of little middle class people and we are poor black women. The middle class never understands the poor because they always need to use them as you want to use poor black women's children to gain power for yourself. You'll run the black community with your kind of black power—You on top!" Indeed, for Pat Robinson and her comrades, notably Patricia Haden and Donna Middleton, a revolutionary Black movement without an understanding of class struggle was worthless, and a class movement that did not consider gender and sexuality was equally worthless. In 1973 they, along with many anonymous Black people, published a remarkable little book titled *Lessons from the Damned*, which attempted to provide a thorough analysis of the forces arrayed against the Black poor. In a section titled "The Revolt of Poor Black Women," they spoke eloquently of how their own families contributed to the exploitation of Black women and youth. Not everything can be blamed on the Man: "Inside families and inside us we have found the seeds of fascism that the traditional left does not want to see. Fascism was no big, frightening issue for us. It was our daily life. The fascism of our parents, and our brothers and sisters, forced them to beat the hell out of us, put us out, deny us food and clothing. Finally, they cooperated with the white system's fascism and had us put away in institutions." Just as Grace Lee Boggs and Jimmy Boggs had long insisted that no revolution could succeed until oppressed people took responsibility for their behavior and struggled to transform themselves, Robinson, Haden, and Middleton called on Black women and men in the movement to dig deep "into our class and racial experience" to understand why women and youth feel the need "to subordinate themselves to men and adults." "We must learn," they write, "why we have loved our chains and not wanted to throw them off. Only we, the politically conscious oppressed, can find out how we were molded, brainwashed, and literally produced like any manufactured product to plastically cooperate in our own oppression. This is *our* historical responsibility."

Haden, Middleton, and Robinson were unequivocal in their support for revolution, but they insisted that revolution must take place on three levels: overthrowing capitalism, eliminating male supremacy, and transforming the self. Like many of their male comrades in the Black freedom movement, they praised those Third World revolutionaries who were "putting out the United States Army and capitalist investors as they did in China and Cuba." At the same time, they were suspicious of all forms of Black cultural nationalism, which they dismissed as just another "hustle." Revolution, they argued, was supposed to usher a brand new beginning; it was driven by the power of a freed imagination, not the dead weight of the past. As they wrote in "A Historical and Critical Essay for Black Women" (circa 1969): "All revolutionaries, regardless of sex, are the smashers of myths and the destroyers of illusion. They have always died and lived again to build new myths. They dare to dream of a utopia, a new kind of synthesis and equilibrium."

Not all Black feminists shared the same commitment to radical critique. In fact, the left wing of the NBFO abandoned the movement after a year because it failed to address the needs of the poor and spoke exclusively to heterosexual women. Women active in the Black lesbian community had worked very hard to build an inclusive movement that addressed the needs of all—irrespective of class or sexual orientation. So in 1974 a group of radical Black feminists in Boston broke with the NBFO and formed the Combahee River Collective. (The Combahee was the name of the river in South Carolina where Black abolitionist Harriet Tubman led a military campaign during the Civil War—the only such campaign planned by a woman. It resulted in the emancipation of more than 750 slaves.) The women who formed the collective came from different movements in the Boston area, including the Committee to End Sterilization Abuse and the campaign to free Ella Ellison—a Black woman inmate who, like Joan Little in North Carolina, was convicted of murder for killing a prison guard in self-defense. Nearly all the women had worked together to bring attention to a series of unsolved murders of Black women in Boston.

In 1977, three collective members—Barbara Smith, Beverly Smith, and Demita Frazier—issued "A Black Feminist Statement." Because they found themselves fighting many oppressions at once—racism, sexism, capitalism, and homophobia—they regarded radical Black feminism as fundamental to any truly revolutionary ideology. They understood the racial and sexual dimensions of domination, arguing that the history of white men raping Black women was "a weapon of political repression." At the same time, they rejected the idea that all men were oppressors by virtue of biology and broke with lesbian separatists who advocated a politics based on sexuality. In their view, such an analysis "completely denies any but the sexual sources of women's oppression, negating the facts of class and race." And while they did not see Black men as enemies and called for broad solidarity to fight racism, they did acknowledge patriarchy within Black communities as an evil that needed eradication. Black people as a whole, they argued, could not be truly free as long as Black women were subordinate to Black men.

As socialists, the collective did not believe that a nonracist, nonsexist society could be created under capitalism, but at the same time they believed that socialism was not enough to dismantle the structures of racial, gender, and sexual domination. The core of their vision was manifest in their political practice. Combahee members immediately saw connections between class, race, and gender issues by working in support of "Third World women" workers, challenging health care facilities for inadequate or unequal care, and organizing around welfare or day care issues. Although a broad vision of freedom informed the group's work, its political positions remained flexible and subject to change. They knew that the very process of struggle, in the context of a democratic organization, would invariably produce new tactics, new strategies, and new analyses. "We believe in collective process and a nonhierarchical distribution of power within our own group and in our vision of a revolutionary society. We are committed to a continual examination of our politics as they develop through criticism and self-criticism as an essential aspect of our practice." Finally, as Black feminist Ann Julia Cooper had suggested some eighty-five years earlier, the collective insisted that

Black and Third World women's position at the bottom of the race/class/gender hierarchy put them in a unique position to see the scope of oppression and dream a new society. "We might use our position at the bottom," they asserted, "to make a clear leap into revolutionary action. If black women were free, it would mean that everyone else would have to be free since our freedom would necessitate the destruction of all systems of oppression."

New Knowledge, New Dreams

The Combahee River Collective's "Statement" remains one of the most important documents of the Black radical movement in the twentieth century. It isn't just a brilliant text drafted by very smart Black women; it is a product of a collective social movement. The Black radical imagination, as I have tried to suggest throughout this book, is a collective imagination engaged in an actual movement for liberation. It is fundamentally a product of struggle, of victories and losses, crises and openings, and endless conversations circulating in a shared environment. Julia Sudbury's recent book, *Other Kinds of Dreams: Black Women's Organisations and the Politics of Transformation*, gives us a brilliant example of how activists produce new knowledge and open new vistas for inquiry. She looks at Black, Asian, and Arab women's organizations in England and reveals how, through their work, study, and discussion, they came to see how racism is gendered, sexism is racialized, and class differences are reproduced by capitalism and patriarchy. Through personal narratives, local interventions, and research on the impact of specific policies negatively affecting their respective communities, these activists developed new modes of analyses and formulated new, imaginative, transformative strategies. For example, Black Women for Wages for Housework challenged existing academic and policy-oriented knowledge regarding who made up the working class by arguing that children, women, and Black men represented "the most comprehensive working class struggle." They saw recognition and reparations for women's unpaid labor, then, as the primary site of any global challenge to capitalism and imperialism. "Counting black and Third World people's contribution to every economy—starting by counting women's unwaged work—is a way of refusing racism, claiming the wealth back from military budgets, and establishing our entitlement to benefits, wages, services, housing, healthcare, an end to military-industrial pollution—not as charity but as rights and reparations owed many times." Imagine what such a formulation could mean for the reparations movement.

Sudbury further demonstrates how seemingly local struggles extended into the international arena because many of the women in her study were immigrants with deep ties to their homelands. Working across cultural and ethnic lines introduced various women activists to many different kinds of struggles as well as more expansive solidarities. Groups like Akina Mama wa Afrika have applied their analysis of structural adjustment programs to West African women in prisons in England, while Southall Black Sisters have raised their voices against the confinement of women associated with the rise of Islamic fundamentalism on a global scale. They also published and circulated their ideas in various independent forums that fell outside, and yet profoundly shaped, formal academic institutions and circuits of knowledge. During the 1970s and 1980s, for example, these activists founded the Black/Brown Women's "Liberation Newsletter," *Outwrite*, *Mukti* (an Asian feminist magazine), *Zami* (a Black feminist bimonthly), and "We Are Here" (a short-lived Black feminist newsletter). They also established publishing cooperatives and grassroots intellectual centers, such as Black Womentalk and the Afro-Caribbean Educational Project Women's Centre.

Sudbury offers an important cautionary note about where we seek out the voices of radical Black women. In England during the 1970s and 1980s, for example, rastafari women were among the most militant and vocal Black activists. This may seem counterintuitive given the common assumptions circulating about the subordination of women in the rastafari culture. However, these women were at the forefront of a new, more secularized rastafari movement that proved more enabling for women. And there are many reasons why rastafari might be attractive to women who may share the dreams of Black radical feminists. Rastas, after all, promoted a vision of community that shunned materialism and artificial drugs and foods and strove for an equal and just society in which people lived in harmony with nature. And the fact that rastafari encouraged female-only spaces enabled Black women to hold political discussions among themselves, allowing them to focus their attention on issues that might affect women differently or exclusively. Finally, as Sudbury points out, rastafari women also challenged what had become the dominant radical feminist paradigm, particularly around sexuality. Whereas many radical feminists fought the veiling of women and women's bodies, and encouraged free expression of sexuality, many rastafari women regarded the traditional covering of the head and body as a means to resist the sexual commodification and degradation of African women's bodies. Of course, veiling can be deeply constricting and reinforce women's subordination, but the rastafari women's explanation for embracing the practice also points to our need to have a more sophisticated understanding of how expressions of women's sexuality take place in a racist context. Once again, movements in struggle produce new knowledge and new questions.

Although we tend to associate contemporary Black feminist thought with academia, some of the most radical thinkers are products of social movements. Today Angela Davis is a distinguished professor at the University of California at Santa Cruz, as well as a an international voice for prisoners' rights, an active supporter of social justice in all realms of life, and a leading radical Black feminist theorist. Three decades earlier, Davis was the nation's most celebrated political prisoner, having served eighteen months in prison (from 1970 to 1972) for being implicated in a failed prison break from a courthouse in California, for which she was acquitted. A child of the civil rights movement, Davis grew up in a Birmingham, Alabama, neighborhood where Black-owned homes were firebombed so frequently that it was nicknamed "Dynamite Hill." She proved to be a brilliant student, completing a Ph.D. in philosophy while an active member of SNCC and later the Black Panther Party in southern California. She not only encountered sexist attitudes on the part of several male leaders, but also realized that SNCC and other Black Power organizations did not have an adequate critique of capitalism. She found such a critique in Marxism.

In 1968, she joined the CPUSA, a decision that eventually led to her dismissal from a teaching post at the University of California at Los Angeles a year later. (Although Davis won the suit, the Board of Regents eventually drove Davis out by censuring her political activism and monitoring her classes.) Davis never ceased her political work, taking up a wide range of issues from police brutality and prisoners' rights to women's liberation and the politics of reproduction. As a result, she produced two seminal volumes of essays that remain key texts in the development of Marxist feminism, *Women, Race, and Class* (1981) and *Women, Culture, and Politics* (1989). Much of this work examines the intersection of race, gender, and class, and the challenges to building a class-conscious, antiracist feminist movement over the past century. She also looks at the intersection of forces oppressing women, including various forms of sexual violence. Furthermore, Davis's own prison experience and her continued work on behalf of prisoners' rights has compelled her to embark upon a massive study of the prison-industrial complex on a global scale. Her writings on prisons have long been key texts in the world abolitionist movement. She examines the relationship between the formation of prisons and the demand for labor under capitalism and situates these developments squarely within the history of modern slavery. One of the strongest aspects of her work is her investigation into the way punishment has been racialized historically. The critical question for Davis centers on how Black people have been criminalized and how this ideology has determined the denial of basic citizenship rights to Black people. Since most leading theorists of prisons focus on issues such as reform, punishment, discipline, and labor under capitalism, discussions of the production of imprisoned bodies often play down or marginalize race. Davis not only makes race and gender central to her inquiry, but also looks at the prisons and the making of prisoners transnationally—from the prisons in socialist Cuba and the virtual dungeons of Brazil to the so-called liberal practices of the Netherlands.

The radical Black feminist movement, not unlike other feminists, also redefined the source of theory. It expanded the definition of who constitutes a theorist, the voice of authority speaking for Black women, to include poets, blues singers, storytellers, painters, mothers, preachers, and teachers. Black women artists are often embraced from all parts of the diaspora—Maryse Condé, Buchi Emecheta, Toni Morrison, Ntozake Shange, Sonia Sanchez, Alice Walker, Gloria Naylor, Paule Marshall, Toni Cade Bambara, Jayne Cortez, June Jordan, Betye Saar, Faith Ringgold, Adrian Piper, Camille Billops, Howardena Pindell, Sweet Honey in the Rock, Abbey Lincoln, Bessie Smith, Ma Rainey—the list can go on for pages. Angela Davis, Michelle Gibbs, and Hazel Carby are just a few Black radical feminists who have claimed Black women blues singers for feminist thought. Davis's *Blues Legacies and Black Feminism* demonstrates how Black women blues singers created a poetics of sexual freedom and power, a politics of protest veiled beneath songs of love and loss, as well as a politics of class critical of alienated wage labor and poverty. Black blues women sang sad and lonely songs, but they also imagined a world free of low-wage, backbreaking labor and full of pleasurable leisure.

Finally, radical Black feminism offers one of the most comprehensive visions of freedom I can think of, one that recognizes the deep interconnectedness of struggles around race, gender, sexuality, culture, class, and spirituality. Among other things, radical Black feminists have sought to create a healthier environment for poor and working-class women and to reduce women's dependence on a capitalist and patriarchal health care system. Black radical feminists have also played critical roles in making lesbian, gay, bisexual, transgendered, and transsexual movements more visible to Black communities and in teaching us how sexual identities get defined (and policed). Their opposition to compulsory heterosexuality also offers emancipatory possibilities for us all. Poets June Jordan and Cheryl Clarke have made eloquent pleas for bisexuality and lesbianism, respectively, as radical challenges to heterosexual domination. For Jordan, sexual freedom is the foundation of all other struggles for freedom:

> If you can finally go to the bathroom wherever you find one, if you can finally order a cup of coffee and drink it wherever the coffee is available, but you cannot follow your heart—you cannot respect the response of your own honest body in the world—then how much of what kind of freedom does any one of us possess?

> Or conversely, if your heart and your honest body can be controlled by the state, or controlled by community taboo, are you not then, and in that case, no more than a slave ruled by outside force?

Cheryl Clarke makes a bold argument both against homophobia and for women's autonomy, self-love, and independence from men. She does not argue that all women ought to become lesbian but rather that they reject "coerced heterosexuality as it manifests itself in the family, the state, and on Madison Avenue. The lesbian-feminist struggles for liberation of all people from patriarchal domination through heterosexism and for the transformation of all sociopolitical structures, systems, and relationships that have been degraded and corrupted under centuries of male domination." Furthermore, lesbian, gay, bisexual, transgendered, and transsexual movements contribute to the freedom of all by challenging all claims to what is "normal." Sexuality may be one of the few conceptual spaces we have to construct a politics of desire and to open our imagination to new ways of living and seeing.

Today's mic-hogging, fast-talking, contentious young (and old) lefties continue to hawk little books and pamphlets on revolution, always with choice words or documents from Marx, Mao, even Malcolm. But I've never seen a broadside with "A Black Feminist

Statement" or even the writings of Angela Davis or June Jordan or Barbara Omolade or Flo Kennedy or Audre Lorde or bell hooks or Michelle Wallace, at least not from the groups who call themselves leftist. These women's collective wisdom has provided the richest insights into American radicalism's most fundamental questions: How can we build a multiracial movement? Who are the working class and what do they desire? How do we resolve the Negro Question and the Woman Question? What is freedom?

Barbara Smith, one of the founding members of the Combahee River Collective, is among the radical voices that have addressed these questions. Since the heyday of the civil rights movement, she has been telling white people that fighting racism is necessary for their own survival and liberation, not some act of philanthropy to help the downtrodden Negroes of the ghetto. She has been telling Black activists that fighting homophobia is their issue because the policing of sexuality, no matter to whom it is directed, affects everyone. And she has been sharply critical of lesbian and gay movements for the narrowness of their political agendas. She knows what it will take to win freedom. "As a socialist and an alert Black woman, it is clear to me that it is not possible to achieve justice, especially economic justice, and equality under capitalism because capitalism was never designed for that to be the case. . . . The assaults from the present system necessitate that most activists work for reforms, but those of us who are radicals understand that it is possible to do so at the very same time that we work for fundamental change—a revolution."

Now there's the *real* question: Can we all get along long enough to make a revolution? Perhaps, but history tells us that it will mean taking leadership from some very radical women of color, and if that's the case I'm not holding my breath. What the old-guard male militants really need to do is give up the mic for a moment, listen to the victims of democracy sing their dreams of a new world, and take notes on how to fight for the freedom of all.

KEEPIN' IT (SUR)REAL:
DREAMS OF THE MARVELOUS

It's always night or we wouldn't need light.

    —Thelonious Monk, quoted in *Time* magazine, 1964

Monk's statement should be taken as more than a clever observation about physics. As one of the greatest "jazz" pianists and composers of the twentieth century, Monk often began work after the sun disappeared over the horizon; thus he understood the power and ubiquity of night. "The night time is the right time," a time to reveal and fulfill desire, a time to dream, the world of the unknown, the hallucinatory. It was nineteenth-century poet Isidore Ducasse—known to his readers as Comte de Lautréamont—who wrote in his *Poésies* (1870): "It is only by admitting the night physically that one is able to admit it morally." For Black folk, however, the night represents pleasure *and* danger, beauty *and* ugliness. Besides its Blackness, with all its mystery and elegance, richness and brilliance, the night is associated with hooded Klansmen and burning crosses, the long night of slavery, the oppression of dark skin. Yes, "it's always night," which is why we absolutely *need* light: the light of social movements ("I've got the light of freedom"), the light of hope ("facing a rising sun/of a new day begun"), the light of spirit ("this little light of mine/I'm gonna let it shine").

Monk meets Lautréamont on the night train to freedom. It is one of many chance encounters that reveal a deep affinity between Black life and culture and surrealism. Neither man would have identified himself as a surrealist, although Lautréamont, along with another nineteenth-century French poet named Arthur Rimbaud, are considered the spiritual fathers of surrealism before the movement was declared after World War I. And yet they embody the basic principles of surrealism, a living, mutable, creative vision of a world where love, play, human dignity, an end to poverty and want, and imagination are the pillars of freedom.

What is surrealism? Its definition is as rich and evasive as the night itself. Here is one answer from the Chicago Surrealist Group (1976):

> Surrealism is the exaltation of freedom, revolt, imagination and love. . . . [It] is above all a revolutionary movement. Its basic aim is to lessen and eventually to completely resolve the contradiction between everyday life and our wildest dreams. By definition subversive, surrealist thought and action are intended not only to discredit and destroy the forces of repression, but also to emancipate desire and supply it with new poetic weapons. . . . Beginning with the abolition of imaginative slavery, it advances to the creation of a free society in which everyone will be a poet—a society in which everyone will be able to develop his or her potentialities fully and freely.

By plunging into the depths of the unconscious and lessening "the contradiction between everyday life and our wildest dreams," we can enter or realize the domain of the Marvelous. Surrealism is no mere artistic movement like cubism or impressionism, and it is not primarily concerned with art. Surrealism is about making a new life. As Franklin Rosemont explains in *André Breton— What Is Surrealism? Selected Writings*:

> Surrealism, a unitary project of total revolution, is above all a method of knowledge and a way of life; it is lived far more than

it is written, or written about, or drawn. Surrealism is the most exhilarating adventure of the mind, an unparalleled means of pursuing the fervent quest for freedom and true life beyond the veil of ideological appearances. Only the social revolution — the leap, in the celebrated expression of Marx and Engels, 'from the realm of necessity to the realm of freedom' — will enable the true life of poetry and mad love to cast aside, definitively, the fetters of degradation and dishonour and to flourish with unrestrained splendour.

Some of these principles, one might argue, were present in Afrodiasporic culture before surrealism was ever named. In this chapter I explore how Black revolt shaped the development of surrealism as a self-conscious political movement, as well as the impact surrealism has had on modern political and cultural movements throughout the African diaspora. Surrealism, I contend, offers a vision of freedom far deeper and more expansive than any of the movements discussed thus far. It is a movement that invites dreaming, urges us to improvise and invent, and recognizes the imagination as our most powerful weapon.

"Surrealism and Us"

Surrealism may have originated in the West, but it is rooted in a conspiracy against Western civilization. Surrealists frequently looked outside Europe for ideas and inspiration, turning most notably to the "primitives" under the heel of European colonialism. Indeed, what later became known as the Third World turned out to be the source of the surrealists' politicization during the mid-1920s. The Paris Surrealist Group and the extreme Left of the French Communist Party were drawn together in 1925 by their support of Abd-el-Krim, leader of the Rif uprising against French colonialism in Morocco. In tracts like "Revolution Now and Forever!" the surrealists actively called for the overthrow of French colonial rule. That same year, in an "Open Letter" to writer and French ambassador to Japan, Paul Claudel, the Paris group announced, "We profoundly hope that revolutions, wars, colonial insurrections, will annihilate this Western civilization whose vermin you defend even in the Orient." Seven years later, the Paris group produced its most militant statement on the colonial question to date. Titled "Murderous Humanitarianism" (1932) and drafted mainly by René Crevel and signed by (among others) André Breton, Paul Eluard, Benjamin Peret, Yves Tanguy, and the Martinican surrealists Pierre Yoyotte and J. M. Monnerot, it was first published in Nancy Cunard's massive anthology, *Negro* (1934). The document is a relentless attack on colonialism, capitalism, the clergy, the Black bourgeoisie, and hypocritical liberals. Arguing that the very humanism upon which the modern West was built also justified slavery, colonialism, and genocide, the writers called for action: "We surrealists pronounced ourselves in favor of changing the imperialist war, in its chronic and colonial form, into a civil war. Thus we placed our energies at the disposal of the revolution, of the proletariat and its struggles, and defined our attitude towards the colonial problem, and hence towards the color question."

In other words, the revolts of the colonial world and its struggles for cultural autonomy animated surrealists as much as reading Freud or Marx. And they discovered in the cultures of Africa, Oceania, and Native America a road into the Marvelous and confirmation of their most fundamental ideas. For example, the surrealist practice of "pure psychic automatism"—sometimes described as automatic writing—was much more than a modern "technical" invention, for it quickly led to the recognition that entire cultures had methods of thought and communication that transcended the conscious. Surrealist automatism, which dates back to 1919, was neither "stream of consciousness writing" nor an experimental writing strategy but a state of mind—a plunge below the surface of consciousness. Related more to shamanism and trance states than to "modernity" as it was understood in the West, automatism was a struggle against the slavery of rationalism, a means to allow the imagination to run free.

Early on, surrealists discovered this kind of imaginative freedom in African-American music. The attraction to Black music must have seemed natural, for as the Chicago Surrealist Group reflected in a special surrealist supplement to *Living Blues* magazine in 1976, "The surrealists could hardly have failed to recognize aspects of their combat in blues (and in jazz), for freedom, revolt, imagination and love are the very hallmarks of all that is greatest in the great tradition of Black music." Natural, yes, but not immediate. Some surrealists—Jacques Baron, René Crevel, Robert Desnos, Michel Leiris—appreciated jazz from the start, but others—including André Breton, author of the 1924 *Surrealist Manifesto*—initially could not see how music might be a medium for the kind of freedom they found in the literary and plastic arts. Even the great painter Giorgio de Chirico proclaimed, "No Music." The winds shifted in 1929 when Belgian surrealist Paul Nougé published an essay titled *Music Is Dangerous*, which offered a critical defense of music as one of many artistic forces "capable of bewitching spirit." And a few years later, in an essay titled "Hot Jazz" in Nancy Cunard's *Negro* anthology, Robert Goffin, a nonsurrealist critic, directly related surrealism to jazz. Although Goffin reinforced the then common perception of Black music as a spontaneous, emotion-driven folk form, which was thus devoid of the kind of creative intellectual work one associates with "Western" arts, he nevertheless placed Black musicians squarely within the pantheon of surrealism's founders. "What Breton and [Louis] Aragon did for poetry in 1920," noted Goffin, "Chirico and Ernst for painting in 1930, had been instinctively accomplished as early as 1910 by humble Negro musicians, unaided by the control of that critical intelligence that was to prove such an asset to the later initiators."

Meanwhile, from the early 1930s on, Black surrealists such as Etienne Léro and René Menil praised jazz and Black vernacular musics as key elements of their revolutionary project; Egyptian surrealist Georges Henein published a substantial lecture on jazz in 1935. During and after World War II, Black music gained enthusiastic support from such important surrealist figures as the Chilean Roberto Matta, the Romanian Victor Brauner, the Sicilian-American Philip Lamantia, and many others. By 1945

André Breton—having heard live jazz in Harlem during his years in New York as a refugee from Nazi-overrun France—had thoroughly revised his earlier views on music.

It is no surprise that Thelonious Monk turned out to be one of the surrealists' major heroes. Monk's music appealed especially to the surrealists' struggle for complete freedom and the overthrow of bourgeois concepts of beauty and art. He made music that destroyed many Western ideas about music making, turning conventional rules of composition, harmony, and rhythm on their heads. He stripped romantic ballads of their romanticism and took his listeners on wild harmonic rides filled with surprising dissonances. His admirers included the important surrealist theorist Gérard Legrand—who wrote the first surrealist book on jazz, *Puissances du Jazz* (1953), Romanian poet Gellu Naum, and poet-critic Georges Goldfayn, who suggested that painters and poets had much to learn from Monk by listening to how he interpreted a song. Victor Brauner did a striking symbolic "picto-portrait" of Monk in 1948 (years before Monk became well known in the United States). Claude Tarnaud wrote a poem for Monk in which he imagined him in a combo with Rimbaud, Brauner, and de Chirico.

Although Black music has long served as a model for Black poetry and prose, Ted Joans—who studied trumpet, sang bebop, and earned a B.A. in fine arts from Indiana University before moving to New York's Greenwich Village in 1951—has always understood modern jazz, from bebop to the avant-garde, as essentially surrealist. He often describes the way Charlie Parker or Cecil Taylor alters or improvises on melodic lines, or scat singing, as "surrealizing" a song. Joans's own poetry not only celebrates and interrogates the music, life, and meaning of jazz brilliantly, but also takes on the characteristics of jazz performance—another way of "surrealizing a song." One can find many examples of this in collections of his poetry, especially *Black Pow-Wow, Funky Jazz Poems, Afrodisia,* and his recent volume of selected works, *Teducation.* Just listen to "The Sax Bit," Joans's homage to that obscure European instrument that Black people made famous:

This bent metal serpent / holy horn with lids like beer
    mug / with phallic tail why did they invent you
    before Coleman Hawkins was born ?
This curved shiney tune gut / hanging lynched like / J
    shaped initial of jazz / wordless without a reed when
    Coleman Hawkins first fondled it / kissed it with Black
    sound did Congo blood sucking Belges frown ?
This tenor / alto / bass / baritone / soprano / moan / cry &
    shout-a-phone ! sex-oh-phone / tell-it-like-damn-
    sho-is-a-phone ! What tremors ran through Adolphe
    Saxe the day Bean grabbed his ax ?
This golden mine of a million marvelous sounds / black
    notes with myriad shadows / or empty crooked tube of
    technical white poor-formance / calculated keys that
    never unlock soul doors / white man made machine saved
    from zero by Coleman Hawkins !
This saxophone salvation / modern gri gri hanging from
    jazzmen's necks placed there by Coleman Hawkins
    a full body & soul sorcerer whose spirit dwells eternally
    in every saxophone NOW and all those sound-a-phones
    to be

The surrealists' discovery of the Marvelous in Black music extends well beyond jazz. Jazz's very heart, body, and soul—the
blues—was the subject of one of the most important surrealist
texts to come out of the United States. Paul Garon's *Blues and
the Poetic Spirit* (first published in 1975; revised and expanded in
1996) argues, among other things, that the blues *is* poetry or, more
specifically, the poetic expression of the Black working class. Insisting that blues artists are much greater poets than T. S. Eliot
or Ezra Pound, or any number of European poets for that matter,
Garon regards the blues as "true poetry"—for what is poetry but
the revolt of the spirit? Unlike dozens of other scholars of the
blues, Garon is less interested in what the blues may tell us about
social reality than in comprehending desire. "Fantasy alone," he
writes, "enables us to envision the real possibilities of human

existence, no longer tied securely to the historical effluvia passed off as everyday life; fantasy remains our most pre-emptive critical faculty, for it alone tells us what can be. Here lies the revolutionary nature of the blues: through its fidelity to fantasy and desire, the blues generates an irreducible and, so to speak, habit-forming demand for freedom and what Rimbaud called 'true life.'"

Desire and sexuality, and their relationship to revolt, have always been central themes in the music, but were too often avoided by well-meaning defenders of the race concerned about reinforcing stereotypes of Black promiscuity. Surrealists, on the other hand, had a long-standing interest in sexual liberty and the power of the erotic, which must have rendered the blues all the more attractive.

Organized surrealism came late to the English-speaking world, and largely because of the language barrier, awareness of the power of the blues came late to surrealism. One can only imagine how the movement's own sexual revolt might have benefited had it embraced the poetry of Black women's blues in the 1920s and 1930s. During this period, leading surrealist women in Europe and the United States, such as Toyen, Valentine Penrose, Leonora Carrington, Meret Oppenheim, Claude Cahun, and Mary Low proposed a more revolutionary sexuality and resisted the subjugation of women to men's desires. In searching for models, they might have drawn on women's blues, for as Angela Davis and Hazel Carby have argued, artists such as Bessie Smith, Ma Rainey, Alberta Hunter, Memphis Minnie, Lucille Bogan, and Ida Cox created a poetics of sexual freedom and power, a poetics to articulate desire, as well as pain, loss, alienation, and dislocation. The music captures the magical, transformative quality of the erotic—something even the best scholarship on the blues rarely addresses because prevailing critical frameworks seem unable to move beyond social realism.

Besides embracing the erotic and working through new visions of love, Black musician-poets have relentlessly critiqued alienated wage labor. Their utopias are always free of "work"—meaning low-wage, unfulfilling, backbreaking labor—and full of pleasurable leisure. This is not to suggest that people do not want to "work," but that the work they are forced to do is not fulfilling, creative, or enjoyable. Blues poets, drawing on the everyday language of the Black working class, often invoke the word *work* to mean nonwaged activity: musical performance, dancing, sex, etc. But one also finds in the blues a strong desire for freedom from toil. Ma Rainey sings:

> I've got those misery blues.
> I've got to go to work now,
> Get another start,
> Work is the thing that's breaking my heart
> So I've got those mean ol' misery blues.

Part of what made the blues so attractive to surrealists was its humor. "Misery" does not define the blues, contrary to popular belief. The blues is often characterized by blues artists themselves as "happy music," stories replete with punch lines and double-entendres. Charlie Campbell's "Goin' Away Blues" tells his listeners, "I don't want a woman who wears a number nine/I wake up in the morning, I can't tell her shoes from mine." Even songs of poverty, loss, and tragedy are filled with absurdities meant to elicit laughter—what André Breton ironically called "black humor." In the wild and wacky world of Black humor—and here the double-entendre is quite deliberate—the blues is just the tip of the iceberg. The absurdity of racism and the fragile and strange world of white supremacy produced a deep wellspring of jokes, hilarious folktales, and humorous word games (e.g., "the dozens") that cut to the heart of our past and present slavery. Consider the yarn about a Southern white dentist charging a Black patient two thousand dollars to pull a tooth while his white patients paid only fifty dollars. Why? Because in the South a Negro doesn't dare open his mouth to a white man, which meant that the dentist had to pull the tooth through the anus!

Freedom Dreams from the Jungle

As European surrealists found renewal in the cultures and revolts of the "colored" and colonial world, several young intellectuals from that world discovered surrealism. The first known group to embrace surrealism was Martinican students sojourning in Paris. In 1932 Etienne Léro, René Menil, J. M. Monnerot, Pierre Yoyotte, his sister Simone Yoyotte, and a few others published one issue of a journal they called *Légitime Défense* (Self-Defense). In it they declared their commitment to surrealism and communist revolution, critiqued the French-speaking Black bourgeoisie, celebrated several Black American writers like Langston Hughes and Claude McKay, and published poetry and automatic writing by several members of the group. Although the journal was promptly suppressed by the colonial authorities, it had its impact. Like other journals of the Black Renaissance (e.g., *La Revue du Monde Noir, Fire!, African Times and Orient Review*, and, a bit later, *L'Étudiant Noir*), the editors of *Légitime Défense* denounced racism (paying special attention to the Scottsboro case) and affirmed their African past as well as the cultures of the diaspora. Members of the group also made major critical contributions to surrealism's theoretical development: J. M. Monnerot produced a stinging critique of the "civilized mentality" for *Le Surréalisme au service de la révolution* (1933), and Pierre Yoyotte wrote a penetrating essay on the significance of surrealism in the struggle against fascism, published in a special surrealist issue of the Belgian journal *Documents* (1934).

Aimé Césaire was part of a different intellectual circle centered around a journal called *L'Étudiant Noir*, whose editors included Leopold Senghor from Senegal and Leon Gotran Damas, a childhood friend of Césaire's from French Guiana. All three men were outstanding poets, and together they would help found the "Negritude" movement celebrating the African cultural heritage in the Francophone world. In *L'Étudiant Noir*'s March 1935 issue, Césaire published a passionate tract against assimilation in which he first coined the term *Negritude*. It is more than ironic that at the moment Césaire's piece appeared, he was hard at work absorbing as much French and European humanities as possible in preparation for his entrance exams for L'École Normale Superieure. The exams took their toll, for sure, though the psychic and emotional costs of having to imbibe the very culture Césaire publicly rejected must have exacerbated an already exhausting regimen. After completing his exams during the summer of 1935, he took a short vacation to Yugoslavia with a fellow student. While visiting the Adriatic coast, Césaire was overcome with memories of home after seeing a small island from a distance. Moved, he stayed up half the night working on a long poem about Martinique of his youth, the land, the people, the majesty of the place. The next morning when he inquired about the little island, he was told it was called Martinska. A magical chance encounter, to say the least. The words he penned that moonlit night were the beginnings of what would subsequently become his most famous poem of all: "Cahier d'un retour au pays Natal" (Notebook of a Return to My Native Land). The next summer he did return to Martinique, but was greeted by an even greater sense of alienation. He returned to France to complete his thesis on African-American writers of the Harlem Renaissance and their representations of the South, and then on July 10, 1937, married Suzanne Roussy, a fellow Martinican student with whom he had worked on *L'Étudiant Noir*.

The couple returned to Martinique in 1939 and began teaching in Fort-de-France. Joining forces with René Menil, Lucie Thesée, Aristide Maugée, Georges Gratiant, and others, they launched the journal *Tropiques*. The appearance of *Tropiques* coincided with the fall of France to the fascist Vichy regime, which put the colonies of Martinique, Guadeloupe, and Guiana under Vichy rule. The effect was startling; any illusions Césaire and his comrades might have harbored about color-blind French brotherhood were shattered when thousands of French sailors arrived on the island. Their racism was blatant and direct. As literary critic A. James Arnold observed, "The insensitivity of this military regime also made it difficult for Martinicans to ignore the fact that they were a colony like any other, a conclusion that the official policy of assimilation had masked somewhat. These conditions contributed to radicalizing Césaire and his friends, preparing them for a more anticolonialist posture at the end of the war." The official policy of the regime to censor *Tropiques* and interdict the publication when it was deemed subversive also hastened the group's radicalization. In a notorious letter dated May 10, 1943, Martinique's chief of information services, Lieutenant de Vaisseau Bayle, justified interdicting *Tropiques* for being "a revolutionary review that is racial and sectarian." Bayle accused the editors of poisoning the spirit of society, sowing hatred, and ruining the morale of the country. Two days later, the editors penned a brilliant polemical response:

> To Lieutenant de Vaisseau Bayle:
>
> Sir,
>
> We have received your indictment of Tropiques.
>   "Racists," "sectarians," "revolutionaries," "ingrates and traitors to the country," "poisoners of souls," none of these epithets really repulses us.
>   "Poisoners of Souls," like Racine, . . .
>   "Ingrates and traitors to our good Country," like Zola, . . .
>   "Revolutionaries," like the Hugo of "Chatiments."
>   "Sectarians," passionately, like Rimbaud and Lautréamont.
>   Racists, yes. Of the racism of Toussaint-Louverture, of Claude McKay and Langston Hughes against that of Drumont and Hitler.
>   As to the rest of it, don't expect for us to plead our case, nor vain recriminations, nor discussion.
>   We do not speak the same language.
>
> Signed: Aimé Césaire, Suzanne Césaire, Georges Gratiant, Aristide Maugée, René Menil, Lucie Thesée.

But for *Tropiques* to survive, they had to camouflage their boldness, passing the publication off as a journal of West Indian folklore. Yet, despite the repressions and the ruses, *Tropiques* survived the war as one of the most important and radical surrealist publications in the world, lasting from 1941 to 1945. The essays and poems it published by the Césaires, René Menil, and others reveal the evolution of a sophisticated anticolonial stance as well as a vision of a postcolonial future. Theirs was a conception of freedom that drew on modernism and a deep appreciation for precolonial African modes of thought and practice; it drew on surrealism as the strategy of revolution of the mind and Marxism as revolution of the productive forces. It was an effort to carve out a position independent of all these forces, a kind of wedding of Negritude, Marxism, and surrealism; this group's collective efforts would have a profound impact on international surrealism, in general, and on André Breton, in particular. *Tropiques* also published Breton, as well as texts by Pierre Mabille, Benjamin Peret, Victor Brauner, Jorge Cáceres, and other surrealists.

The influence of surrealism on Aimé Césaire has been called into question many times, by critics as different as Jean-Paul Sartre (1948) and Jahnheinz Jahn (1958). The question of his surrealism, however, is generally posed only in terms of André Breton's influence on Césaire. In this view, surrealism is treated as "European thought" and, like Marxism, is considered alien to non-European cultural traditions. But such a "diffusionist" interpretation seems too simplistic, too one-sided, overlooking the possibility that the Césaires (Aimé and Suzanne) were creative innovators of surrealism — that they actually introduced fresh surrealist ideas to Breton and his colleagues. I don't think it is too much to argue that the Césaires not only embraced surrealism — independently of the Paris Group, I might add — but also expanded it, enlarged its perspectives, and contributed enormously to theorizing the "domain of the Marvelous." Aimé Césaire, after all, has never denied his surrealist leanings. As he explains: "Surrealism provided me with what I had been confusedly searching for. I have accepted it joyfully because in it I have found more of a confirmation than a revelation." Surrealism, he explained, helped him to summon up powerful unconscious forces. "This, for me, was a call to Africa. I said to myself: it's true that superficially we are French, we bear the marks of French customs; we have been branded by Cartesian philosophy, by French rhetoric; but if we break with all that, if we plumb the depths, then what we will find is fundamentally black." And in another interview with Jacqueline Leiner, he was even more enthusiastic about Breton's role: "Breton brought us boldness, he helped us take a strong stand. He abridged our hesitations and research. I realized that the majority of the problems I encountered had already been resolved by Breton and surrealism. I would say that my meeting with Breton was confirmation of what I had arrived at on my own. This saved us time, let us go quicker, farther. The encounter was extraordinary."

We know far less about Suzanne Césaire, though judging from her all-too-brief writings, it is not too much to proclaim her as one of surrealism's most original theorists. Unlike critics who boxed surrealism into narrow avant-garde aesthetic tendencies alongside futurism or cubism, Suzanne Césaire linked it to broader movements such as romanticism, socialism, and Negritude. Surrealism was a state of mind, or in Franklin Rosemont's words, a "permanent readiness for the Marvelous." In a 1941 issue of *Tropiques*, she imagined new possibilities in terms that were foreign to Marxists; she called on readers to embrace "the domain of the strange, the marvelous and the fantastic, a domain scorned by people of certain inclinations. Here is the freed image, dazzling and beautiful, with a beauty that could not be more unexpected and overwhelming. Here are the poet, the painter and the artist, presiding over the metamorphoses and the inversions of the world under the sign of hallucination and madness." And yet when she speaks of the domain of the Marvelous, she also has her sights on the chains of colonial domination, never forgetting the crushing reality of everyday life in Martinique and the rest of the world. In "Surrealism and Us: 1943," she writes with boldness and clarity:

> Thus, far from contradicting, diluting, or diverting our revolutionary attitude toward life, surrealism strengthens it. It nourishes an impatient strength within us, endlessly reinforcing the massive army of refusals.
>
> And I am also thinking of tomorrow.
>
> Millions of black hands will hoist their terror across the furious skies of world war. Freed from a long benumbing slumber,

the most disinherited of all peoples will rise up from plains of ashes.

Our surrealism will supply this rising people with a punch from its very depths. Our surrealism will enable us to finally transcend the sordid antinomies of the present: whites/Blacks, Europeans/Africans, civilized/savages—at last rediscovering the magic power of the mahoulis, drawn directly from living sources. Colonial idiocy will be purified in the welder's blue flame. We shall recover our value as metal, our cutting edge of steel, our unprecedented communions.

One painter who succeeded in creating the kind of art Suzanne Césaire demanded, of producing what Breton called "convulsive beauty," was the Cuban-born Wifredo Lam. The eighth child born to an eighty-four-year-old Chinese father (Lam Yam) and "mulatto" mother of Indian, African, and Spanish descent, Lam grew up in an environment that, in his view, prepared him for surrealism by exposing him to African culture. His godmother, Mantonica Wilson, practiced Santeria and was consulted far and wide for remedies for physical and spiritual afflictions. And as a young man, Lam knew revolt firsthand: While studying art in Madrid, he participated in the defense of republican Spain during the civil war. After leaving Spain for France in 1938, he befriended Pablo Picasso, whose interest in African art turned out to be a considerable factor in Lam's work as well as his politics. "What made me feel such empathy with [Picasso's] painting more than anything else," Lam remembered, "was the presence of African art and the African spirit I discovered in it. When I was a little boy, I had seen African figures in Mantonica Wilson's house. And in Pablo's work I seemed to find a sort of continuity." Picasso also brought Lam to the Surrealist Group in Paris, introducing him to such critical figures as André Breton, Michel Leiris, Benjamin Péret, Joan Miró, Dora Maar, Tristan Tzara, and Paul Eluard, among others.

Bringing together his interest in African figures, his memory of his Cuban homeland, and surrealism, Lam's work became less naturalistic and more totemlike, less androcentric and more magical in its fusions of human and animal forms. In his efforts to depict the spirit world of Santeria, his figures became mythic, larger than life, even majestic in character. Lam's politics, like those of the *Tropiques* group, were rooted in a combination of surrealism, Negritude, Marxism, and an intense love of his native land. He detested the "picturesque" imagery of Cuba "for the tourists" as well as social realism, and instead sought to represent "the Negro spirit, the beauty of the plastic art of the blacks. In this way I could act as a Trojan horse that would spew forth hallucinating figures with the power to surprise, to disturb the dreams of the exploiters. I knew I was running the risk of not being understood either by the man in the street or by the others. But a true picture has the power to set the imagination to work, even if it takes time."

Lam beautifully executes this vision in what may be his most famous painting, "The Jungle." Completed in 1943, it depicts four monsterlike creatures with enormous feet and masks rising in the jungle surrounded by spirits. Critic Alain Jouffroy has called it "the first revolutionary statement in a plastic art of a Third World that is already conscious of the need for all cultures to make common cause, the prophetic announcement of that awakening on a world scale." Lam himself thought of it as a representation of revolt but from the depth of the unconscious. "My idea was to represent the spirit of the Negroes in the situation in which they were then. I have used poetry to show the reality of acceptance and protest."

A Poetics of Anticolonialism

Another powerful "revolutionary statement . . . of a Third World that is already conscious of the need for all cultures to make common cause" found voice in Aimé Césaire's *Discourse on Colonialism* (1950). Césaire's first nonfiction book, *Discourse* was very much a product of its time and a reflection of the changing political landscape. By the end of the war, Césaire became more directly involved in politics, joining the Communist Party and successfully running for mayor of Fort-de-France and deputy to the French National Assembly on the Communist ticket. His main concern, however, was not proletarian revolution but the colonial question. In 1946, he succeeded in getting the National Assembly to pass a law changing the status of Martinique, Guadeloupe, Guiana, and Réunion from colonies to "departments" within the French Republic. He believed that the assimilation of the old colonies into the republic would guarantee equal rights, but it turned out not to be the case. In the end, French officials were sent to the colonies in greater numbers, often displacing some of the local Black Martinican bureaucrats. It was a painful lesson for Césaire, perhaps the main catalyst for *Discourse on Colonialism*.

A fusion of ideas drawn from surrealism, communism, Negritude, and national liberation movements, as well as Césaire's imagination, *Discourse* might best be described as a declaration of war. I would almost call it a "Third World manifesto" but hesitate because it is primarily a polemic against the old order bereft of the kind of propositions and proposals that accompany manifestos. Yet *Discourse* speaks in revolutionary cadences, capturing the spirit of its age just as Marx and Engels did 102 years earlier in their little manifesto. It appeared just as the old empires were on the verge of collapse, thanks in part to a world war against fascism that left Europe in a material, spiritual, and philosophical shambles. It was the age of decolonization and revolt in Africa, Asia, and Latin America. Five years earlier (1945) Black people from around the globe gathered in Manchester, England, for the Fifth Pan-African Congress to discuss the freedom and future of Africa. Five years later (1955), representatives from the nonaligned nations gathered in Bandung, Indonesia, to discuss the freedom and future of the Third World. Mao's revolution in China was a year old, while the Mau Mau in Kenya were just gearing up for an uprising against their colonial masters. The French encountered insurrections in Algeria, Tunisia, Morocco, Cameroon, and Madagascar, and suffered a

humiliating defeat by the Viet Minh at Dien Bien Phu. Revolt
was in the air. India, the Philippines, Guyana, Egypt, Guate-
mala, South Africa, Alabama, Mississippi, Georgia, Harlem, you
name it: Revolt! *Discourse on Colonialism* was indisputably one
of the key texts in this tidal wave of anticolonial literature produced during the postwar period—works that include W. E. B.
Du Bois's *Color and Democracy* (1945) and *The World and Africa*
(1947), Frantz Fanon's *Black Skin, White Masks* (1952); George
Padmore's *Pan-Africanism or Communism? The Coming Struggle for Africa* (1956); Albert Memmi's *The Colonizer and the
Colonized* (1957); Richard Wright's *White Man Listen!* (1957);
Jean-Paul Sartre's essay "Black Orpheus" (1948); and journals
such as *Présence Africaine* and *African Revolution*. As with much
of the radical literature produced during this epoch, *Discourse*
placed the colonial question front and center. Although, remaining somewhat true to his Communist affiliation, Césaire never
quite dethroned the modern proletariat from its exalted status as
a revolutionary force, he made the European working class practically invisible. This was a book about colonialism, its impact
on the colonized, on culture, on history, on the very concept of
civilization itself, and most importantly, on the colonizer. In the
finest Hegelian fashion, Césaire demonstrates how colonialism
worked to "decivilize" the colonizer: Torture, violence, race hatred, and immorality constituted a dead weight on the so-called
civilized, pulling the master class deeper and deeper into the
abyss of barbarism. The instruments of colonial power relied on
barbaric, brutal violence and intimidation, and the end result
was the degradation of Europe itself. Hence Césaire could only
scream: "Europe is indefensible."

Europe was also dependent. Anticipating Fanon's famous
proposition in *The Wretched of the Earth* that "Europe is literally
the creation of the Third World," Césaire revealed over and over
again the colonizers' sense of superiority and their sense of mission as the world's civilizers, a mission that depended on turning
the Other into barbarians. The Africans, the Indians, the Asians
could not possess civilization or a culture equal to that of the

imperialists, or the latter had no purpose, no justification for the exploitation and domination of the rest of the world. The colonial encounter, in other words, required a reinvention of the colonized, the deliberate destruction of their past, what Césaire called "thingification." *Discourse*, then, had a double-edged meaning: It was Césaire's discourse on the material and spiritual havoc created by colonialism, and it was a critique of colonial discourse. Anticipating the explosion of work we now call "postcolonial studies," Césaire revealed how the circulation of colonial ideology—an ideology of racial and cultural hierarchy—was as essential to colonial rule as police and corvée labor. Moreover, as a product of the post–World War II period, *Discourse* went one step further by drawing a direct link between the logic of colonialism and the rise of fascism. Echoing a number of Black radicals, including W. E. B. Du Bois, George Padmore, and C. L. R. James (see chapter 2), Césaire provocatively pointed out that Europeans tolerated "Nazism before it was inflicted on them, that they absolved it, shut their eyes to it, legitimized it, because, until then, it had been applied only to non-European peoples; that they have cultivated that Nazism, that they are responsible for it, and that before engulfing the whole of Western, Christian civilization in its reddened waters, it oozes, seeps, and trickles from every crack." So the real crime of fascism was the application of colonial procedures to white people "which until then had been reserved for the Arabs of Algeria, the coolies of India, and the blacks of Africa."

The very idea that there was a superior race lay at the heart of the matter, and this is why elements of *Discourse* also drew on Negritude's impulse to recover the history of Africa's accomplishments. Taking his cue from Leo Frobenius's injunction that the "idea of the barbaric Negro is a European invention," Césaire set out to prove that the colonial mission to "civilize" the primitive was just a smoke screen. If anything, colonialism resulted in the massive destruction of whole societies—societies that not only functioned at a high level of sophistication and complexity, but that could offer the West valuable lessons about how we might live together and

remake the modern world. Indeed, Césaire's insistence that precolonial African and Asian cultures "were not only ante-capitalist . . .
but also *anti-capitalist*" anticipated romantic claims advanced
by African nationalist leaders such as Julius Nyerere, Kenneth
Kaunda, and Senghor himself that modern Africa could establish
socialism on the basis of precolonial village life.

Discourse was not the first place Césaire made the case for the
barbaric West following the path of the civilized African. In his
introduction to a book by liberal French scholar Victor Schoelcher, *Esclavage et colonisation* (1948), he wrote:

> The men they took away knew how to build houses, govern em-
> pires, erect cities, cultivate fields, mine for metals, weave cotton,
> forge steel.
>   Their religion had its own beauty, based on mystical connec-
> tions with the founder of the city. Their customs were pleasing,
> built on unity, kindness, respect for age.
>   No coercion, only mutual assistance, the joy of living, a free
> acceptance of discipline.
>   Order—Earnestness—Poetry and Freedom.

Reading this passage and the book itself deeply affected one of
Césaire's brightest students, Frantz Fanon. It was a revelation for
him to discover cities in Africa and "accounts of learned blacks."
"All of that," he noted in *Black Skin, White Masks* (1952), "ex-
humed from the past, spread with its insides out, made it possible
for me to find a valid historical place. The white man was wrong,
I was not a primitive, not even a half-man, I belonged to a race
that had already been working in gold and silver two thousand
years ago."

Negritude turned out to be a miraculous weapon in the struggle to overthrow the "barbaric Negro." And yet despite Césaire's
construction of precolonial Africa as an aggregation of warm,
communal societies, he never called for a return. Unlike his old
friend Senghor, Césaire's Negritude was future oriented and
modern. His position in *Discourse* was unequivocal: "For us the

problem is not to make a utopian and sterile attempt to repeat the past, but to go beyond. It is not a dead society that we want to revive. We leave that to those who go in for exoticism. . . . It is a new society that we must create, with the help of our brother slaves, a society rich with all the productive power of modern times, warm with all the fraternity of olden days."

Then comes the shocking next line:

"For some examples showing that this is possible, we can look to the Soviet Union."

Now, given everything he had written thus far, everything that he had lived, why would he hold up Stalinism circa the 1950s as an exemplar of the new society? Certainly, his praise for the U.S.S.R. was a logical manifestation of his Communist Party membership. But why would a great poet and major voice of surrealism and Negritude join the Communist Party in the 1940s? Actually, once we consider the context of the postwar world, his decision is not shocking at all. First, remember that Communist parties worldwide, especially in Europe, were at their height immediately after the war, and Joseph Stalin spent the war years as an ally of liberal democracy. Second, several leading writers and artists committed to radical social change, particularly in the Caribbean and Latin America, became Communists—including Césaire's friends, Jacques Romain, Nicolas Guillén, and René Depestre.

Thus given Césaire's role as Communist leader, we should not be surprised by *Discourse*'s nod to the Soviet Union, or even the final closing lines of the text where he named proletarian revolution as our savior. What is jarring, however, is how incongruous these statements were in relation to the rest of the text. After demonstrating how Europe was a dying civilization, one on the verge of self-destruction in which the chickens of colonial violence and tyranny had come home to roost, and the white working class looked on in silent complicity, he proposed proletarian revolution as the final solution! Yet throughout the book he anticipated Fanon, implying that there was nothing worth saving in Europe, that the European working class had too often joined

forces with the European bourgeoisie in support of racism, imperialism, and colonialism, and that the uprisings of the colonized
might point the way forward. Ultimately, *Discourse* was a challenge to, or revision of, Marxism that drew on surrealism and
the antirationalist ideas of his early poetry and explorations in
Negritude. It was fairly unmaterialist and quite surrealist in the
way it cried out for new spiritual values to emerge out of the study
of what colonialism sought to destroy.

Césaire's position vis-à-vis Marxism became even clearer less
than one year after the third edition of *Discourse* appeared. In
October 1956, Césaire penned his famous letter to Maurice
Thorez, secretary general of the French Communist Party (CP),
tendering his resignation from the party. Besides its stinging re-
buke of Stalinism, the heart of the letter dealt with the colonial
question—not just the Party's policies toward the colonies but
the colonial relationship between the metropolitan CP and the
Martinican party. Arguing that people of color needed to exercise self-determination, he warned against treating the "colonial
question . . . as a subsidiary part of some more important global
matter." Racism, in other words, could not be subordinate to the
class struggle. His letter was an even bolder, more direct assertion
of Third World unity than *Discourse*. Although he still identified
himself as a Marxist and was still open to alliances, he cautioned
that there "are no allies by divine rights." If following the Communist Party "pillages our most vivifying friendships, wastes the
bond that weds us to other West Indian islands, the tie that makes
us Africa's child, then I say communism has served us ill in having
us swap a living brotherhood for what looks to have the features
of the coldest of all chill abstractions." More important, Césaire's
investment in a Third World revolt that would pave the way for a
new society certainly anticipated Fanon. He had practically given
up on Europe and the old humanism and its claims of universality, opting instead to redefine the "universal" in a way that did
not privilege Europe. Césaire explains, "I'm not going to entomb
myself in some strait particularism. But I don't intend either to
become lost in a fleshless universalism. . . . I have a different idea

of a universal. It is of a universal rich with all that is particular, rich with all the particulars there are, the deepening of each particular, the coexistence of them all."

What Césaire articulates in *Discourse,* and more explicitly in his letter to Thorez, distills the spirit that swept through African intellectual circles in the age of decolonization. This pervasive spirit was what Negritude was all about then; it was never a simple matter of racial essentialism. Critic, scholar, and filmmaker Manthia Diawara beautifully captured the atmosphere of the era and, implicitly, what these radical critiques of the colonial order such as *Discourse on Colonialism* meant to a new generation:

> The idea that Negritude was bigger even than Africa, that we were part of an international moment which held the promise of universal emancipation, that our destiny coincided with the universal freedom of workers and colonized people worldwide— all this gave us a bigger and more important identity than the ones previously available to us through kinship, ethnicity, and race. . . . The awareness of our new historical mission freed us from what we regarded in those days as the archaic identities of our fathers and their religious entrapments; it freed us from race and banished our fear of the whiteness of French identity. To be labeled the saviors of humanity, when only recently we had been colonized and despised by the world, gave us a feeling of righteousness, which bred contempt for capitalism, racialism of all origins, and tribalism.

In light of recent events—genocide in East Africa, the collapse of democracy throughout the continent, the isolation of Cuba, the overthrow of progressive movements throughout the so-called Third World—some might argue that the moment of truth has already passed, that Césaire and Fanon's predictions proved false. We face an era in which fools are calling for a renewal of colonialism, in which descriptions of violence and instability draw on the very colonial language of "barbarism" and "backwardness" that Césaire critiqued in *Discourse.* But this is all a mystification; the fact is, while colonialism in its formal sense might have been dismantled, the colonial state was not. Many of the problems of democracy are products of the old colonial state, whose primary difference with the current states is the absence of Black faces. It has to do with the rise of a new ruling class—the class Fanon warned us about—that is content with mimicking the colonial masters, whether they are the old-school British or French officers, the new jack American corporate rulers, or the Stalinists whose sympathy for the "backward" countries often mirrored the very colonial discourse Césaire exposed. Corruption runs rampant; violence and intimidation are employed to keep order and "motivate" workers; profits for big capital take precedence over the problems of poverty, health, and safety for the poor.

We are hardly in a postcolonial moment. The official apparatus might have been removed, but the political, economic, and cultural links established by colonial domination still remain, with some alterations. *Discourse* was less concerned with the specifics of political economy than with a way of thinking. Its lesson was that colonial domination required a whole way of thinking, a discourse in which everything that was advanced, good, and civilized was defined and measured in European terms. *Discourse* called on the world to move forward as rapidly as possible, and yet called for the overthrow of a master class's ideology of progress, one built on violence, destruction, and genocide. Both Fanon and Césaire warned the "colored" world not to follow in Europe's footsteps, and not to go back to the ancient way, but to carve out a new direction altogether. What we've been witnessing, however (and here I must include Césaire's own beloved Martinique), hardly reflects the imagination and vision captured in these brief pages: the same old political parties, the same armies, the same methods of labor exploitation, the same education, the same tactics of incarceration, exiling, and killing artists and intellectuals who dare to imagine a radically different way of living, who dare to invent the Marvelous before our very eyes.

In the end, *Discourse* was never intended to be a road map or a blueprint for revolution. It is poetry and therefore revolt. It is an act of insurrection, drawn from Césaire's own miraculous weapons, molded and shaped by his work with *Tropiques* and its challenge to the Vichy regime, by his imbibing of European culture and his sense of alienation from both France and his native land. It is a rising, a blow to the master who appears as owner and ruler, teacher and comrade. It is revolutionary graffiti painted in bold strokes across the great texts of Western civilization; it is a hand grenade tossed with deadly accuracy, clearing the field so that we might write a new history with what's left standing. *Discourse* is hardly a dead document about a dead order. If anything, it is a call for us to plumb the depths of the imagination for a different way forward. Just as Césaire drew on Comte de Lautréamont's *Chants de Maldoror* to illuminate the cannibalistic nature of capitalism *and* the power of poetic knowledge, *Discourse* offers new insights into the consequences of colonialism and a model for dreaming a way out of our postcolonial predicament. Although we still need to overthrow all vestiges of the old colonial order, destroying the old is just half the battle.

The Noise of Our Living: In the Wilderness of North America

Surrealism's influence in the Black world extends well beyond the formally colonized people. In North America, it is reflected in the work of Black artists as diverse as Frank London Brown, Bob Kaufman, Jayne Cortez, Ted Joans, Will Alexander, and Richard Wright.

Richard Wright?

Only a handful of critics have acknowledged Wright's surrealist influences, and yet it is hard to comprehend some of his most radical political impulses without surrealism. As early as 1940, Kenneth Burke characterized *Native Son* as a "surrealistic" novel, and more recently, Eugene E. Miller's insightful study, *Voice of a Native Son: The Poetics of Richard Wright* (1990), argued that Wright's fascination with surrealism was more than a passing flirtation. According to Miller, the manuscript version of

Wright's *American Hunger* reveals that he knew about Dadaism (a short-lived forebear of surrealism founded in 1916, emphasizing humor, irreverence, and a critique of bourgeois conceptions of "art"). Also, Wright's poem "Transcontinental" (1935) was modeled on surrealist Louis Aragon's celebrated pro-Communist poem "Red Front." Moreover, in an essay titled "Personalism" written some time between 1935 and 1937, Wright advocated the use of "any and all techniques, including those of Dada and Surrealism, in order to express a writer's deepest subjective feelings."

Wright's most sustained discussion of surrealism appears in his unpublished "Memories of My Grandmother." Surrealism, he suggests, helped him understand the character and strengths of African-American folk culture and clarify "the mystery" of the way his grandmother—like blues singers—used language and composition. The blues juxtaposed elements that had no rational connection, and it possessed no narrative sequence. Wright found the blues structure analogous to the surrealists' use of the "exquisite corpse," the chance encounter, the juxtaposing of seemingly unrelated things in order to reveal the Marvelous.

Wright indirectly acknowledged the influence of surrealism on his most famous novel, *Native Son*, in his classic essay "How Bigger Was Born." In Wright's novel, Bigger Thomas is the protagonist whose degradation under racism and capitalism compels him to murder and rape, but just as he is about to face his own execution he recognizes the redeeming power of working-class collective action through the Communist Party. Wright did not try to pass off *Native Son* as social realism or proletarian realism, and he did not characterize it as mere social commentary. Rather, it is a psychological journey that attempts to communicate what's incommunicable; it is about alienation and yearning for something, but Wright isn't sure exactly what it is. In trying to make sense of Bigger, Wright succumbed to the power of imagination:

> While writing, a new and thrilling relationship would spring up under the drive of emotion, coalescing and telescoping alien facts into a known and felt truth. That was the deep fun of the job: to feel within my body that I was pushing out to new areas

of feeling, strange landmarks of emotion, tramping upon foreign soil, compounding new relationships of perceptions, making new and—until that very split second of time!—unheard-of
and unfelt effects with words. It had a buoying and tonic impact
upon me; my senses would strain and seek for more and more of
such relationships; my temperature would rise as I worked. That
is writing as I feel it, a kind of significant living.

For Wright, Black people did not have to go out and find surrealism, for their lives were already surreal. He suggested that it
was exactly the forced exclusion of Black people that produced
a different way of looking at the world and of feeling it—an idea
made evident in his 1941 text *Twelve Million Black Voices*. Wright
used Farm Security Administration photographs to drive his narrative. The text captured the surrealist character of Black life and
turned to poetry as a means to elucidate alienation and its impact
on the psyche. "The noise of our living," he writes, "boxed in
stone and steel, is so loud that even a pistol shot is smothered."
In the foreword, Wright announced that he was not interested in
celebrating the Black middle class, the success stories who were
"like single fishes that leap and flash for a split second above the
surface of the sea." He really wanted to write a "history" that attempted, as Baudelaire put it, to "plunge to the bottom of the
abyss, Hell or Heaven . . . to the bottom of the Unknown in order
to find the new!" His world was the world of the 90 percent, the

tragic school that swims below in the depths, against the current,
silently and heavily, struggling against the waves of vicissitudes
that spell a common fate. It is not, however, to celebrate or exalt
the plight of the humble folk who swim in the depths that I
select the conditions of their lives as examples of normality, but
rather to seize upon that which is qualitative and abiding in Negro experience, to place within full and constant view the collective humanity whose triumphs and defeats are shared by the
majority, whose gains in security mark an advance in the level
of consciousness attained by the broad masses in their costly and
tortuous upstream journey.

I don't think it is an exaggeration to declare *Twelve Million Black Voices* a surrealist text. Employing dream imagery, Wright conveyed to his readers the long nightmare that is Black life in America and held out the possibility of a new dream, one rooted in African-American folk values which he attributes to the absurd and impoverished life Black people have had to endure. Unlike the "lords of the land," slavery's descendants never had the option of creating a culture based on property ownership, accumulation, and exploitation. Instead, Black families were held together "by love, sympathy, pity, and the goading knowledge that we must work together to make a crop." "That is why we black folk laugh and sing when we are alone together," Wright mused. "Our scale of values differs from that of the world from which we have been excluded; our shame is not its shame, and our love is not its love." The implications of black folk culture as the basis for a new politics was made explicit in Wright's most surreal passage, rendered ironically as a sermon. It reads like a piece of automatism, spoken from the unconscious, free of traditional form or punctuation. In this breathtaking tale of good versus evil, Satan versus God, Jesus *"dies upon a cross to show Man the way back up the broad highway to peace and thus Man begins to live for a time under a new dispensation of Love and not Law. . . ."* The congregation's response was as important as the sermon itself: The people "sway in our seats until we have lost all notion of time and have begun to float on a tide of passion. The preacher begins to punctuate his words with sharp rhythms, and we are lifted far beyond the boundaries of our daily lives, upward and outward, until drunk with our enchanted vision, our senses lifted to the burning skies, we do not know who we are, what we are, or where we are. . . ." But the hope of a new dispensation keeps their souls nourished until tomorrow.

Wright's engagement with surrealism seemed to parallel that of many other Black intellectuals. They have found in surrealism confirmation of what they already know—for them it is more an act of recognition than a revolutionary discovery. As we have already seen, Aimé Césaire insisted that surrealism brought him back to African culture. Ted Joans wrote Breton that he "chose" surrealism because he recognized its fundamental ideas and camaraderie in jazz. Wifredo Lam said he was drawn to surrealism because he already knew the power of the unconscious, having grown up in the Africanized spirit world of Santeria. The contemporary Senegalese artist Cheikh Tidiane Sylla is even more explicit about how surrealism reveals what is already familiar in African culture. "In the ecologically balanced tribal cultures of Africa," he wrote in *Arsenal/Surrealist Subversion* (1989), "the surrealist spirit is deeply embedded in social tradition. The 'mysticism' prevalent in all Black African philosophy presupposes a highly charged psychic world in which every individual agrees to forget himself or herself in order to concentrate on the least known instances of the mind's movement—a thoroughly emancipatory experience." He further asserted that in Africa the practice of poetry was always a way of life, whereas in the West surrealism was the product of a long philosophical and political struggle "to recover what the traditional African has never lost."

In other words, all these Black artists with whom the surrealists identify suggest that a thorough understanding and an acceptance of the Marvelous existed in the lives of Blacks and non-Western peoples—before Breton, before Rimbaud, before Lautréamont—in music, dance, speech, the plastic arts, and above all philosophy. We are, after all, talking about cultures that valued imagination, improvisation, and verbal agility, from storytelling, preaching, and singing to toasting and the dozens. Indeed, when I first read Lautréamont's injunction that "Poetry must be made by all," I was reminded of Olaudah Equiano, a former slave who wrote in his *Interesting Narrative* (1792) that the world from which he was stolen was "almost a nation of dancers, musicians, and poets [where] every great event . . . is celebrated in public dances . . . accompanied with songs and music." For all of the problems and exploitations and oppressions one finds in precolonial Africa, there remained a deep longing for that world, for it was remembered and experienced as a world that kept us whole. Richard Wright's *Twelve Million Black Voices* located the heart of African "civilization" in the imagination: "We smelted iron, danced, made music, and recited folk poems; we sculptured, worked in glass, spun cotton and wool, wove baskets and cloth. . . ." In her poem "I Wonder Who," Jayne Cortez goes one step further than Wright, juxtaposing Africa's creativity and self-reliance against the corruption of neocolonial schemes of "modernization":

> We have been calling across fields
> & falsetto snapping & moaning
> in deep Shona deep Edo deep Mandingo
> before the erection
> of artificial systems
>
> & we have been building granaries
> pounding grain
> going from dry stream
> to dry stream
> since the beginning of
> the illumination of stars
>
> We have been pulling tons of wood
> up the road
> in the rain
> in malaria land
> for thousands of years
>
> & we have been ploughing across deserts
> linking events
> & circulating information
> since the division of night & day
> day & night. . . .

The second half of the poem asks, Who will get rid of Africa's oppressors, the "Presidents Ministers and Chiefs," "all the non-serious scholars & serious expert invaders of indigenous cultures," the white settler regimes, the mercenaries sent by the forces of imperialism to foil revolutionary movements? The beauty and peace Africa might one day enjoy, again, is musically illustrated in her recording of "I Wonder Who," which is backed by Salieu Suso's and Sarjo Kuyateh's magnificent *kora* playing.

Cortez, after all, is first and foremost an activist. In 1963, SNCC leader James Forman persuaded her to go to Mississippi, where she attended mass meetings and met with grassroots organizers, including Fannie Lou Hamer. She returned to Los Angeles that year and founded Friends of SNCC, a gathering of movement supporters that attracted a broad array of figures from the performing and visual arts. Friends of SNCC succeeded in drawing celebrities and raising money, but Cortez wanted to focus her energies on grassroots organizing. In 1964 she created Studio Watts with Jim Woods, a community theater in the heart of South Central Los Angeles's Black community that performed highly politicized street theater and poetry readings before the Watts rebellion of 1965. Studio Watts grew rapidly, attracting committed artists. Cortez and others broke with Jim Woods in 1967 and formed the Watts Repertory Theatre Company, becoming one of the most dynamic community arts projects in the nation. Although she relocated to New York soon after the WRTC was founded, she returned in 1968 and 1970 to direct Jean Genet's moving play *The Blacks*.

As with Césaire, Richard Wright, Wifredo Lam, and others, it was surrealism that discovered Cortez rather than the other way around. Surrealism was less a revelation than a recognition of what already existed in the Black tradition. For Cortez surrealism is merely a tool to help create a strong revolutionary movement and a powerful, independent poetry.

Jayne Cortez dreams anti-imperialist dreams. It is not enough to imagine what kind of world we would like; we have to do the work to make it happen. Today, in an era when many young people believe that surrealism is merely an aesthetic or a hip style, Cortez exemplifies the revolutionary commitment that has always been at the heart of the Black radical imagination. We hear in her performances with her band Firespitters (which plays all manner of Afrodiasporic music) a vibrant poetic imagery drawn from the deep well of the blues. This is certainly evident in collections such as *Pissstained Stairs and the Monkey Man's Wares* (1969), *Celebrations and Solitudes* (1975), *Coagulations* (1984), *Everywhere Drums* (1990), *Poetic Magnetic* (1991), and *Somewhere in Advance of Nowhere* (1996). She wages poetic war against imperialism, racism, sexism, fascism, consumerism, and environmental injustice, while schooling those who don't know to some of our great artists—from Nicolas Guillén to Babs Gonzalez. She creates magnetic images of convulsive beauty, to be sure, but they are fighting words. Poems such as "Stockpiling" and "War Devoted to War" reveals the connection between war and capitalism, whereas "Rape" and "If the Drum Is a Woman" are antiwar "songs" about the vicious and violent assault on women's bodies. But Cortez is a true radical feminist; she refuses to write women as victims. One of the greatest lyrical paeans to the resistance of women to all forms of domination is Cortez's "Sacred Trees." Using trees as a metaphor for all women, she laments their abuse and exploitation while celebrating their strength, longevity, and rebellion. Women here are the forest; they grow, resist, and lay the foundation for new dreams, a new life:

> . . . everytime I think about us women
> I think about the trees
> I think about
> the subversive trees laden in blood
> but not bleeding
> the rebellious trees encrusted
> but not cracking
> the abused trees wounded
> but still standing
> I think about the proud trees
> the trees with beehive tits buzzing
> the transparent trees
> the trees with quinine breath hovering

the trees swaying & rubbing their
stretched marked bellies
in the rain
the crossroad trees coming from
the tree womb
 of tree seeds
Trees. . . .

"There It Is" is a warning to the liberals and fence-sitters who
don't believe that we are fighting for our lives:

The enemies polishing their penises between
oil wells at the pentagon
the bulldozers leaping into demolition dances
the old folks dying of starvation
the informers wearing out shoes looking for crumbs
the lifeblood of the earth almost dead in
the greedy mouth of imperialism
And my friend
they don't care
if you're an individualist
a leftist a rightist
a shithead or a snake. . . .

To call this "protest poetry" misses the point. It is a complete
revolt, a clarion call for a new way of life. Cortez not only lifts the
proverbial rug covering the mess created by our global systems of
domination, but she also opens our imaginations to new possibilities in some unlikely places: "A promenading surface of erotic
strokes/Rebellions carried on the felt tip of an evening sunset"
(from "In a Stream of Ink"). And in the tradition of the great blues
poets from whom she descends, Jayne Cortez understands and
embraces the transformative, magical quality of the erotic. Listen
to "Say It":

Say it
and peel off that grey iguana skin mask

Say it
and clean out your cockpit of intoxicated spiders
Tear the sexual leaves of grief from your heart
Pluck the feathers of nostalgia from your nipples
Push the slowmoving masochistic mudslide
of contralto voices
from your afternoon skull of anxiety
Say it
and let the tooth chips fall from
your hole of rebellious itches. . . .

Ted Joans has the distinction of being acknowledged by André
Breton as the only African-American surrealist he ever met. He is
the author of more than thirty books of poetry, prose, and collage,
including *Black Pow-Wow, Beat Funky Jazz Poems, Afrodisia, Jazz
Is Our Religion, Sure, Really, I Is, Double Trouble, Wow,* and *Teducation.* Perhaps his best known statement is a poem titled "The
Truth." He warns us not to fear the poets, for they speak the truth;
they are our seers, clairvoyants, visionaries. And yet, to the enemies of freedom, poets, like Joans and Cortez, are dangerous.
Joans knows this all too well, which is why he calls one series of
poems "hand grenades," poems meant to "explode on the enemy
and the unhip." Although his subjects range from love to poverty,
Africa to the blues, race to rhinos, all his writing, like his life,
is a relentless revolt. Back in 1968, Joans dispatched his nearly
forgotten "Black Flower" statement, a Black surrealist manifesto
in support of a Black freedom movement for dignity and spiritual
unity. He envisaged a movement of Black people in the United
States bringing down American imperialism from within using
the weapon of poetic imagery, "black flowers" sprouting all over
the land.

While some of his poems blow up like a bomb, others spring to
life like a fake snake in a can. His imagery is rich with humor, joy,
and sensuality, characteristics Joans finds fundamental to surrealism's liberatory ethic. He makes us laugh with the "Flying Rats of
Paris" or the darkly humorous "Deadnik." Or he might douse us

with the fragrance of freedom, as he does with his radically erotic "Successexful":

> Our noble implements
> That liberate love
> That marvelous Joy
> Propelled in sudanic sun
> Wide open is desire
> Ushered by
> Red filter tip toes
> Under brown roasted surface eyes
> our own thighcology.

When Joans speaks of "Our noble implements," he is not just thinking of genitalia; he is referring to the imagination. Fantasy, imagination, dreaming—these are the characteristics that distinguish surrealism from the kinds of social critiques at the core of leftist politics. In fact, it is quite possible that Black dissatisfaction with socialist realism had to do precisely with the suppression of key elements of Black culture that surrealism embraces: the unconscious, the spirit, desire, humor, magic, and love. At the same time, ironically, the fact that relatively few Black radicals actually took part in the international surrealist movement may well be because of its very familiarity; its revolutionary core was recognized as having always existed in African and Black diasporic life. Thus in 1948 Ralph Ellison wrote of Harlem as "a world so fluid and shifting that often within the mind the real and the unreal merge, and the marvelous beckons from behind the same sordid reality that denies its existence."

Revolution of the Mind

The idea of a revolution of the mind has always been central to surrealism as well as to Black conceptions of liberation. By revolution of the mind, I mean not merely a refusal of victim status. I am talking about an unleashing of the mind's most creative capacities, catalyzed by participation in struggles for change. As the

Black radical thinker Cedric Robinson pointed out nearly two decades ago in his *Black Marxism: The Making of the Black Radical
Tradition*, the focus of Black revolt "was always on the structures
of the mind. Its epistemology granted supremacy to metaphys-
ics not the material." Likewise, as the surrealist writer and blues
scholar Paul Garon put it: "Human freedom depends not only
on the destruction and restructuring of the economic system, but
on the restructuring of the mind. New modes of poetic action,
new networks of analogy, new possibilities of expression all help
formulate the nature of the supersession of reality, the transformation of everyday life as it encumbers us today, the unfolding and
eventual triumph of the marvelous."

Juxtaposing surrealism and Black conceptions of liberation is
no mere academic exercise; it is an injunction, a proposition,
perhaps even a declaration of war. I am suggesting that the Black
freedom movement take a long, hard look at our own surreality
as well as surrealist thought and practice in order to build new
movements, new possibilities, new conceptions of liberation.
Surrealism can help us break the constraints of social realism
and take us to places where Marxism, anarchism, and other
"isms" in the name of revolution have rarely dared to venture.
From the 1920s on, surrealism has recognized the decadence
of Western civilization, and has never ceased to sharpen its critique of the West's institutions and value systems, but it has always refused to fall into the trap of cynicism or technotopias
or fatalism and false prophets. After all, surrealists have consistently opposed capitalism and white supremacy, have promoted
internationalism, and have been strongly influenced by Marx
and Freud in their efforts to bridge the gap between dream and
action. In other respects, surrealism is night to Marxism's day:
It breaks the chains of social realism and rationality, turning to
poetry as a revolutionary mode of thought and practice. In many
ways surrealism has real affinities with aspects of Afrodiasporic
vernacular culture, including an embrace of magic, spirituality,
and the ecstatic — elements Marxism has never been able to deal
with effectively.

At the same time, surrealism is not some lost, esoteric body of thought longing for academic recognition. It is a living practice and will continue to live as long as we dream. Nor is surrealism some atavistic romanticization of the past. Above all, surrealism considers love and poetry and the imagination powerful social and revolutionary forces, not replacements for organized protest, for marches and sit-ins, for strikes and slowdowns, for matches and spray paint. Surrealism recognizes that any revolution must begin with thought, with how we imagine a New World, with how we reconstruct our social and individual relationships, with unleashing our desire and building a new future on the basis of love and creativity rather than rationality (which is like *rationalization*, the same word they use for improving capitalist production and limiting people's needs).

By superseding existing reality, we must break with the current injunction to "keep it real." Of course, in contemporary hip-hop lingo the power of "keepin' it real" means many things: It is a challenge to commercialism, a recognition of the ghetto as a site of creativity, a call for solidarity with oppressed classes. But if we believe in revolution, the critical moral of this essay is that we need to move beyond the real and make it surreal. And in the "wonderful world" according to Ted Joans, this is what being hip is all about. Go ahead Ted, take us out with a final chorus of "Let's Play Something":

> LET'S PLAY THAT WE ALL HIP, very hip and wise/ thus we are hipsters and hipstresses/ we use machinery and do not allow the machinery to use or mis-use us/ as hipsters we are spiritually involved with life/ and we dig good food/ good sex/ and the finest of arts and we travel all over this wonderful world/ for the entire earth is ours/ we love those whom wished to be loved/ we kiss but do not kill/ we work at jobs that give us thrills/ we abuse all money/ and we pick up on all knowledge that we can use/ we experience all great kicks/ we avoid conformity/ disaffiliated with any organized goof/ thus digging freedom/ freedom/ freedom now/ freedom for all/ and create a new life that is an eternal

surreal ball/ marvelous for yellow ones/ black ones/ living/ sharing/ caring and healthy creating/ a new hip world where nobody is hungry where nobody is oppressed and where there is hope

YEAH LADIES AND GENTLEMEN BOYS AND GIRLS LET'S PLAY THAT YES LET'S PLAY THAT FOR REAL LET'S PLAY THAT WE ARE ALL HIPSTERS AND REALLY BEGIN TO LIVE!!

"WHEN HISTORY WAKES":
A NEW BEGINNING

Fall 2021

*When History wakes, image becomes deed, the poem is achieved:
poetry goes into action.*

—Octavio Paz[1]

*Struggle is social practice and when you engage in social practice,
you gain new insights. You find out that there was much more
involved than you had originally perceived to be the case when
you began your struggle.*

—James Boggs, "Thinking Dialectically, Not Biologically"[2]

The epilogue in the first edition of *Freedom Dreams* was a brief
meditation on what we might build upon the smoldering ashes
of New York's World Trade Center. I had originally written a very
different essay to close the book but discarded it after the 9/11
attacks and the US invasion of Afghanistan. For this edition, however, I decided to restore the original epilogue. It proved to be
rather prescient, especially since Black Spring 2020 portended
the kind of movement I'd conjured up in that first essay. It was

inspired entirely by Octavio Paz's line "poetry goes into action." I conclude with a few brief reflections on moments over the past twenty years when life imitates art, and art imitates life.

Aside from minor copyedits, I chose not to alter the story, change historical details, or update the language. The only significant change was to reduce the duration of the story from seven hundred years to one hundred years. Not that I'm any more optimistic, but it feels as though the pace of change has accelerated since 2001. And given the climate catastrophe before us, I seriously doubt the planet can survive seven centuries without decolonization and ending capitalism.

The following is a slightly embellished version of a dream I had the night of February 26, 2000. That day my family and I had marched down Fifth Avenue in Manhattan with several thousand people to protest the acquittal of the four officers who fatally shot an unarmed and compliant African named Amadou Diallo. We had to march. The verdict angered us to no end, proving once again that police forces were not established to "serve and protect" but to control aggrieved, exploited populations—communities of color, unruly working people. We live in a country built on empire and slavery; violence is endemic, not because we are violent people but because it flows directly from the state and is deeply enmeshed in the nationalist ideology of Manifest Destiny. The Diallo murder and its "legal" aftermath, like the Three-Fifths Compromise; the Dred Scott *decision;* Plessy v. Ferguson; *the lynching of Emmett Till; the deaths of Addie Mae Collins, Denise McNair, Carole Robertson, and Cynthia Wesley in the vicious bombing of a Birmingham Church; the assassinations of Malcolm, Medgar, Martin; COINTELPRO and the destruction of Black movements; the Ku Klux Klan's open assassination of Communist Workers' Party members in Greensboro; the beating of Rodney King; the death sentence of Mumia Abu-Jamal; the thousands and thousands of victims of lynchings and formalized police violence in the last two centuries—all are historical markers, more reminders that we still must live in fear of the master. We are not safe, and therefore nor is anyone else.*

At the same time, the anger we brought to that demonstration turned to exhilaration. It was perhaps the most diverse march I ever attended—no group was dominant. Latinos; Asian Americans; Black people from all parts of the globe; Arabs; Palestinians; Europeans and native-born white people; a rainbow of gays, lesbians, and transgender people; young and old, walking, dancing, rolling in wheelchairs. Sectarian-left posturing seemed at a minimum, and the main speakers were people who had lost loved ones at the hands of the police. As expected, the police moved in on the crowds, divided the marchers, and carted hundreds away to jail. Nevertheless, I came away from February 26th with renewed hope.

My dream, then, is a bundle of emotions. The question of state violence and the need for ordinary people to do the work of changing our culture were foremost in my mind. I confess that had I simply sat down one afternoon and mapped out the next thousand years, the result would not have been so apocalyptic. But this is a dream, an explosive utterance from deep in the unconscious, and an uncontrollable journey full of pathos and humor, not unlike the blues. If you read this as a completely thought-out, rational argument, you've missed the point.

FEBRUARY 26, 2000: The threat of rain didn't stop anyone from showing up. They gathered near the Plaza Hotel, the stopover for the super-duper bourgeoisie, and made their way down Fifth Avenue, past the upscale shops carrying every designer fashion, every fur, and every mineral imaginable. Slogans echoed off the high-rise buildings denouncing Mayor Giuliani, the NYPD, and the criminal justice system. Marchers held up wallets to show the cops that what Diallo held up that night was his ID, not a gun.

Somewhere around Forty-Fourth Street, a seventeen-year-old poet named Tishawna Mai Song Suheir Teresde Ojo persuaded a gathering of young people to break from the march to continue a conversation they started in front of FAO Schwarz. They had come to read poetry dedicated to Diallo and were inspired by the events of the past year, but something seemed amiss. Marching and sloganeering and leafleting seemed so inadequate, and poetry felt dead. The young people concluded that they needed to lift their poems off the page and make them live. Calling themselves Maroon Poets (MPs), the tiny multiracial gathering created a structure without leaders. Their model of thought and action was the cypher, a circle anyone can enter and in which anyone can speak. They also saw the cypher as a weapon, an ever-expanding circle that can surround oppressors and either squeeze them to death or incorporate them into the circle.

Initially, the MPs concentrated on the problem of police violence. They questioned why state violence was legal in the first place and wondered why the same administration that ran the police department could objectively police and prosecute the cops. They never relented, constantly reminding the people that Amadou Diallo was just the tip of the iceberg in a wave of police killings. Other groups reached out to the MPs, including the revolutionary Brooklyn collective FIST (Forever In Struggle Together), the Coalition Against Police Brutality, the Audre Lorde Project, CAAAV Organizing Asian Communities, the National Congress for Puerto Rican Rights, and the Malcolm X Grassroots Movement, among others. And as word of their deeds spread beyond New York, their ranks began to swell. All over the cities of North America, MPs seized billboards and wrote the names of those murdered by police:

> *Eleanor Bumpurs. Michael Stewart. Anthony Baez. Michael Wayne Clark. Yong Xin Huang. Benjamin Nunez. Kuthurima Mwaria. Julio Nunez. Maria Rivas. Mohammed Assassa. Leonard Lawton. Aswon "Keshawn" Watson. Nathaniel Gains. Dion Hawthorne. Lori Leitner. Donald Fleming. Kenneth Arnold. Paul Mills.*

They made huge projections on the sides of skyscrapers with the names of other people murdered by the police:

Rudy Buchanan. Kim Groves. Ivory McQueen. Stanley "Rock" Scott. Donnell "Bo" Lucas. Tommy Yates. Darryl Edwards. Gilberto Cruz. Kenny Johnson. Jorge Guillen. Eric Smith. Angel Castro Jr. Bilal Ashraf. Maneia By. Anthony Starks. Johnny Gammage. Malice Green. Gary Glenn. Jose Itturalde. James Johnson. Darlene Tiller. Crystal Lujan. Bobby Mitchell. Vickey Finklea. Roy Hoskins. Donnie Alexander. Mark Anthony Longo. Osiris E. Galan. Torrey Donovan Jacobs.

The MPs aerosol art contingent covered city walls, streets, subways, and buses with more names:

Yvon Guerrier. Alvin Barroso. Marcillus Miller. Brenda Forester. David Ortiz. Arturo Jimenez. Miguel Ruiz. Josie Gay. Damian Garcia. Manuel Hernandez. Eliberto Saldana. Elzie Coleman. Tracy Mayberry. De Andre Harrison. John Daniels Jr. Michael Bryant. Jose Manuel Sanchez. Justice Hasan Netherly. Sonji Taylor. Fernando Herrera Jr. Dwight Stiggons. Hue Truong. Salomon Hernandez. Raphael and Luke Grinnage. Baraka Hall. Carolyn Adams. Dannette Daniels. Andre Jones. Tama T. Ava. Leon Fisher. James Quarles. Kuan Chung Kao. Brandon Auger. Tyisha Miller. Devon Nelson. LaTanya Haggerty. Robert Russ.

The MPs issued a series of demands to city, state, and federal governments, including the elimination of all firearms and the complete dismantling of police departments and the criminal "justice" system as we know it. They proposed creating community-based institutions for public safety structured along nonmilitary lines that practiced restorative justice and would be run by elected community boards. The public safety workers would have to attend intensive workshops on race, gender, sexuality, and antiviolence intervention, and study how capitalism, racism, and patriarchy create and maintain inequality. The institutions of public safety must reflect the racial and ethnic makeup of the communities they serve and maintain an equal gender balance in all areas of work. Public safety workers would be required to reside in the neighborhood in which they work and conduct a study of that community in all of its historical, social, economic, and psychological dimensions — sort of like writing an honors thesis before graduating from the "academy of public safety." And no one would be able to complete their training without studying, writing, and reading poetry. All public safety workers would be expected to conduct a few regular poetry readings in open neighborhood forums.

The MPs recruited others to the Maroon cause: singers, waiters, chefs, sanitation workers, technicians, and even computer hackers (many of whom decided after the antiglobalization demonstrations in the '90s that working for freedom is more fulfilling than pulling pranks). The Maroon hackers turned out to be especially valuable for one of their major campaigns. When the MPs realized that persuasion and even mass protest were not enough to eliminate the police, the hackers broke into all law enforcement data bases, erased the names of all people who had been arrested or surveilled by police, and replaced them with the names of police officers. The utter chaos allowed incarcerated people to sue for their immediate release and demand the restoration of their basic civil rights (the right to vote, protections from employment discrimination, etc.).

The MPs continued to grow and extend their work beyond the issue of state violence and the criminal justice system. The movement's vision had expanded as well; cyphers popped up all over the world uniting around the slogan "Freedom and Love Now." Committed to waging a permanent, protracted revolution, the MPs rejected all the Enlightenment -isms: capitalism, socialism, liberalism, republicanism, etc., and set out to invent new ideas. They scoured the ancient practices of the oppressed, discovering shamanism, Pocomania, Sufism, candomblé, Hinduism, and Mayan and Aztec and Pueblo and Iroquois religions, not to mention the traditions of Jubilee. They studied how ancient peoples developed powers of the mind — powers allegedly enabling them to travel through space and bring back the dead.

Though they had no fixed address, struggling people always took care of the MPs. Many took refuge on Native reservations, home to thousands of MPs. They spoke every language in the world and listened attentively to everything that was said before speaking. They made their own clothes, let their hair grow wild and natural, made an effort to eat food without chemicals, and embraced veganism.

FEBRUARY 25, 2002: On the second anniversary of the Amadou Diallo verdict (declared White Day of Mourning) the MPs released the Maroon Poets Manifesto, flooding the internet and plastering it on city walls around the world. Benetton ads and posters advertising new releases by Juvenile, Marc Anthony, and Jennifer Lopez were rendered invisible by the MPs' bold proclamations. The manifesto read:

> We recognize the decadence of Western Civilization; its motive force has ALWAYS been violence;
>
> Its riches are derived from conquest, the violent removal of people from the land who are then turned into laborers to enrich the idle few;
>
> It maintains peace through war and any challengers to its social order are met with violence: lynching, rape, incarceration, chain gangs, exile, harassment. And by semantic sleight of hand, you call it JUSTICE.
>
> It has promoted the myth of a master race; the myth of civilization; the myth of national destiny (the source of virtually all modern wars); the myth that progress can be measured by the power to destroy and kill efficiently; the myth that a massive, modern slave society invented freedom.
>
> It has perpetuated an even older myth, older than the West itself: the idea of male supremacy; the myth that the world belongs to men and the home to women. It has built whole economies based on female dependency and unpaid female labor; cultural systems that police gender and sexual identities; philosophical systems that "scientifically" justify women's subordination.
>
> We call for the destruction of Western Civilization, and on its ashes a new beginning; a new society based on freedom, imagination and love.

We not only want to discredit and destroy all forces of repression against all of humanity (women, people of color/the colonized, youth, queer people, all working people, etc.), but also to emancipate desire and supply it with new poetic weapons. . . .

We call for the abolition of imaginative slavery, the creation of a free society in which everyone will be a poet—a society in which everyone will be able to develop his or her potentialities fully and freely.

FALL 2004: George W. Bush is reelected to the presidency, this time under the newly formed Law and Order Party, and he vows to crush the MPs. With David Duke as head of the FBI, the Bush administration launches Poetelpro, an all-out assault on the MPs. He also declares a temporary dictatorship on the grounds that America was in a state of emergency.

But the MPs are ready. All those years of studying the ancient sciences of the mind, along with modern sound technology pioneered by the hip-hop generation, prepared them for war. They developed the ability to pirate any microphone, loudspeaker, TV station, or radio station without being visible or detected. Highly trained MPs broke into all of these venues and warned the people of impending fascism, reminding listeners and viewers how fascism started in Germany. They explained how some bona fide gangsters went unchecked because they beat and murdered the most degraded segments of society—Jews and communists, gays and lesbians, Roma and Africans. They reminded listeners that these thugs became an organization, built a following, and gained state power, which enabled them to establish a more efficient killing machine. Too many people were caught napping because they were not the victims . . . at least, not yet.

The transmissions apparently were effective. Although white people had been part of the MPs since the beginning, most coming out of the police brutality protests, they were always a tiny minority. Now they were beginning to recruit former supporters of the Law and Order Party. War was no longer impending; it had arrived.

SPRING 2044: War raged on for forty years. The MPs established liberated zones throughout North America, turning the former ghettoes and barrios into safe havens. Empty lots become gardens; streets are blocked off for community theater; stores were taken over and turned into cooperatives where volunteers could work in exchange for consumer goods. Restaurants became public kitchens where community cooks prepared food for whomever wants it. Local governments were formed in which everyone over the age of nine was eligible to vote or run for office. Tiny libraries sprang up on every block and stayed open twenty-four hours a day.

2050–2090: The liberated zones grow, spreading from the urban areas to the deserts and mountains and farmlands of the nation. The MPs in the Southwest build underground laboratories called Cyphernautics, where they develop new technologies to harness the power of the mind. They can employ mental energy to bend steel, twisting the barrels of guns into knots. They can dematerialize if necessary, drawing on their power of invisibility to move without being seen.

More importantly, in the liberated zones new poets are born and raised by entire communities without violence. The only violence they know is the ongoing war being waged against them by the dwindling anti-poet minority.

AUGUST 2091: The final bold act takes place during a celebration of the three-hundredth anniversary of Boukman's rebellion in Haiti, marking the beginning of the Haitian Revolution. Following Lautréamont's injunction "Poetry must be made by all," they declare everyone a poet and call for a 100 Million Poets March on Washington. They come in waves, not to demonstrate or express outrage or to atone, but to remove the government and dismantle the old and useless state that claimed to govern the country. Swiftly, painlessly, bloodlessly, they bring the last bastion of oppressive power into their fold. Washington, DC, remembered a

millennia ago as our one and only Chocolate City, will hence-
forth be known as the world's last liberated zone.

Nearly a century after Amadou Diallo is buried, History
Begins. . . .

*So this was my original dream, with a few minor revisions. Not the
outrageous details of this story, but the very idea that our dreams
and our poetry could be a critical source of new knowledge, that we
could invent from the unconscious, that we could, for once, take our
imaginations seriously.*

*George Clinton used to say that we needed to dance our way,
out of our constrictions. He was being funny but dead serious.
Whether we call it dancing, or dreaming, or making poetry, we
need to embrace and understand what these semi-free spaces offer
us, and to recognize that the hardest work we have before us is
imagining. If we want a new society, we have no choice but to su-
persede the dominant reality—to imagine a different relationship
not only to the economy but also to time, to work, to the natural
world, to each other.*

Poetarian Revolution Is Here

This is what revolution looks like. It begins with what Fred Moten
and Stefano Harney call "fugitive planning." It is woven from the
spontaneous revolts of poets who set the world in motion with
their words, their bodies, their songs, their art. Revolutions are
not singular events but long dreams, shared by aggrieved communities, nurtured in fugitive spaces, and enacted by social movements. Even in dark times, revolutions are nourished in liberated
zones, the spaces we create where we can "grow our souls," as
Grace Lee Boggs aptly put it. "This is what true revolutions are
about. They are about redefining our relationships with one another, to the Earth and to the world; about creating a new society
in the places and spaces left vacant by the disintegration of the
old, about hope, not despair; about saying yes to life and no to

war; about finding the courage to love and care for the peoples of the world as we love and care for our own families."[3]

What Grace proposes is no dream. MPs and liberated zones are everywhere, hiding in plain sight, turning image into deed, turning poetry into action. We've already seen many examples of real-life MPs—artists turning "freedom dreams" from noun to verb—in the introduction to this volume. Indeed, if you skipped over Aja Monet's brilliant foreword to this volume, bookmark this page and go back and read it immediately. She and her crew are the original "Maroon Poets," the poem in action, the defenders of the dream who understood freedom to mean everything: "freedom to imagine . . . freedom from police, prisons, and poverty, freedom of movement, freedom of mind, freedom to be." The scholar, activist, and poet Alexis Pauline Gumbs offered one of the clearest articulations of what it means to create liberated zones in which abolition is practiced, where the world we want is constantly in rehearsal, built on memories, experiences, and an ethic of care. These practices become the "freedom seeds" for a different future. She asks, "What if abolition is something that sprouts out of the wet places in our eyes, the broken places in our skin, the waiting places in our palms, the tremble holding in my mouth when I turn to you? What if abolition is something that grows? What if abolishing the prison industrial complex is the fruit of our diligent gardening, building and deepening of a movement to respond to the violence of the state and the violence in our communities with sustainable, transformative love?"[4]

Gumbs helped create a community like this in Durham, North Carolina, called UBUNTU, a women-of-color, survivor-led coalition to end gendered violence. And there are others. Allow me to turn to two such examples of emergent liberated zones, formed since the publication of this book, that mirror the kind of slow and rooted revolutionary insurgency I had imagined twenty years ago.

The story of Jackson, Mississippi, takes up where I left off in chapter 4, when the provisional government of the Republic of New Afrika established its base in Mississippi and demanded reparations and territory as the basis for establishing an independent

Black nation. Although the demand for reparations never disappeared, the group purchased land, set up cooperative farms, built institutions, and, despite relentless state repression, took root in the city of Jackson. Black radicals had been slowly building power there for four decades, but the promise of Jackson didn't come on the radar of most "progressives" until 2013, when the late Chokwe Lumumba, a radical lawyer and leader in the New Afrikan People's Organization (NAPO) and the Malcolm X Grassroots Movement (MXGM), was elected mayor. Lumumba had moved to Mississippi from Detroit in 1971.

In the aftermath of Hurricane Katrina, the MXGM developed the "Jackson Plan," designed to "build a base of autonomous power in Jackson that can serve as a catalyst for the attainment of Black self-determination and the democratic transformation of the economy."[5] The plan included establishing a "solidarity economy," akin to the Mondragon Corporation in Spain's Basque region, through worker cooperatives; eco-friendly community gardens; the building of inexpensive, energy-efficient housing; and the development of community and conservation land trusts to make land available to the community and house the homeless. The result was Cooperation Jackson, a project focused on addressing the needs of Jackson's poor and working-class communities through cooperative economic strategies that can ensure a sustainable future. The group purchased several vacant lots and abandoned homes in order to develop sustainable, energy efficient, low-income housing. It also plans to develop a zero-waste, highly energy-efficient "eco-village."

The Jackson plan also included a political strategy of creating People's Assemblies, open meetings to discuss community needs, ensure full democratic participation, and mobilize working people to win political power. The People's Assemblies were not only responsible for Chokwe Lumumba's victory and the election of Jackson's current mayor— Lumumba's son, Chokwe Antar Lumumba—but for creating a structure for participatory budgeting. They succeeded in passing a 1 percent sales tax to aid the city in fixing its poor physical infrastructure, although the revenue generated still falls far short of what is required just to repair the aging water system. A chief coordinator of the People's Assemblies is Rukia Lumumba, founding director of the People's Advocacy Institute (PAI), co-leader of the Electoral Justice Project of the Movement for Black Lives, and daughter of the late Chokwe Lumumba. She founded PAI to advance a transformative justice agenda that resists mass criminalization, builds collective political and economic power, and develops new forms of governance that promote participatory democracy, environmental sustainability, community wealth, safety, and racial, gender, and sexual equality.

The struggle to turn the former seat of the Confederacy into a model of social justice and Black liberation is certainly no cakewalk; white supremacy and class rule are alive and well in the state of Mississippi. State government has tried to erode local political power and financially starve the city by reallocating revenues from the city's 1 percent sales tax to other state initiatives and introducing legislation that would strip the city of control of the Jackson-Medgar Wiley Evers International Airport and all related commerce. As I write these words, Mississippi Republicans are still fighting to replace the predominantly Black Jackson Municipal Airport Authority (JMAA) with a larger authority composed of city, state, and regional representatives. But so far, the city and its People's Assemblies have prevailed. Jackson's revolutionaries remain undeterred. Once the seat of the Confederacy, Jackson is a city of freedom dreamers. Rukia Lumumba put it best: "I'm not scared to dream big. I'm not living in scarcity. I'm dreaming as big as I can because . . . I know for a fact that we can live in a world where joy is abundant and everyone feels safe."[6]

Detroit is the place and space to begin anew.

—Grace Lee Boggs

Detroit is also a city of freedom dreamers committed to turning the poster child for industrial abandonment, where foreclosure is the new enclosure, where unelected emergency managers impose Third World–style austerity measures, into a flourishing, sustainable, humane, caring, beloved community. If Detroit offers a map to a liberated future, then all roads lead back to where this book began: to James and Grace Lee Boggs, the community they mentored, and the generations that followed. They envisioned a transformed urban economy that would promote self-sufficiency, ecological sustainability, and human interaction—in a phrase, a new commons. They emphasized community development, values of cooperation, mutual aid, nonviolence, equality, and love. It is a vision shared and shaped by dedicated comrades such as Shea Howell, Rich Feldman, Larry Sparks, Tawana "Honeycomb" Petty, Frank Joyce, Wayne and Myrtle Curtis, Kim Sherrobi, Dr. Gloria House/Aneb Kgositsile, Invincible/ill Weaver, adrienne maree brown, Stephen Ward, and many others who continue to fight for Detroit—against the privatization of water; against the state's use of emergency managers to strip residents of local governance; against efforts by developers to replace community-based urban agriculture with profit-driven commercial farms and properties; against a way of thinking that sees youth as criminals, corporations as saviors, neighborhoods as "blight," and communities as an aggregation of human capital.

They call themselves solutionaries. They fight water shutoffs, create their own alternative sources of energy (wind, solar), run freedom schools, build collective economic power and sustainability through cooperatives and time banking, and turn empty lots into urban farms to deal with food insecurity, joblessness, and community alienation. Charity Hicks was one of the great solutionaries. Her mantra for social justice movements was to "wage love." She believed in the commons: "The commons is not just how I survive and adapt, but how we are all surviving and adapting."[7] A native of Detroit's Eastside and a beloved activist known for her work on environmental justice and food security, she helped found the Great Lakes Commons network and the People's Water Board Coalition, which had been fighting the city's mass water shutoffs for nonpayment of bills since 2008.

Detroiters saw steady increases in their water bills, some households shelling out as much as 20 percent of their income for water—far in excess of the 2–4 percent suggested by the EPA and various international agencies. By 2014, nearly half had fallen behind on their monthly payments. In 2006, the Detroit City Council approved a water affordability plan that would have capped costs, but it was never implemented. To address the crisis, the People's Water Board Coalition, the Michigan Welfare Rights Organization (MWRO), We the People of Detroit, and allied groups called for a moratorium on shutoffs, which the city ignored. Why? First, the Detroit Water and Sewerage Department (DWSD) was already running a deficit, and when the unelected emergency financial managers in charge of the city of Flint (in succession: Ed Kurtz, Darnell Earley, and Gerald Ambrose) decided to switch its water source from the Detroit River to the polluted Flint River, it put DWSD into deeper debt. Bondholders pressured the department to keep raising rates and cutting off service to delinquent customers. Despite clear evidence of contamination and an offer from DWSD to slash its rates if Flint would return, Ambrose stayed the course, since he had signed an agreement with the private firm Veolia to build a treatment plant and manage the Flint River water supply. Meanwhile, in 2013, Detroit residents were also stripped of democracy when corporate lawyer Kevyn Orr was appointed emergency financial manager of their city. As he pushed even harder to raise rates and shut off water to delinquent households, he began accepting bids from Veolia and other companies to take over DWSD, which ultimately was dissolved and replaced by the suburban-controlled Great Lakes Water Authority in 2015.[8]

Charity Hicks had been following and resisting the privatization of water in Flint, Highland Park, and Detroit for years. In the spring of 2014, as Kevyn Orr arranged to sell the city's water supply, his regime deployed a private company to shut off water to tens of thousands of homes—a decision that the United Nations deemed a violation of human rights. When the trucks showed up in Hicks's community, she scrambled to warn neighbors and urged them to collect as much water as possible, in pots, pans, buckets, bathtubs, anything they could find. She asked the driver to delay the shutoffs to allow families time to gather water, but he refused. Hicks then determined that the crew lacked proper documentation to turn off her water, especially since she was not past due. The driver then called the police and had *Hicks* arrested and jailed overnight. Her arrest galvanized the movement, prompting some to dub her the "Rosa Parks of the Detroit water struggle." Less than two weeks later, on May 31, 2014, Charity Hicks was struck by a hit-and-run driver while waiting at a bus stop in Midtown Manhattan. She had gone to New York to give a talk at the Left Forum about the water struggle. She lay in a coma for over a month before succumbing to her injuries on July 8.[9]

Friends and comrades described Hicks as a larger-than-life figure who motivated people with almost shaman-like qualities. But they also remembered her as a master gardener who understood that sustainability begins with food security. Her politics were shaped by Detroit's tradition of urban gardening, which had begun to take on greater social and political significance in 1992 when the Boggses launched Detroit Summer, a multicultural, intergenerational youth project designed to "rebuild, redefine and respirit" the city from the ground up.[10] Young people partnered with retired autoworker Gerald Hairston, founder of the Gardening Angels, whose slogan was "we cannot free ourselves unless we feed ourselves," and planted community gardens in vacant lots. They also picked up trash, created huge murals on buildings, renovated houses, and formed coops to produce local goods for the needs of the community. They transformed abandoned lands into mini-farms bearing names like Wellness gardens, Hope Takes Root gardens, and Kwanzaa gardens. Since then, urban farm collectives have flourished. Keep Growing Detroit, an organization committed to making the city food-sovereign, helps secure seeds and plants for over 1,600 community gardens. Malik Yakini founded and directs the Detroit Black Community Food Security Network

(DBCFSN) to promote urban agriculture, healthy diets, cooperatives, environmental justice, sustainability, self-reliance and
self-determination, and "respect for life and nature." Through
its "Food Warriors" program, DBCFSN trains young people in
the techniques of sustainable farming, encourages healthy life-
styles, and builds intergenerational community solidarity.[11]

In other words, the Detroit farm movement is not just about
producing food and training future generations to carry on the
tradition. It is a largely Black working-class movement to create a
"new commons," a sustainable future, and a hedge against gentrification and dispossession. The neoliberal city leaders backing
water privatization and hyper-policing have tried to displace these
more radical urban agriculture projects with white gentrifiers by
offering them "stipends to move into the Detroit area and grow
gardens" while "accidentally" razing some of the Black-run gardens.[12] The Ohana Family Garden, for example, not only raises
vegetables, flowers, and bees, but renovates apartments to provide a safe place for young mothers. Feedom Freedom Growers,
founded by Myrtle Thompson-Curtis and Wayne Curtis, is as
much a school and community center as it is an organic farm.
Their doors are open to anyone who wants to learn to grow food,
discuss social transformation, and make art. They launched a
monthly "Arts in the Garden" program, which soon expanded
to the Emory Douglas Family Youth Arts Program, offering art
classes using natural materials either at the farm or at neighboring
Hope Community Church. For Wayne Curtis, a former member of the Black Panther Party, the program is a way of bringing
people together to build an alternative to the dominant culture:
"Culture to me is, what do you do in order to exist in a particular environment? This particular environment is capitalism. So
what do we do to transform this system and survive at the same
time? So this creates a culture of resistance and sustainability,
and transformation. That's what we're initiating."[13]

A culture of resistance, sustainability, and transformation has
grown up almost as fast as cultivated vegetation, and the seeds
have been sown by Detroit's abundance of Maroon Poets. Today's

MPs have deep roots in the Motor City—this is where poet Dudley Randall founded Broadside Press and helped launch the revolutionary Black Arts Movement over a half century ago. It is home to poet-activist Dr. Gloria House/Aneb Kgositsile, a long-time fixture in the Boggs' circle of dedicated solutionaries. Known affectionately as "Mama Aneb," Dr. House embodies all the characteristics of the MP: an organic intellectual rooted in social movements and community, generating art and ideas that address pressing needs and advance a revolutionary future. A SNCC organizer in Alabama before moving to Detroit in 1967, Dr. House protested police repression (for which she lost her job at the *Detroit Free Press*), cofounded the Detroit Independent Freedom Schools Movement, and helped build movements such as Detroiters Resisting Emergency Management and We the People of Detroit to fight water shutoffs, and co-edits *Riverwise*, the publication of the Boggs Center.[14] Her book *Tower and Dungeon: A Study of Place and Power in American Culture* examines the relationship between the downtown Renaissance Center, constructed after the 1967 rebellion, and Jackson State Prison, built in 1842. She describes the buildings as "two faces of the same cultural commitment, deeply inscribed in the American landscape. At one end, we have towers of wealth protected by police forces; on the other, we have overcrowded dungeons for dispensable populations. Tower and dungeon—two armed camps serving the same interests, built on the basis of violent dispossession of the people, and maintained by threat of further violence."[15] She continued exploring the relationship between capitalism, dispossession, and violence with the We the People of Detroit Community Research Collective, through which she led a collaborative research project exposing how corporate plunder, the dismantling of democratic governance, and neoliberal privatization were the real reasons for Detroit's water *and* debt crises. Two decades of corporate-driven policies resulted in the displacement of historic Black neighborhoods, the privatization of resources, a shift in power from the city to the suburbs, and the birth of a movement to resist the neoliberal onslaught and remake the city.[16]

In 2010, Dr. House delivered a breathtaking talk and poem at the US Social Forum that offered ten lessons from her political work in Detroit with Grace Lee Boggs. She instructed activists to focus on the "aspirations, hopes and needs" of the people we fight for, of the most vulnerable; respect people's culture and religious and spiritual practices; learn from the youth; stay independent of corporate and foundation funding; educate and raise our children "to be creators of a new world"; and be principled and guided by love, honesty, and grace. But it is the last lesson that encapsulates the key principles guiding Detroit's revolutionary praxis:

> Trust that no matter how insurmountable a social change task appears, there are ways to resist and to eventually create alternative ways of living. Though the impact of the global economy of the transnational corporations has dismantled vital aspects of our cities and communities world-wide, remember that the wrecked terrain that has been left offers us a field of opportunity for rethinking, recreating, claiming a higher quality of human life. Of course, this requires our greatest effort of collective work and responsibility, of hope, and of unswerving faith in the people's ability to make "a way out of no way!"[17]

Dr. House and Grace mentored generations of radicals, in the movement, at the university, and in freedom schools they helped to create. Among them are three poets who exemplify everything I imagined the MPs to be: adrienne maree brown, Invincible/ ill Weaver, and Tawana "Honeycomb" Petty. brown describes herself as a "writer, facilitator, coach, mentor, mediator, pleasure activist, sci-fi scholar, doula, healer, tarot reader, witch, cheerleader, singer, philosopher, queer Black multiracial lover of life living in Detroit."[18] She has worked with and led many different national anti-racist, social justice, and media organizations, but much of her political life resides in her adopted city. She was the founding facilitator of the Detroit Narrative Agency (DNA), which counters dominant media representations with stories of the city's movement toward justice and liberation. She also facilitated or co-facilitated the Detroit Food Justice Task Force, Detroit

Future, and the Detroit Digital Justice Coalition. She also served as executive director of the Ruckus Society, an antiglobalization and environmental justice organization that trains activists in militant tactics of civil disobedience. Her workshops, podcasts, and many books, including *Emergent Strategy: Shaping Change, Changing Worlds, Holding Change: The Way of Emergent Strategy Facilitation and Mediation,* and *We Will Not Cancel Us and Other Dreams of Transformative Justice,* are models of effective and ethical movement building.

Poet, rapper, and performance artist Invincible/ill Weaver is currently working on a series of art projects inspired by Dr. House's *Tower and Dungeon,* including a collaborative installation with Detroit activist Siwatu-Salama Ra, who turned her letters and other writing she did while in prison (and pregnant) into kites, lifting up her story and that of other incarcerated mothers and their families.[19] Born in Champaign, Illinois, Invincible came into the Boggs-House radical orbit through Detroit Summer, remaining a principal organizer for a decade and cofounding Detroit Future Youth Network. In 2008, they cofounded Emergence Media with artist-musician Wesley Taylor and organizer Mike Medow, and in 2010 launched an insurgent, visionary arts collective called Complex Movements. "It was inspired by conversations I was having with Grace Lee Boggs," Invincible explained to me. "She was speaking frequently then about quantum scales of changemaking as a way to describe organizing on hyperlocal levels; and critical connections (relationship building globally across hyperlocal small-scale projects and interconnected communities) as more effective than critical mass (which she used as a metaphor for mass rallies with unified slogans and charismatic leaders)."[20] This, of course, is the MPs' model of movement building and culture changing, which I had absorbed from Grace over the course of two decades.

In 2016, Invincible, Wesley Taylor, sound designer Waajeed, producer Sage Crump, and performance artist Lo5 (Carlos Garcia) collaborated on a project called *Beware of the Dandelions,* an astounding art installation in the form of a mobile cypher that functions as a hip-hop performance, visual arts exhibition, and workshop space for people to share their organizing strategies and imagine the world they are trying to build. As participants draw on these shared experiences, the lyrics for all eleven tracks move us through a story of revolt against corporate power, environmental destruction, genetically modified food, industrial farming, land enclosure, "the water hoarders," and prisons. Songs like "Apple Orchard," "Channel," "Doubt," "Man Made Drought," and "False Solutions" recount how the commodification of resources have forced people into "hubs" and a precarious life, and how underground revolutionaries resist the "groundskeepers" who control the land and resources. Dandelions are an apt metaphor. Dismissed as weeds, dandelions are strong, resilient, and possess life-giving value. They are unstoppable, pushing through cracks in the sidewalk in search of sunlight.[21]

Tawana "Honeycomb" Petty was born and raised in Detroit, a city she genuinely loves even when it doesn't love her back. At age nine she lost her father to AIDS back in the 1980s, when few understood the disease and fewer cared. She survived poverty and sexual assault and witnessed her share of violence, despair, and hopelessness. But she discovered art, poetry, and revolution early in life, and with guidance from the Boggses, Dr. House, Charity Hicks, Ron Scott, and others, she emerged as a principal force in the remaking of her hometown. Petty is a warrior in the water wars, an anti-racist organizer, a leader in the ongoing effort to rethink public safety, a single mother and teacher raising up a new generation of solutionaries, a writer, and a poet. She writes unapologetically about being a Black woman, premature death and the struggle to live, real love and the traps of desire, capitalism and its crimes, and the revolutionaries who taught her.[22] As a "revolutionary poet," she understood her task to

peel poems
off the scabs
of our existence
clench them tightly

between gums
worn out from resistance
we barely exist
through the pain
in our stories
yet embody
the wisdom
of Ancestors
before us[23]

Petty imparts such wisdom to young people through spoken-word performance and arts education workshops. She and fellow poet-organizer Jamii Tata run an intergenerational workshop called Poetry as Visionary Resistance: Literacy By Any Means Necessary, designed, in Petty's words, "to re-spirit community members who had been dehumanized through the five-decade assault on the city. This included the children who were now on the frontlines of that assault."[24] Tata, too, is a modern Maroon Poet, a self-proclaimed "artivist" who uses poetry, storytelling, technology, and his considerable organizing experience to educate and mobilize youth. In 2005, Tata founded Know Allegiance Nation (KAN), which he describes as "a village building enterprise that seeks to build a nation of knowledge seekers." Their space in North Detroit houses the Operation Rebel Community Radio station, Uhuru Sasa Farms, a variety of youth literacy programs, and KAN Books, a worker co-operative bookstore oriented toward writers of color and local authors.[25] Similar to the cyphers, libraries, and liberated zones of the MPs, KAN functions as a space of assembly for an insurgent community. This is where the people gathered for Poetry as Visionary Resistance, to learn about the history of poetic rebellion in the Black Arts movement, perform for each other, share ideas, and collaborate on collective poems imagining a liberated Detroit. One participant described the workshop as "a space to heal."[26]

Having "a space to heal," from the trauma of daily life under predatory racial capitalism and from the trauma we often inflict on each other, is fundamental to "growing our souls." But Detroit's revolutionaries understand that in order to reduce and possibly end the harm, they must reimagine and remake public safety. This had been a priority of the Boggses at least since the 1970s and '80s. They worked closely with Save Our Sons and Daughters (SOSAD), a local organization founded by the late Clementine Barfield in 1987 after she had lost her teenaged son to gun violence a year earlier. SOSAD was to be a vehicle "to reduce violence, foster a culture of healing and hope, and create meaningful pathways for young people's development."[27] Working with Barfield and SOSAD inspired Detroit Summer and their focus on confronting drug dealers and crack houses, rehabilitating abandoned houses, and "reclaiming our neighborhoods as places of safety and peace for ourselves and our children."[28] Simultaneously, police violence plagued Detroit's Black community. In 1992, two plainclothes officers fatally beat thirty-five-year-old Malice Green, and the campaign surrounding his case led Ron Scott, Dr. Gloria House, and Marge Parsons to form the Detroit Coalition Against Police Brutality. From its formation in 1996, the coalition demanded accountability and community control over police by making the chief and the police commissioner elected offices. More significantly, they proposed creating "peace zones for life," a process for conflict resolution and mediation *free of police*—particularly in instances of domestic disputes. Grievances would be submitted to participants' "neighbors or persons whom they trust; thereby, remaining outside the police/criminal justice system and eliminating conflict within our communities."[29]

A little more than a decade later, it became clear that more needed to be done to address community violence without involving the police. Police intervention in domestic conflicts always risked a lethal outcome. Sandra Hines, a social worker active in the Detroit Coalition Against Police Brutality, began holding meetings at Feedom Freedom Growers to discuss how to reduce violence and establish physical space where neighbors may resolve conflicts before they become violent.[30] Scott, Hines,

and others took their original idea and transformed it into Peace
Zones 4 Life, a tangible institution that organizes conflict resolution centers and neighborhood watches, and recruits artists
to promote a culture of peace "through visual and performing
arts" that "moves us through pain to a deeper understanding of
ourselves, our responsibilities to one another and our visions for
the future."[31]

Today, most of the organizations within the orbit of the Boggs
Center have moved inexorably toward a politics of abolition.[32]
As police power grows and community power erodes, genuine
public safety has become increasingly elusive. Even before the
rebellions of spring 2020, Detroit's solutionaries were fighting to
end Project Green Light (PGL). First introduced in 2016, PGL is
a public-private partnership between the Detroit Police Department (DPD) and tech companies producing facial-recognition
technology. The name, Green Light, is a blatant appropria-
tion of the feminist anti-violence strategy of the 1970s of creating safe spaces for women assaulted or threatened on the street.
Safe houses were identifiable by a fluorescent green light bulb
placed in a window or on a porch.[33] By contrast, the DPD en-
listed churches, schools, gas stations, clinics, and liquor stores to
serve not as designated places of safety but as spaces of heightened surveillance, equipped with cameras and facial-recognition
technology. By 2019, PGL had spread to over 550 locations across
the city.[34] The BYP100 Detroit Chapter, Boggs Center, Detroit
Justice Center, and Feedom Freedom Collective took the lead
in this fight, bringing several different organizations together to
form the Black Out Green Light Coalition and Green Light
Black Futures coalition. The latter, an initiative of BYP100, began hosting workshops in political education around the dangers
of hyper-surveillance "designed to make space for participants to
dream of a world where oppressions such as mass surveillance,
food insecurities, and poor education are not factors."[35] As a
counter, Myrtle Thompson-Curtis of Feedom Freedom Growers proposed replacing green lights with "green chairs," an old
idea introduced by activists in Milwaukee around 1980 to re-

cruit neighborhood residents, especially elders, to resurrect the tradition of keeping watch from their porches. The practice had virtually stopped in the face of rising crime, organized abandonment, and heightened security. It worked in Milwaukee and in Michigan, where Shea Howell introduced the idea nearly twenty years ago to address racial tensions between older white residents and Black youth walking to and from school. Children and their parents felt safer, and neighbors got to know each other. As Thompson-Curtis explained, the green chair initiative promoted collective and "personal accountability and revolutionary love for self and others, with each of us being responsible as our first line of defense. Let us sit on the porches in our green chairs and look out for one another."[36]

This abolitionist, community-oriented approach to public safety and transformative justice informs the work of the Detroit Justice Center (DJC), founded in 2017 by native Detroiter and radical attorney Amanda Alexander. The DJC is dedicated to ending mass incarceration, dramatically reducing the police presence, and building popular economic power through community land trusts and worker cooperatives. Alexander's vision is clearly inspired by the Boggs Center and the multiplicity of movements fighting to transform the city. In a 2019 talk titled "Centering Our Freedom Dreams," Alexander described how "Detroiters have shown me every day what it means to be a *solutionary*—to create visionary solutions in the face of devastation. When grocery stores leave, Detroiters teach each other how to farm and they share seeds. When politicians and developers try to build a new jail, many Detroiters say stop—let's build places where we can heal instead."[37] The DJC uses a three-pronged strategy to creating just communities that entails "defense" (handling legal challenges to keep people out of jail, in their homes, and employed), "offense" (building economic security, sustainability, and power), and "dreaming." Dreaming means creating space for collectively imagining alternatives to precarity, poverty, prisons, and premature death, and then planning to bring them to fruition. For example, as a coalition of organizations fought plans to build a new jail and youth detention center slated to cost the county a half billion dollars, young people participating in the DJC's Just Cities Lab dreamed up ways to make better use of the money that could be described as abolitionist. Their proposals included raising teacher salaries, investing in affordable and accessible housing, building a regional transit system, "restorative justice centers," a "mental health spa" where people could get free therapy and support, a financial assistance center that would use the money to give grants to families in need "without filling out a lot of paperwork."[38]

These are not dreams to be left on web pages or colored Post-its or reams of butcher paper to simply decorate the halls of crumbling schools. They fuel social movements, just as movements animate new visions of liberation. The struggle to liberate Detroit from rapacious racial capitalism and reverse its catastrophic impact on the earth culminates in the work of the Eastside Solutionaries, a collective formed by leaders from a variety of community-based organizations, including the Boggs Center, Eastside Community Network, Detroit Justice Center, Feedom Freedom Growers, Sustainable Community Farms, and Breathe Free Detroit. They are an incredible cross-generational assembly of folks currently implementing an ambitious plan to create a city where work is non-exploitative, non-ableist, and oriented toward making and doing things communities need; where food, housing, and energy are affordable and green; where essential resources from water to the internet are free and held in common; and where "restorative justice . . . community healing, and education" are social priorities.[39]

Through the creative use of community benefit agreements, community land trusts, government and foundation grants, investments in the community by Fiat-Chrysler (the leading employer), a community tax on corporations and businesses, and the creation of a community improvement fund, the Eastside Solutionaries plan to reverse the process of gentrification by making some ten thousand low- and middle-income, energy efficient homes available in East Detroit. A community improvement fund would support home upgrades and repair, protect homes built or renovated on community land trusts, providing a hedge against future foreclosures, and help sustain educational and cultural institutions, such as the public library and a proposed "Music and Art House" that could train residents—especially youth—in art, music, video, and digital production. The Eastside Solutionaries have already partnered with other groups to create green energy alternatives, including Soulardarity, a collective specializing in making solar and other renewable energy sources available to communities, and Ryter Cooperative Industries (RCI), which helps low-income and marginalized communities create their own energy infrastructure via wind and solar power. These alternative power stations reduce dependence on the "grid," turning people from energy consumers to energy producers.[40] Sculptor Carlos Nielbock, a collective member, used his considerable talents to build windmills that allow users to charge cellular and other electronic devices.[41]

Image becomes deed. Detroit, like Jackson, is becoming a liberated zone, where poets and solutionaries of every generation are unafraid to build what they haven't seen or fight a system that has wreaked havoc on the land and our lives for five centuries. They understand that freedom dreaming is not a luxury or a fantasy, and that our very survival depends on turning dreams of decolonization, redistribution, reparation, and abolition into action. Long before COVID-19 inspired writer, critic, and revolutionary Arundhati Roy to famously described the pandemic as "a portal, a gateway between one world and the next,"[42] Detroit's freedom dreamers had been digging their own portal to the next world, not waiting for a crisis or opportunity to seize the moment. They haven't stopped digging.

> "I also wanted to let you know that our east side community land trust has decided to name itself: Freedom Dreams."
>
> —Email from Rich Feldman, June 20, 2021

Notes from "When History Wakes"

1. Octavio Paz, "Hacia el poema" (Towards the poem), 1950.

2. James Boggs, "Think Dialectically, Not Biologically," in *Pages from a Black Radical's Notebook: A James Boggs Reader*, ed. Stephen M. Ward (Detroit: Wayne State University Press, 2011), 266.

3. Grace Lee Boggs, "The Beloved Community of Martin Luther King," *YES Magazine*, May 21, 2004, https://www.yesmagazine.org/issue /hope-conspiracy/2004/05/21/the-beloved-community-of-martin-luther-king.

4. Alexis Pauline Gumbs, "Freedom Seeds: Growing Abolition in Durham, North Carolina," in *Abolition Now! Ten Years of Strategy and Struggle Against the Prison Industrial Complex*, ed. CR-10 Publications Collective (Oakland, CA: AK Press, 2008), 145.

5. Kali Akuno, "The Jackson-Kush Plan: The Struggle for Black Self-Determination and Economic Democracy," in *Jackson Rising: The Struggle for Economic Democracy, Socialism and Black Self-Determination in Jackson, Mississippi*, ed. Kali Akuno and Ajamu Nangwaya (Montreal: Daraja Press, 2017).

6. Carolyn Copeland, "'I'm Dreaming as Big as I Can': A Q&A with Human Rights Activist Rukia Lumumba," *Prism*, March 24, 2020, https://prism reports.org/2020/03/24/im-dreaming-as-big-as-i-can-a-qa-with-human-rights -activist-rukia-lumumba.

7. "Remembering Charity Hicks," *Commons Magazine*, July 22, 2014, https:// www.onthecommons.org/magazine/commoner/remembering-charity-hicks.

8. The most thorough study of the Detroit water crisis is We the People of Detroit Community Research Collective, *Mapping the Water Crisis: The Dismantling of African-American Neighborhoods in Detroit: Volume One* (Detroit: We the People of Detroit Community Research Collective, 2016). See also "Detroit Needs Water Affordability," *Food and Water Watch: Issue Brief* (May 2015), https://foodandwaterwatch.org/wp-content/uploads /2021/03/Detroit-Water-Plan-IB-May-2015.pdf; Emily Holden, Ron Fonger, and Jessica Glenza, "Revealed: Water Company and City Officials Knew About Flint Poison Risk," *Guardian*, December 10, 2019, https://www .theguardian.com/us-news/2019/dec/10/water-company-city-officials-knew -flint-lead-risk-emails-michigan-tap-water; Leana Hosea and Sharon Lerner, "From Pittsburgh to Flint: The Dire Consequences of Giving Private Companies Responsibility for Ailing Public Water Systems," *The Intercept*, May 20, 2018, https://theintercept.com/2018/05/20/pittsburgh-flint-veolia-privatization -public-water-systems-lead/; Josiah Rector, "Neoliberalism's Deadly Experiment," *Jacobin*, October 2016, https://www.jacobinmag.com/2016/10/water -detroit-flint-emergency-management-lead-snyder-privatization.

9. "Remembering Charity Hicks," *Commons Magazine*; Shea Howell, "Who's Water? Our Water!," paper delivered to Central States Communica-

tion Association, April 15, 2016, in author's possession. In a strange twist, the driver who struck Hicks and fled, Thomas Shanley, was on parole for a prior drug conviction. He was also the son of a police officer who died of a heart attack while on duty. His mother paid his legal expenses with money she embezzled from a charity set up to help the families of slain officers. Ashley Southall, "Police Widow Spent $410,000 on Herself That Should Have Gone to Slain Officers' Families, Officials Say," *New York Times*, March 21, 2019, https://www.nytimes.com/2019/03/21/nyregion/lorraine-shanley-nypd-charity -theft.html.

10. Grace Lee Boggs, "These Are the Times That Grow Our Souls," Animating Democracy, https://animatingdemocracy.org/sites/default/files/documents /reading_room/Grace_Lee_Boggs_Grow_Our_Souls.pdf, accessed November 19, 2021.

11. Malik Yakini, "Progress, Challenges, and Lessons from D-Town Farm," *Riverwise* 5 (Winter–Spring 2018): 13–15; DBCFSN, "Core Values," https:// www.dbcfsn.org/mission-vision-values; Jessica High Hester, "Farming for Their Lives," *City Lab*, August 29, 2016, https://www.citylab.com/life/2016/08 /detroit-urban-farmers-growing/497027; Eric Thomas Campbell, "Farm Collectives Show the Future of Progress," *Riverwise* 6 (Spring–Summer 2018), https://riverwisedetroit.org/article/farm-collectives-show-the-future-in -progress/; Tepfirah Rushdan, "A Brief History of Urban Agriculture in Detroit," *Riverwise* 5 (Winter–Spring 2018): 26–27.

12. Tawana Petty, *Petty Propolis Reader: My Personal and Political [R]evolution* (Detroit: Tawana Petty, 2017), 6.

13. Eric Thomas Campbell, "Expressions of an Emerging Community: Arts Program Builds Culture of Resistance and Family," *Riverwise* 5 (Winter–Spring 2018): 19–20.

14. Nichole Christian, ed., *A Life Speaks: Gloria House, 2019 Kresge Eminent Artist* (Troy, MI: Kresge Foundation, 2019) 8, 16, 32–33. House also has a long history with Broadside Press, which published her first collections of poetry and which she eventually would run after it merged with Lotus Press.

15. Gloria House/Aneb Kgositsile, *Tower and Dungeon: A Study of Place and Power in American Culture* (Detroit: Casa de Unidad Press, 1991), 54. *Tower and Dungeon* is a revision of her doctoral dissertation, "Tower and Dungeon: A Study in American Spatial Politics," (PhD diss., University of Michigan, 1986). Thanks to Invincible/ill Weaver for drawing my attention to *Tower and Dungeon*, a remarkable yet underappreciated work of scholarship.

16. We the People of Detroit Community Research Collective, *Mapping the Water Crisis*.

17. Gloria House, PhD (aka Aneb Kgositsile), "Ten Lessons from Years of Activism in Detroit Community Struggles and International Solidarity, and

'Lessons in Grace,' a Poem Celebrating the Life of Grace Lee Boggs," at http://adriennemareebrown.net/2010/06/24/10-lessons-from-detroit-for-movement-building.

18. adrienne maree brown, *Emergent Strategy: Shaping Change, Changing Worlds* (Chico, CA: AK Press, 2017), 22–23.

19. "Kites on Kites: Shadows to the Sky," https://vimeo.com/396804671.

20. Invincible/ill Weaver email to author, July 29, 2021; "Invincible," https://emergencemedia.org/pages/invincible.

21. Complex Movements, "Narrative Sharing and Narrative Shifting with Digital Technology," *Howlround Theater Commons*, June 10, 2019, https://howlround.com/narrative-sharing-and-narrative-shifting-digital-technology; Complex Movements, *Beware of the Dandelions—Soundtrack* (Dirty Teck Reck/Emergence Media, 2016).

22. She is the author of four books: *Introducing Honeycomb: A Collection of Poems, Haikus, and Quotes* (Detroit: Urban Guerrilla Entertainment, 2011); *Coming Out My Box: Poems, Articles, and Essays* (Detroit: Tawana Petty, 2016); *Petty Propolis Reader: My Personal and Political Evolution* (Detroit: Tawana Petty, 2017); *Towards Humanity: Shifting the Culture of Anti-Racism Organizing* (Detroit: Tawana Petty, 2018).

23. Petty, *Coming Out My Box*, 16.

24. Tawana "Honeycomb" Petty, "Poetry as Visionary Resistance," *Riverwise* no. 6 (Spring–Summer 2018): 12–13.

25. "Know Allegiance Nation," https://knowallegiance.wordpress.com/; "KAN Books," https://kanbooks.org/about.

26. Petty, "Poetry as Visionary Resistance," 12.

27. Stephen M. Ward, *In Love and Struggle: The Revolutionary Lives of James and Grace Lee Boggs* (Chapel Hill: University of North Carolina Press, 2016), 330.

28. Ward, *In Love and Struggle*, 330.

29. Ron Scott, *How to End Police Brutality: An Organizer's Manual* (Detroit: Detroit Coalition Against Police Brutality, 2015); Petty, *Petty Propolis Reader*, 20; Scott Kurashige, *The Fifty-Year Rebellion: How the U.S. Political Crisis Began in Detroit* (Oakland: University of California Press, 2017), 135; Grace Lee Boggs, *The Next American Revolution: Sustainable Activism for the Twenty-First Century*, ed. Scott Kurashige (Oakland: University of California Press, 2011), 103–4.

30. Zak Rosen, "Our Neighborhoods, Our Streets: The March to Peace in Detroit," Michigan Radio, October 26, 2016, https://stateofopportunity.michiganradio.org/families-community/2016-10-26/our-neighborhoods-our-streets-the-march-to-peace-in-detroit.

31. Ron Scott and Sandra Hines, Detroit Coalition Against Police Brutality, "Peace Zones for Life," *New Work Culture Reader* (Detroit: Boggs Center, unpublished manuscript), 122.

32. Shea Howell, "Not One More," *Riverwise* 12 (Spring 2020): 6; River-wise Editorial Board, "Community Policing: A Matter of Survival," *Riverwise* 12 (Spring 2020): 4.

33. Janis Kelly and Tacie Dejanikus, "Roxbury Organizing," *Off Our Backs* 9, no. 9 (October 31, 1979): 7; Victoria Law, "Protection Without Police: North American Community Responses to Violence in the 1970s and To-day," *Upping the Anti* 12 (August 17, 2017), https://uppingtheanti.org/journal /article/12-protection-without-police.

34. Noah Urban, Jacob Yesh-Brochstein, Erica Raleigh, and Tawana Petty, "A Critical Summary of Detroit's Project Green Light and Its Greater Context," Detroit Community Technology Project, June 9, 2019, https:// detroitcommunitytech.org/system/tdf/librarypdfs/DCTP_PGL_Report.pdf; Bill Wylie-Kellerman, "Fighting Racist Surveillance in Detroit," *Riverwise* 12 (Spring 2020): 11–13.

35. Atinusewakaraiye "Tinu" Roland, "'She Safe, We Safe': A New Focal Point for Black Liberation," *Riverwise* 12 (Spring 2020): 10; see also Green Light Black Futures Coalition Members, Rayshaun Phillips, Rumi Weaver, and Keysha Wall, "Open Letter to Detroiters: Challenging Project Green Light and Facial Recognition for a Better Future," *Riverwise* 11 (Winter 2020): 8–9.

36. Myrtle Thompson-Curtis, "Green Chairs, Not Green Lights: Building Community From Our Front Porches," Feedom Freedom flier, 2019; "Safe or Just Surveilled? Tawana Petty on the Fight Against Facial Recognition Sur-veillance," *Logic* 10 (May 4, 2020), https://logicmag.io/security/safe-or-just -surveilled-tawana-petty-on-facial-recognition.

37. Amanda Alexander, "Centering Our Freedom Dreams: The Fight Ahead for Just Communities," Detroit Justice Center, September 25, 2019, https://www.detroitjustice.org/blog/centeringourfreedomdreams. She gave this speech at the Smart on Crime conference at John Jay College in New York City.

38. Alexander, "Centering Our Freedom Dreams"; Amanda Alexan-der, "What Can We Build Instead of Jails?" *Riverwise* 7 (Summer–Fall 2018): 8; Sebastian Johnson, "Imagining Safety Without Prisons: Seek-ing a Holistic Solution to Violence in Detroit," *Detroit Free Press*, Octo-ber 20, 2019, https://www.freep.com/story/opinion/2019/10/20/detroit-mass -incarceration/4011031002.

39. "Who Are We?" *East Side Solutionaries Collective* 1 (Summer 2021): 1; "Our Communities Are Up to Us: Our Future Is Now!," East Side Proposals for FCA Community Benefits Engagements Working Document, March 28, 2019, in author's possession.

40. Eric Thomas Campbell, "Self-Empowerment Through Solar En-ergy," *Riverwise* 5 (Winter–Spring 2018): 11–12; Ari Dural, "The Power of So-lar," *East Side Solutionaries Collective* 1 (Summer 2021): 2.

41. Larry Gabriel, "The (CAN)Arts Recreations: Windmills Breathe Life in to Grassroots Energy Potential," *Riverwise* 5 (Winter–Spring 2018): 13–15.

42. Arundhati Roy, "The Pandemic Is a Portal," *Financial Times*, April 3, 2020, https://www.ft.com/content/10d8f5e8-74eb-11ea-95fe-fcd274e920ca.

SOURCES

"When History Sleeps": A Beginning

Baker, Lee D. *From Savage to Negro: Anthropology and the Construction of Race, 1896–1954*. Los Angeles and Berkeley: University of California Press, 1998.

Baraka, Amiri [Jones, LeRoi]. *Black Music*. New York: Quill, 1967.

Boggs, Grace Lee. *Living for Change*. Minneapolis: University of Minnesota Press, 1998.

Bush, Rod. *We Are Not What We Seem: Black Nationalism and Class Struggle in the American Century*. New York: New York University Press, 1999.

Carby, Hazel. *Race Men*. Cambridge: Harvard University Press, 1998.

———. *Reconstructing Black Womanhood*. New York: Oxford University Press, 1987.

Césaire, Aimé. "Poetry and Knowledge." In *Refusal of the Shadow: Surrealism and the Caribbean*, edited and translated by Michael Richardson and Krzysztof Fijalkowski, 134–46. London: Verso, 1996.

Chau-Jua, Sundiata Keita. "The Black Radical Congress and the Reconstruction of the Black Freedom Movement." *Black Scholar* 28, nos. 3/4 (1998): 3–22.

Chicago Surrealist Group. "Surrealism and Blues." *Living Blues*, no. 25 (January/February, 1976), 19.

Davis, Angela Y. *Blues Legacies and Black Feminism: Gertrude "Ma" Rainey, Bessie Smith, and Billie Holiday*. New York: Pantheon, 1998.

Du Bois, W. E. B. *Black Reconstruction in America: An Essay toward a History of the Part Which Black Folk Played in the Attempt to Reconstruct Democracy, 1860–1880*. New York: Harcourt, Brace, 1935.

Giroux, Henry A. *Beyond the Corporate University: Culture and Pedagogy in the New Millennium*. Lanham, Md.: Rowman & Littlefield, 2001.

Giroux, Henry A. *Disturbing Pleasures: Learning Popular Culture.* New York: Routledge, 1994.

———. *Fugitive Cultures: Race, Violence, and Youth.* New York: Routledge, 1996.

———. *Impure Acts: The Practical Politics of Cultural Studies.* New York: Routledge, 2000.

———. *Stealing Innocence: Youth, Corporate Power, and the Politics of Culture.* New York: St. Martin's Press, 2000.

Hall, James C. *Mercy, Mercy Me: African-American Culture and the American Sixties.* New York: Oxford University Press, 2001.

Harding, Vincent. *There Is a River: The Struggle for Black Freedom in America.* New York: Random House, 1983.

Hersch, Charles. *Democratic Artworks: Politics and the Arts from Trilling to Dylan.* Albany, N.Y.: State University of New York Press, 1998.

James, Joy. *Transcending the Talented Tenth: Black Leaders and American Intellectuals.* New York: Routledge, 1997.

Kelley, Robin D. G. "'But a Local Phase of a World Problem': Black History's Global Vision, 1883–1950." *Journal of American History* 86, no. 3 (December 1999): 1045–77.

———. *Hammer and Hoe: Alabama Communists during the Great Depression.* Chapel Hill, N.C.: University of North Carolina Press, 1990.

———. *Race Rebels: Culture, Politics, and the Black Working Class.* New York: Free Press, 1994.

Kgositsile, Keorapetse. *When the Clouds Clear.* Cape Town, South Africa: Congress of South African Writers, 1990.

Lincoln, Abbey. "Africa." *People in Me.* Philips LP 5100, 1973.

Linebaugh, Peter and Marcus Rediker. *The Many-Headed Hydra: Sailors, Slaves, Commoners, and the Hidden History of the Revolutionary Atlantic.* Boston: Beacon Press, 2000.

Lipsitz, George. *A Life in the Struggle: Ivory Perry and the Culture of Opposition.* Philadelphia: Temple University Press, 1988.

———. *Dangerous Crossroads: Popular Music, Postmodernism, and the Poetics of Place.* New York: Verso, 1994.

Paz, Octavio. *Eagle or Sun?*, translated by Eliot Weinberger. New York: New Directions Books, 1976.

Robinson, Cedric. *Black Marxism: The Making of the Black Radical Tradition.* 1983. Reprint, Chapel Hill, N.C.: University of North Carolina Press, 2000.

Rosemont, Penelope. *Surrealist Experiences: 1001 Dawns, 221 Midnights.* Chicago: Black Swan Press, 2000.

Surrealist Group in Madrid. "Beyond Anti-Racism: The Role of Poetic Thought in the Eradication of White Supremacy." *Surrealism:*

Revolution against Whiteness, special issue of *Race Traitor* 9 (summer 1998): 42–45.

Thompson, E. P. *Making History: Writings on History and Culture*. New York: New Press, 1994.

Ward, Brian. *Just My Soul Responding: Rhythm and Blues, Black Consciousness, and Race Relations*. Los Angeles and Berkeley: University of California Press, 1998.

Woodard, Komozi. *A Nation within a Nation*. Chapel Hill, N.C.: University of North Carolina Press, 1998.

1. Dreams of the New Land

Anderson, Benedict. *Imagined Communities: Reflections on the Origins and Spread of Nationalism*. London and New York: Verso, 1991.

Arrested Development. *Three Years, Five Months, and Two Days in the Life of . . .* Chrysalis compact disk F4 21929, 1992.

Bair, Barbara. *Freedom Is Never a Final Act: Women Emerge from the Garvey Movement*. Chapel Hill, N.C.: University of North Carolina Press, forthcoming.

Barnes, Sandra T., ed. *Africa's Ogun: Old World and New*. Bloomington, Ind.: Indiana University Press, 1989.

Barrett, Leonard. *Soul-Force: African Heritage in Afro-American Religion*. Garden City, N.Y.: Anchor Press, 1974.

Berry, Mary Frances and John Blassingame. *Long Memory: The Black Experience in America*. New York: Oxford University Press, 1982.

Bittle, William E. and Gilbert Geis. *The Longest Way Home: Chief Alfred C. Sam's Back-to-Africa Movement*. Detroit: Wayne State University Press, 1964.

Blackett, R. J. M. *Beating against the Barriers: Biographical Essays in Nineteenth-Century Afro-American History*. Baton Rouge, La.: Louisiana State University Press, 1986.

Blyden, Edward Wilmot. *Black Spokesman: Selected Published Writings of Edward Wilmot Blyden*. New York: Humanities Press, 1971.

———. *Christianity, Islam, and the Negro Race*. Edinburgh: University Press, 1967.

Brundage, W. Fitzhugh, ed. *Under Sentence of Death: Lynching in the South*. Chapel Hill, N.C.: University of North Carolina Press, 1997.

Brundage, W. Fitzhugh. *Lynching in the New South: Georgia and Virginia, 1880–1930*. Urbana, Ill.: University of Illinois Press, 1993.

Campbell, Horace. *Rasta and Resistance: From Marcus Garvey to Walter Rodney*. Trenton, N.J.: Africa World Press, 1987.

Clarke, John Henrik, ed. *Marcus Garvey and the Vision of Africa*. New York: Vintage, 1974.

Clifford, James. "Diasporas." In *Routes: Travel and Translation in the Late Twentieth Century*. Cambridge: Harvard University Press, 1997.

Corbett, John. *Extended Play: Sounding off from John Cage to Dr. Funkenstein*. Durham, N.C.: Duke University Press, 1994.

Cortez, Jayne. *Coagulations: New and Selected Poems*. New York: Thunder's Mouth Press, 1984.

———. *Somewhere in Advance of Nowhere*. New York and London: High Risk Books, 1996.

Del tha Funkee Homosapien. *I Wish My Brother George Was Here*. Elektra audiocassette 9 61133–4, 1991.

Delany, Martin Robison. *The Condition, Elevation, Emigration, and Destiny of the Colored People of the United States, Politically Considered*. 1852. Reprint, New York: Arno Press, 1968.

Drachler, Jacob, ed. *Black Homeland/Black Diaspora: Cross-currents of the African Relationship*. Port Washington, N.Y.: Kennikat Press, 1975.

Drake, St. Clair. *Black Folk Here and There: An Essay in History and Anthropology*, vols. 1 and 2. Los Angeles: Center for Afro-American Studies, University of California, 1987, 1990.

Egerton, Douglas R. "'Its Origin Is Not a Little Curious': A New Look at the American Colonization Society." *Journal of the Early Republic* 5 (winter 1985): 463–80.

Eure, Joseph D. and James G. Spady, eds. *Nation Conscious Rap*. New York: P. C. International, 1991.

Franklin, V. P. *Black Self-Determination: A Cultural History of African-American Resistance*. 2d ed. Brooklyn, N.Y.: Lawrence Hill Books, 1992.

Gaines, Kevin. *Uplifting the Race: Black Leadership, Politics, and Culture in the Twentieth Century*. Chapel Hill, N.C.: University of North Carolina Press, 1996.

Gilroy, Paul. *The Black Atlantic: Modernity and Double Consciousness*. Cambridge: Harvard University Press, 1993.

Griffith, Cyril W. *The African Dream: Martin R. Delany and the Emergence of Pan-African Thought*. University Park, Pa.: Pennsylvania State University Press, 1975.

Hager, Steve. *Hip Hop: The Illustrated History of Break Dancing, Rap Music, and Graffiti*. New York: St. Martin's Press, 1984.

Hair, William Ivy. *Carnival of Fury: Robert Charles and the New Orleans Race Riot of 1900*. Baton Rouge, La.: Louisiana State University Press, 1976.

Hall, Gwendolyn Midlo. *Africans in Colonial Louisiana: The Development of Afro-Creole Culture in the Eighteenth Century*. Baton Rouge, La.: Louisiana State University Press, 1992.

Hall, Stuart. "Cultural Identity and Diaspora," in *Identity: Community, Culture, Difference.* London: Lawrence & Wishart, 1990.

Hanchard, Michael. "Identity, Meaning, and the African-American." *Social Text* 8, no. 24 (1990): 31–42.

Harding, Vincent. *There Is a River: The Black Struggle for Freedom in America.* New York: Harcourt, Brace, 1983.

Harris, Joseph E., ed. *Global Dimensions of the African Diaspora.* Washington, D.C.: Howard University Press, 1982.

Harris, Sheldon, ed. *Paul Cuffe: Black America and the African Return.* New York: Simon and Schuster, 1972.

Herskovits, Melville J. *The Myth of the Negro Past.* Boston: Beacon Press, 1941.

Hill, Robert A. "Chief Alfred Sam and the African Movement." In *Pan-African Biography.* Los Angeles: University of California and Crossroads Press, 1987.

Hill, Robert and Barbara Bair, eds. *Marcus Garvey: Life and Lessons.* Berkeley and Los Angeles: University of California Press, 1987.

Hinks, Peter. *"To Awaken My Afflicted Brethren": David Walker and the Problem of Antebellum Slave Resistance.* University Park, Pa.: University of Pennsylvania Press, 1997.

James, Winston. *Holding Aloft the Banner of Ethiopia: Caribbean Radicalism in Early Twentieth-Century America.* London and New York: Verso, 1998.

Jayne Cortez and the Firespitters. *Cheerful and Optimistic.* Bola Press compact disk BP9401, 1994.

Kelley, Robin D. G. and Tiffany Patterson. "Unfinished Migrations: Reflections on the African Diaspora and the Making of the Modern World." *African Studies Review* 43, no. 1 (April 2000): 11–45.

Knight, Franklin. *The African Dimension in Latin American Societies.* New York: Macmillan Press, 1974.

Lemelle, Sidney J. and Robin D. G. Kelley, eds. *Imagining Home: Class, Culture, and Nationalism in the African Diaspora.* London and New York: Verso, 1994.

Linebaugh, Peter and Marcus Rediker. *The Many-Headed Hydra: Sailors, Slaves, Commoners, and the Hidden History of the Revolutionary Atlantic.* Boston: Beacon Press, 2000.

Litwack, Leon F. *Trouble in Mind: Black Southerners in the Age of Jim Crow.* New York: Knopf, 1998.

Lock, Graham. *Blutopia: Visions of the Future and Revisions of the Past in the Work of Sun Ra, Duke Ellington, and Anthony Braxton.* Durham, N.C.: Duke University Press, 1999.

Lynch, Hollis R. *Edward Wilmot Blyden: Pan-Negro Patriot, 1832–1912.* London: Oxford University Press, 1964.

Magubane, Bernard M. *The Ties that Bind: African-American Consciousness of Africa*. Trenton, N.J.: Africa World Press, 1987.

Martin, Tony. *Race First: The Ideological and Organizational Struggles of Marcus Garvey and the Universal Negro Improvement Association*. Westport, Conn.: Greenwood Press, 1976.

Miller, Floyd. *The Search for a Black Nationality: Black Emigration and Colonization, 1787–1863*. Urbana, Ill.: University of Illinois Press, 1975.

Mintz, Sidney and Richard Price. *The Birth of African-American Culture: An Anthropological Perspective*. Boston: Beacon Press, 1992.

Moses, Wilson J. *Afrotopia: The Roots of African-American Popular History*. Cambridge: Cambridge University Press, 1998.

———. *Alexander Crummell: A Study of Civilization and Discontent*. New York: Oxford University Press, 1989.

———. *The Golden Age of Black Nationalism, 1850–1925*. 1978. Reprint, New York: Oxford University Press, 1988.

Moses, Wilson J., ed. *Classical Black Nationalism: From the American Revolution to Marcus Garvey*. New York: New York University Press, 1996.

Mudimbe, V. Y. *The Invention of Africa: Gnosis, Philosophy, and the Order of Knowledge*. Bloomington, Ind.: Indiana University Press, 1988.

Mugge, Robert. *Sun Ra: A Joyful Noise*. Mug Shot Productions, 1980. Film.

Painter, Nell Irvin. *Exodusters: Black Migration to Kansas after Reconstruction*. New York: Knopf, 1976.

Plummer, Brenda Gayle. *Rising Wind: Black Americans and U.S. Foreign Affairs, 1935–1960*. Chapel Hill, N.C.: University of North Carolina Press, 1996.

Poor Righteous Teachers. *Holy Intellect*. Profile audiocassette PCT–11289, 1990.

Raboteau, Albert. *A Fire in the Bones: Reflections on African-American Religious History*. Boston: Beacon Press, 1995.

Raper, Arthur Franklin. *The Tragedy of Lynching*. Chapel Hill, N.C.: University of North Carolina Press, 1933.

Redkey, Edwin S. *Black Exodus: Black Nationalist and Back-to-Africa Movements, 1890–1910*. New Haven: Yale University Press, 1969.

Robinson, Cedric J. "W. E. B. Du Bois and Black Sovereignty." In *Imagining Home: Class, Culture, and Nationalism in the African Diaspora*, edited by Sidney J. Lemelle and Robin D. G. Kelley. London: Verso, 1994.

———. *Black Marxism: The Making of the Black Radical Tradition*. 1983. Reprint, Chapel Hill, N.C.: University of North Carolina Press, 2000.

———. *Black Movements in America*. New York and London: Routledge, 1997.

Rose, Tricia. *Black Noise: Rap Music and Black Culture in Contemporary America*. Hanover, N.H.: University Press of New England, 1994.

Shapiro, Herbert. *White Violence and Black Response: From Reconstruction to Montgomery*. Amherst, Mass.: University of Massachusetts Press, 1988.

Skinner, Elliot P. *African Americans and U.S. Policy toward Africa, 1850–1924: In Defense of Black Nationality*. Washington, D.C.: Howard University Press, 1992.

Sterling, Dorothy. *The Making of an Afro-American: Martin Robison Delany—African Explorer, Civil War Major, and Father of Black Nationalism*. 1971. Reprint, New York: Da Capo, 1996.

Stovall, Tyler. *Paris Noir: African Americans in the City of Light*. Boston and New York: Houghton Mifflin, 1996.

Stuckey, Sterling. *Slave Culture: Nationalist Theory and the Foundations of Black America*. New York: Oxford University Press, 1987.

Sundiata, Ibrahim K. *Black Scandal, America and the Liberian Labor Crisis, 1929–1936*. Philadelphia: Institute for the Study of Human Issues, 1980.

Szwed, John. *Space Is the Place: The Lives and Times of Sun Ra*. New York: Pantheon, 1997.

Tallie, Mariahadessa Ekere. "Barefoot Stroll." In *Listen Up! Spoken Word Poetry*, edited by Zoë Anglesey. New York: Ballantine, 1999.

Taylor, Ula. *The Veiled Garvey*. Forthcoming.

Thomas, Lamont. *Paul Cuffe: Black Entrepreneur and Pan-Africanist*. Urbana, Ill.: University of Illinois Press, 1988.

Thompson, Robert Farris. *Flash of the Spirit: African and Afro-American Art and Philosophy*. New York: Vintage, 1983.

Thompson, Vincent. *The Making of the African Diaspora in the Americas, 1441–1900*. New York: Longman, 1987.

Thornton, John. *Africa and Africans in the Making of the Atlantic World*. New York and Cambridge: Cambridge University Press, 1992.

Thorpe, Earl E. *Black Historians: A Critique*. New York: William Morrow and Co., 1971.

Tolnay, Stewart E. *A Festival of Violence: An Analysis of Southern Lynchings, 1882–1930*. Urbana, Ill.: University of Illinois Press, 1995.

Toop, David. *Rap Attack 2*. Boston: Consortium Press, 1992.

Vincent, Ted [Theodore]. *Keep Cool: The Black Activists Who Built the Jazz Age*. London and East Haven, Conn.: Pluto Press, 1995.

Vincent, Theodore. *Black Power and the Garvey Movement*. Berkeley: Ramparts Press, 1971.

Weinstein, Norman C. *A Night in Tunisia: Imaginings of Africa in Jazz*. New York: Limelight Editions, 1993.

Weisbord, Robert. *Ebony Kinship: Africa, Africans, and the Afro-American*. Westport, Conn.: Greenwood Press, 1973.

Wells-Barnett, Ida B. *On Lynchings: Southern Horrors, a Red Record, Mob Rule in New Orleans, 1862–1931*. New York, Arno Press, 1969.

White, E. Frances. "Africa on My Mind: Gender, Counter Discourse, and African-American Nationalism." *Journal of Women's History* 2, no. 1 (spring 1990): 73–97.

White, Walter. *Rope and Faggot: A Biography of Judge Lynch*. New York: Knopf, 1929.

Woodson, Carter G. "Fifty Years of Negro Citizenship as Qualified by the United States Supreme Court." *Journal of Negro History* 6, no. 1 (January 1921): 1–53.

Wright, Richard. *Twelve Million Black Voices*. 1941. Reprint, New York: Thunder's Mouth Press, 1988.

X-Clan. *To the East, Blackwards*. 4th B'Way audiocassette 444 019–4, 1989.

———. *Xodus: The New Testament*. Polydor audiocassette 314 513225 4, 1992.

2. "The Negro Question": Red Dreams of Black Liberation

African Blood Brotherhood. "Program of the African Blood Brotherhood," *Communist Review* (London) (April 1922): 449–54.

Allen, James S. and Philip Foner, eds. *American Communism and Black Americans: A Documentary History, 1919–1929*. Philadelphia: Temple University Press, 1987.

Allen, Robert. *Reluctant Reformers: Racism and Social Reform Movements in the United States*. Washington, D.C.: Howard University Press, 1983.

Anderson, Jervis. A. *Phillip Randolph: A Biographical Portrait*. New York: Harcourt Brace Jovanovich, 1973.

Ashbaugh, Carolyn. *Lucy Parsons, American Revolutionary*. Chicago: Charles Kerr, 1976.

Billings [Otto Huiswoud]. "Report on the Negro Question." *International Press Correspondence* 3, no. 2 (1923): 14–16.

Briggs, Cyril. "Negro Revolutionary Hero—Toussaint L'Ouverture." *Communist* 8, no. 5 (May 1929): 250–54.

Buhle, Mari Jo. *Women and American Socialism, 1870–1920*. Urbana, Ill.: University of Illinois Press, 1981.

Buhle, Paul. *C. L. R. James: The Artist as Revolutionary*. London and New York: Verso, 1988.

———. *From the Knights of Labor to the New World Order: Essays on Labor and Culture*. New York: Garland, 1997.

———. *Marxism in the United States: Remapping the History of the American Left*. London: Verso, 1987.

Buhle, Paul and Harvey Kaye, eds. *The American Radical*. New York: Routledge, 1994.

Buhle, Paul and Robin D. G. Kelley. "Allies of a Different Sort: Jews and Blacks in the American Left." In *Struggle in the Promisedland: The History of Black/Jewish Relations in the U.S.*, edited by Jack Salzman and Cornel West. New York: Oxford University Press, 1997.

Bunche, Ralph J. "French and British Imperialism in West Africa." *Journal of Negro History* 21, no. 1 (January 1936): 31–46.

Bush, Rod. *We Are Not What We Seem: Black Nationalism and Class Struggle in the American Century.* New York: New York University Press, 1998.

Buzz Johnson, ed. *"I Think of My Mother": Notes on the Life and Times of Claudia Jones.* London: Karia Press, 1985.

Commission on the National and Colonial Questions. "Theses on the National and Colonial Question Adopted by the Second Congress of the Comintern Congress." In *The Communist International, 1919–1943, Documents,* vol.1, edited by Jane Degras. London: Oxford University Press, 1956.

Dawson, Michael C. *Black Visions: The Roots of Contemporary African-American Political Ideologies.* Chicago: University of Chicago Press, 2001.

Du Bois, W. E. B. "The African Roots of War." *Atlantic Monthly* 115 (May 1915): 707–14.

——. "The Color Line Belts the World." In *W. E. B. Du Bois: A Reader,* edited by David Levering Lewis. New York: Henry Holt, 1995.

——. *The Autobiography of W. E. B. Du Bois.* Edited by Herbert Aptheker. New York: International Publishers, 1968.

——. *The World and Africa.* New York: International Publishers, 1947.

Duberman, Martin Bauml. *Paul Robeson.* New York: Knopf, 1989.

Dudziak, Mary L. *Cold War Civil Rights.* Princeton: Princeton University Press, 2000.

Esedebe, P. Olisanwuch. *Pan-Africanism: The Idea and Movement, 1776–1963.* Washington, D.C.: Howard University Press, 1982.

Foner, Philip. *American Socialism and Black Americans: From the Age of Jackson to World War II.* Westport, Conn.: Greenwood Press, 1977.

Ford, James. *The Negro and the Democratic Front.* New York: International Publishers, 1938.

Franklin, V. P. *Living Our Stories, Telling Our Truths: Autobiography and the Making of the African American Intellectual Tradition.* New York: Oxford University Press, 1996.

Gaines, Kevin. *Uplifting the Race: Black Leadership, Politics, and Culture in the Twentieth Century.* Chapel Hill, N.C.: University of North Carolina Press, 1996.

Geiss, Immanuel. *The Pan-African Movement.* London: Methuen and Co., 1974.

Gosse, Van. *Where the Boys Are: Cuba, Cold War America, and the Making of a New Left.* London: Verso, 1993.

Haithcox, John. *Communism and Nationalism in India: M. N. Roy and Comintern Policy, 1920–1939.* Princeton, N.J.: Princeton University Press, 1971.

Harding, Vincent. "Beyond Chaos: Black History and the Search for the New Land." In *Amistad 1*, edited by John A. Williams and Charles F. Harris. New York: Random House, 1970.

Harrison, Hubert Henry. *When Africa Awakes: The "Inside Story" of the Stirrings and Strivings of the New Negro in the Western World*. 1920. Reprint, Baltimore: Black Classic Press, 1997.

Haywood, Harry. *Black Bolshevik: Autobiography of an Afro-American Communist*. Chicago: Liberator Press, 1978.

Hill, Rebecca. "Fosterites and Feminists, or 1950s Ultra-Leftists and the Invention of AmeriKKKa." *New Left Review* 1, no. 228 (March/April 1998): 67–90.

Hill, Robert. "Racial and Radical: Cyril V. Briggs, the *Crusader* Magazine, and the African Blood Brotherhood, 1918–1922," Introduction to *The Crusader—Facsimile Editions*, edited by Robert Hill. New York: Garland Press, 1987.

Horne, Gerald. *Black and Red: W. E. B. Du Bois and the Afro-American Response to the Cold War, 1944–1963*. Albany, N.Y.: State University of New York Press, 1996.

———. *Communist Front? The Civil Rights Congress, 1946–1956*. London and Toronto: Fairleigh Dickinson University Press, 1988.

Jackson, Esther Cooper and Constance Pohl, eds. *Freedomways Readers: Prophets in Their Own Country*. Boulder, Colo.: Westview Press, 2000.

James, C. L. R. "The Revolutionary Answer to the Negro Problem in the U.S.A." In *The C. L. R. James Reader*, edited by Anna Grimshaw. Oxford: Basil Blackwell, 1992.

James, Winston. *Holding Aloft the Banner of Ethiopia: Caribbean Radicalism in Early Twentieth-Century America*. London: Verso, 1998.

Johnson, Oakley C. "Marxism and the Negro Freedom Struggle (1876–1917)." *Journal of Human Relations* 13, no. 1 (1965): 25–27.

Kanet, Roger E. "The Comintern and the 'Negro Question': Communist Policy in the United States and Africa, 1921–1941." *Survey* 19, no. 4 (autumn 1973): 86–122.

Kelley, Robin D. G. "'Afric's Sons With Banner Red': African-American Communists and the Politics of Culture, 1919–1934." In *Class, Culture, and Nationalism in the African Diaspora*, edited by Sidney J. Lemelle and Robin D. G. Kelley. London: Verso, 1995.

———. *Hammer and Hoe: Alabama Communists during the Great Depression*. Chapel Hill, N.C.: University of North Carolina Press, 1990.

———. *Race Rebels: Culture, Politics, and the Black Working Class*. New York: Free Press, 1994.

Kornweibel, Theodore. *No Crystal Stair: Black Life and the Messenger, 1917–1928*. Westport, Conn.: Greenwood Press, 1975.

Layton, Azza Salama. *International Politics and Civil Rights Policies in the United States, 1941–1960*. Cambridge: Cambridge University Press, 2000.

Lenin, V. I. "New Data on the Laws Governing the Development of Capitalism in Agriculture." In *Collected Works*, vol. 22. Moscow: Foreign Language Publishing House, 1963–70.

———. "On Statistics and Sociology." In *Collected Works*, vol. 23. Moscow: Foreign Language Publishing House, 1963–70.

———. "Russians and Negroes." In *Collected Works*, vol. 18. Moscow: Foreign Language Publishing House, 1963–70.

———. "The Report of the Commission on the National and Colonial Questions, July 26, 1920." In *Lenin on the National and Colonial Questions: Three Articles*, 30–37. Peking: Foreign Languages Press, 1967.

Levine, Bruce Carlan. "Free Soil, Free Labor, and Freimaenner: German Chicago in the Civil War Era." In *German Workers in Industrial Chicago, 1850–1910: A Comparative Perspective*, edited by Hartmut Keil and John B. Jentz, 163–82. DeKalb, Ill.: Northern Illinois University Press, 1983.

Lewis, David Levering. *W. E. B. Du Bois: Biography of a Race, 1863–1919*. New York: Henry Holt, 1993.

Lewis, Gilbert. "Revolutionary Negro Tradition." *Negro Worker* (March 15, 1930): 8.

Lynch, Hollis R. *Black American Radicals and the Liberation of Africa: The Council on African Affairs, 1937–1955*. Ithaca, N.Y.: Center for Research in Africana Studies, 1978.

Magubane, Bernard M. *The Ties that Bind: African-American Consciousness of Africa*. Trenton, N.J.: Africa World Press, 1987.

Maxwell, William J. *New Negro, Old Left: African-American Writing and Communism between the Wars*. New York: Columbia University Press, 1999.

McKay, Claude. *A Long Way from Home*. New York: Lee Furman, 1937.

———. *The Negroes in America*. Translated by Robert J. Winter. Edited by Alan L. McLeod. 1923. Reprint, Port Washington, N.Y.: Kennikat, 1979.

Miller, Sally M. "The Socialist Party and the Negro, 1901–1920." *Journal of Negro History* 56 (July 1971): 220–39.

Moore, Lawrence. "Flawed Fraternity: American Socialist Response and the Negro, 1901–1920." *Journal of Negro History* 33, no. 1 (1969): 1–14.

Naison, Mark. *Communists in Harlem during the Depression*. Urbana, Ill.: University of Illinois Press, 1983.

———. "Marxism and Black Radicalism in America: Notes on a Long (and Continuing) Journey." *Radical America* 5, no. 3 (1971): 4–10.

Patterson, William L., ed. *We Charge Genocide: The Historic Petition to the United Nations for Relief from a Crime of the United States Government against the Negro People*. New York: Civil Rights Congress, 1951.

Perry, Jeffery, ed. *A Hubert Harrison Reader.* Middletown, Conn.: Wesleyan University Press, 2001.

Plummer, Brenda Gayle. *Rising Wind: Black Americans and U.S. Foreign Affairs, 1935–1960.* Chapel Hill, N.C.: University of North Carolina Press, 1996.

Preece, Harold. "Folk Music of the South." *New South* 1, no. 2 (March 1938): 13–16.

Rampersad, Arnold. *The Life of Langston Hughes.* Vols. 1 and 2. New York: Oxford University Press, 1986.

Robeson, Paul. *Here I Stand.* 1958. Reprint, Boston: Beacon Press, 1988.

Robinson, Cedric J. "The African Diaspora and the Italo-Ethiopian Crisis." *Race and Class* 27, no. 2 (autumn 1985): 51–65.

———. "Fascism and the Intersection of Capitalism, Racialism, and Historical Consciousness." *Humanities in Society* 3, no. 6 (autumn 1983): 325–49.

———. *Black Marxism: The Making of the Black Radical Tradition.* 1983. Reprint, Chapel Hill, N.C.: University of North Carolina Press, 2000.

Samuels, David. "Five Afro-Caribbean Voices in American Culture, 1917–1929: Hubert H. Harrison, Wilfred A. Domingo, Richard B. Moore, Cyril Briggs, and Claude McKay." Ph.D. diss., University of Iowa, 1977.

Sherwood, Marika. *Claudia Jones: A Life in Exile.* London: Lawrence & Wishart, 1999.

Singer, Barry. *Black and Blue: The Life and Lyrics of Andy Razaf.* New York and Toronto: Schirmer Books and Maxwell Macmillan Canada, 1992.

Solomon, Mark. *The Cry Was Unity: Communists and African Americans, 1917–1936.* Jackson, Miss.: University Press of Mississippi, 1998.

Stuckey, Sterling. *Slave Culture: Nationalist Theory and the Foundations of Black America.* New York: Oxford University Press, 1987.

Taylor, Theman. "Cyril Briggs and the African Blood Brotherhood: Effects of Communism on Black Nationalism, 1919–1935." Ph.D. diss., University of California, Santa Barbara, 1981.

The Editors of *Freedomways. Paul Robeson: The Great Forerunner.* New York: International Publishers, 1998.

"Theses on the Negro Question." *Bulletin of the Fourth Congress of the Communist International* no. 27 (December 7, 1922): 8–10.

Von Eschen, Penny M. *Race against Empire: Black Americans and Anticolonialism, 1937–1957.* Ithaca, N.Y.: Cornell University Press, 1996.

Woodard, Komozi. *A Nation within a Nation: Amiri Baraka (LeRoi Jones) and Black Power Politics.* Chapel Hill, N.C.: University of North Carolina Press, 1998.

Workers (Communist) Party of America. *Fourth National Convention of the Workers (Communist) Party of America.* Chicago: Literature Department, Workers Party, 1925.

———. *Program and Constitution: Workers Party of America*. New York: Literature Department, Workers Party, 1921.

———. *The Second Year of the Workers Party of America: Theses, Programs, Resolutions*. Chicago: Literature Department, Workers Party, 1924.

3. "Roaring from the East": Third World Dreaming

Allen, Ernest, Jr. Interview with author. June 8, 1997.

Allen, Robert. *Black Awakening in Capitalist America*. Garden City, N.Y.: Doubleday & Co., 1969.

Baldwin, James. *Nobody Knows My Name: More Notes of a Native Son*. New York: Dial Press, 1961.

Baraka, Amiri [LeRoi Jones]. "Cuba Libre." In *Home: Social Essays*. 1966. Reprint, Hopewell, N.J.: The Ecco Press, 1998, 11–62.

———. *The Autobiography of LeRoi Jones/Amiri Baraka*. New York: Freundlich Books, 1984.

———. "Revolutionary Party, Revolutionary Ideology." Speech delivered at Congress of Afrikan People Midwestern Conference. March 31, 1974.

Barksdale, Marcellus C. "Robert Williams and the Indigenous Civil Rights Movement in Monroe, North Carolina, 1961." *Journal of Negro History* 69 (spring 1984): 73–89.

Berry, Mary Frances and John Blassingame. *Long Memory: The Black Experience in America*. New York and Oxford: Oxford University Press, 1982.

Boggs, Grace Lee. *Living for Change*. Minneapolis: University of Minnesota Press, 1998.

Brock, Lisa and Digna Castaneda Fuertes, eds. *Between Race and Empire: African-Americans and Cubans before the Cuban Revolution*. Philadelphia: Temple University Press, 1998.

Brown, Elaine. *A Taste of Power: A Black Woman's Story*. New York: Pantheon Books, 1992.

Brundage, W. Fitzhugh, ed. *Under Sentence of Death: Lynching in the South*. Chapel Hill, N.C.: University of North Carolina Press, 1997.

Burran, James A. "Urban Racial Violence in the South During World War II: A Comparative Overview." In *From the Old South to the New: Essays on the Transitional South*, edited by Walter J. Fraser Jr. and Winfred B. Moore Jr., 167–77. Westport, Conn.: Greenwood Publishers, 1981.

Bush, Rod. *We Are Not What We Seem: Black Nationalism and Class Struggle in the American Century*. New York: New York University Press, 1999.

Capeci, Dominic J. *The Harlem Riot of 1943*. Philadelphia: Temple University Press, 1977.

Capeci, Dominic J., Jr. *Race Relations in Wartime Detroit: The Sojourner Truth Housing Controversy of 1942*. Philadelphia: Temple University Press, 1984.

Communist League. "Dialectics of the Development of the Communist League." Los Angeles: Communist League, 1972. Mimeographed.

Cone, James. *Martin and Malcolm and America: A Dream or a Nightmare?* Maryknoll, N.Y.: Orbis Books, 1991.

Cooper, John C. *The Police and the Ghetto.* Port Washington, N.Y.: Kennikat Press, 1980.

Cruse, Harold. *Rebellion or Revolution?* New York: Morrow, 1968.

Davis, Mike. *City of Quartz: Excavating the Future in Los Angeles.* New York and London: Verso, 1990.

DeCaro, Louis. *On the Side of My People: A Religious Life of Malcolm X.* New York: New York Univeristy, 1996.

Fields, A. Belden. *Trotskyism and Maoism: Theory and Practice in France and the United States.* New York: Praeger, 1988.

Foner, Philip S., ed. *The Black Panthers Speak, The Manifesto of the Party: The First Documentary Record of the Panthers' Program.* Philadelphia: Lippincott, 1970.

Freeman, Don. "Nationalist Student Conference." *Liberator* 4, no. 7 (July 1964): 18.

———. "The Cleveland Story." *Liberator* 3, no. 6 (June 1963): 7, 18.

Gambino, Ferruccio. "The Transgression of a Laborer: Malcolm X in the Wilderness of America." *Radical History Review* 55 (winter 1993): 7–31.

Gibbs, Michelle. Interview with author. April 1997.

Ginzburg, Ralph, ed. *One Hundred Years of Lynching.* Baltimore: Black Classics Press, 1996.

Gosse, Van. *Where the Boys Are: Cuba, Cold War America, and the Making of a New Left.* London: Verso, 1993.

Greenberg, Cheryl. *"Or Does It Explode?" Black Harlem in the Great Depression.* New York and Oxford: Oxford University Press, 1991.

Harlem Branch of the Progressive Labor Party. *The Plot against Black America.* New York, PLP, 1965.

Haynes, Robert V. *A Night of Violence: The Houston Riot of 1917.* Baton Rouge, La.: Louisiana State University Press, 1976.

Heath, G. Louis, ed. *Off the Pigs: The History and Literature of the Black Panther Party.* Metuchen, N.J.: Scarecrow Press, 1976.

Horne, Gerald. *Communist Front? The Civil Rights Congress, 1946–1956.* London and Toronto: Fairleigh Dickinson University Press, 1988.

———. *The Fire This Time: The Watts Uprising and the 1960s.* Charlottesville, Va.: University Press of Virginia, 1995.

James, Joy. *Resisting State Violence: Radicalism, Gender, and Race in U.S. Culture.* Minneapolis: University of Minnesota Press, 1996.

Jones, Charles, ed. *The Black Panther Party Reconsidered.* Baltimore: Black Classic Press, 1998.

Kobler, A. L. "Figures (and Perhaps Some Facts) on Police Killing of Civilians in the United States, 1965–1969." *Journal of Social Issues* 31 (1975): 163–91.

Lemelle, Sidney. Interview with author. May 1997.

Lenin, V.I. "The Report of the Commission on the National and Colonial Questions, July 26, 1920." In *Lenin on the National and Colonial Questions: Three Articles*, 30–37. Peking: Foreign Languages Press, 1967.

Litwack, Leon F. *Trouble in Mind: Black Southerners in the Age of Jim Crow.* New York: Knopf, 1998.

Malcolm X, with Alex Haley. *The Autobiography of Malcolm X.* New York: Grove Press, 1964.

Mao Tse-tung. *Mao Tse-tung on Art and Literature.* Peking: Foreign Languages Press, 1960.

———. *Quotations from Chairman Mao Tse-tung.* Peking: Foreign Languages Press, 1966.

———. *Statement by Comrade Mao Tse-tung, Chairman of the Central Committee of the Communist Party of China, in Support of the Afro-American Struggle against Violent Repression.* Peking: Foreign Languages Press, April 16, 1968.

Marable, Manning. *How Capitalism Underdeveloped Black America.* Boston: South End Press, 1983.

———. *Race, Reform, and Rebellion: The Second Reconstruction in Black America, 1945–1990.* 2d ed. Jackson, Miss.: University Press of Mississippi, 1991.

Matthews, Tracye. "'No One Ever Asks What a Man's Role in the Revolution Is': Gender and Sexual Politics in the Black Panther Party, 1966–1971." Ph.D. diss., University of Michigan, 1998.

Monteiro, Tony. Interview with author. Philadelphia. October 24, 1998.

Moore, Audley. Interview with Mark Naison and Ruth Prago. Oral History of the American Left. Tamiment Library, New York University. May 3, 1974.

Newton, Huey P. *Revolutionary Suicide.* New York: Harcourt Brace Jovanovich, 1973.

O'Brien, Gail Williams. *The Color of Law: Race, Violence, and Justice in the Post–World War II South.* Chapel Hill, N.C.: University of North Carolina Press, 1999.

O'Reilly, Kenneth. *Racial Matters: The FBI's Secret File on Black America, 1960–1972.* New York: The Free Press, 1989.

Peery, Nelson. *The Negro National Colonial Question.* Chicago: Workers Press, 1975.

Plummer, Brenda Gayle. *Rising Wind: Black Americans and U.S. Foreign Affairs, 1935–1960.* Chapel Hill, N.C.: University of North Carolina Press, 1996.

Prashad, Vijay. *Everybody Was Kung Fu Fighting*. Boston: Beacon Press, 2001.

———. *The Karma of Brown Folk*. Minneapolis: University of Minnesota Press, 2000.

Radical Education Project. *An Introduction to the Black Panther Party*. Ann Arbor, Mich.: Radical Education Project, 1969.

Revolutionary Action Movement. *The World Black Revolution*. 1966. Pamphlet.

Rudwick, Elliot. *Race Riot at East St. Louis*. Urbana, Ill.: University of Illinois Press, 1964.

Sackett, R. "Plotting a War on Whitey: Extremist Set for Violence." *Life* 60 (June 10, 1966): 100–100B.

Salaam, Kalamu ya. "Robert Williams: Crusader for International Solidarity." *The Black Collegian* 8, no. 3 (January/February 1978): 53–60.

Sales, Williams, Jr. *From Civil Rights to Black Liberation: Malcolm X and the Organization of Afro-American Unity*. Boston: South End Press, 1994.

Schermerhorn, Tim. Interview with Betsy Esch. May 1998.

Shapiro, Herbert. *White Violence and Black Response: From Reconstruction to Montgomery*. Amherst, Mass.: University of Massachusetts Press, 1988.

Shivji, Issa. *Class Struggles in Tanzania*. New York: Monthly Review Press, 1976.

Simmons, Michael. Interview with author. Philadelphia. October 24, 1998.

Snellings, Rolland [Askia Muhammad Toure]. "Afro American Youth and the Bandung World." *Liberator* 5, no. 2 (February 1965): 4–7.

Spellman, A. B. "The Legacy of Malcolm X." *Liberator* 5, no. 6 (June 1965): 13.

Stanford, Max. "Revolutionary Nationalism and the Afroamerican Student." *Liberator* 5, no. 1 (January 1965): 13–14.

Stanford, Maxwell C. "Revolutionary Action Movement: A Case Study of an Urban Revolutionary Movement in Western Capitalist Society." M.A. thesis, Atlanta University, 1986.

The Crusader 2, no. 21 (December 31, 1960); *The Crusader* 2, no. 6 (August 20, 1960); *The Crusader* 5, no. 4 (May/June 1964); *The Crusader* 8, no. 4 (May 1967); *The Crusader* 9, no. 1 (July 1967); *The Crusader* 9, no. 2 (September/October 1967).

The League of Revolutionary Struggle. "The Revolutionary Communist League (MLM) and the League of Revolutionary Struggle (M-L) Unite!" *Forward: Journal of Marxism-Leninism-Mao Zedong Thought* 3 (January 1980).

Tolnay, Stewart E. *A Festival of Violence: An Analysis of Southern Lynchings, 1882–1930*. Urbana, Ill.: University of Illinois Press, 1995.

Tullis, Tracy. "A Vietnam at Home: Policing the Ghetto in the Era of Counterinsurgency." Ph.D. diss., New York University, 1998.

Tyson, Timothy B. *Radio Free Dixie: Robert Williams and the Roots of Black Power.* Chapel Hill, N.C.: University of North Carolina Press, 1999.

———. "Robert Williams, 'Black Power,' and the Roots of the African American Freedom Struggle." *Journal of American History* 85, no. 2 (September 1998): 540–70.

U.S. National Advisory Commission on Civil Disorders. *Report of the National Advisory Commission on Civil Disorders.* New York: Bantam Books, 1968.

Umoja, Akinyele. "Eye for an Eye: The Role of Armed Resistance in the Mississippi Freedom Movement, 1955–1980." Ph.D. diss., Emory University, 1996.

Van Deburg, William L. *New Day in Babylon: The Black Power Movement and American Culture, 1965–1975.* Chicago: University of Chicago Press, 1992.

Von Eschen, Penny M. *Race against Empire: Black Americans and Anticolonialism, 1937–1957.* Ithaca, N.Y.: Cornell University Press, 1996.

Ward Churchill and Jim Vander Wall. *Agents of Repression: The FBI's Secret Wars against the Black Panther Party and the American Indian Movement.* Boston: South End Press, 1988.

Warden, Donald. "The California Revolt." *Liberator* 3, no. 3 (March 1963): 15.

Watkins, Williams. Interview with author. August 1998.

Williams, Robert F. *Listen, Brother.* New York: World View Publishers, 1968.

———. *Negroes with Guns.* New York: Marzani and Munsell, 1962.

———. "Robert Williams: Interview." *Black Scholar* 1, no. 7 (May 1970): 5–14.

Wood, Joe, ed. *Malcolm X: In Our Own Image.* New York: St. Martin's Press, 1992.

Woodard, Komozi. *A Nation within a Nation: Amiri Baraka (LeRoi Jones) and Black Power Politics.* Chapel Hill, N.C.: University of North Carolina Press, 1998.

Zangrando, Robert L. *The NAACP Crusade against Lynching, 1909–1950.* Philadelphia: Temple University Press, 1980.

4. "A Day of Reckoning": Dreams of Reparations

Allen, Robert L. "Past Due: The African American Quest for Reparations." *Black Scholar* 28, no. 2 (1998): 2–17.

Anderson, James D. *The Education of Blacks in the South, 1860–1935.* Chapel Hill, N.C.: University of North Carolina Press, 1988.

"Audley (Queen Mother) Moore, interview by Cheryl Townsend-Gilkes, June 6 and 8, 1978." In *The Black Women Oral History Project*, vol. 8, edited by Ruth Edmonds Hill. Westport and London: Meckler, 1991.

Banner-Haley, Charles T. *The Fruits of Integration: Black Middle-Class Ideology and Culture, 1960-1990.* Jackson, Miss.: University Press of Mississippi, 1994.

Bell, Derek. *Faces at the Bottom of the Well: The Permanence of Racism.* New York: Basic Books, 1992.

Berlin, Ira, Barbara Fields, Leslie Rowland, and Joseph Reidy. *Slaves No More: Three Essays on Emancipation and the Civil War.* Cambridge and New York: Cambridge University Press, 1992.

Berry, Mary Frances and John Blassingame. *Long Memory: The Black Experience in America.* New York: Oxford University Press, 1982.

Bitker, Boris. *The Case for Black Reparations.* New York: Random House, 1973.

Boggs, Grace Lee. *Living for Change: An Autobiography.* Minneapolis: University of Minnesota Press, 1998.

Bracey, John H., August Meier, and Elliot Rudwick, eds. *Black Nationalism in America.* New York: Bobbs-Merrill, 1970.

Brown, Oscar, Jr. "Forty Acres and a Mule." *Mr. Oscar Brown Jr. Goes to Washington.* Verve compact disk SRF-67540, 1964.

Browne, Robert S. "The Economic Basis for Reparations to Black America." *Review of Black Political Economy* 2, no. 2 (1972): 67–80.

Bush, Rod. *We Are Not What We Seem: Black Nationalism and Class Struggle in the American Century.* New York: New York University Press, 1999.

Carmichael, Stokely and Charles V. Hamilton. *Black Power: The Politics of Liberation in America.* New York: Vintage Books, 1967.

Carnoy, Martin. *Faded Dreams: The Politics and Economics of Race in America.* Cambridge: Cambridge University Press, 1994.

Cell, John. *The Highest Stage of White Supremacy.* New York: Cambridge University Press, 1982.

Cha-Jua, Sundiata Keita. "Slavery, Racist Violence, American Apartheid: The Case for Reparations." *Sage Public Administration Abstracts* 28, no. 3 (2001): 301–445.

Child, L. Maria. *The Freedmen's Book.* 1865. Reprint, New York: Arno Press, 1968.

Clegg, Claude Andrew, III. *An Original Man: The Life and Times of Elijah Muhammad.* New York: St. Martin's Press, 1997.

Cose, Ellis. "The Solidarity of Self-Interest." *Newsweek* (August 27, 2001): 25.

D'Souza, Dinesh. *The End of Racism: Principles for a Multiracial Society.* New York: The Free Press, 1995.

———. *The Virtue of Prosperity: Finding Values in an Age of Techno-Affluence.* New York: Free Press, 2000.

Darity, William, Jr. "Forty Acres and a Mule: Placing a Price Tag on Oppression." In *The Wealth of Races: The Present Value of Benefits from Past Injustice,* edited by Richard F. America. New York: Greenwood Press, 1990.

Du Bois, W. E. B. *Black Reconstruction in America: An Essay toward a History of the Part Which Black Folk Played in the Attempt to Reconstruct Democracy, 1860–1880.* New York: Harcourt, Brace, 1935.

Essien-Udom, E. U. "The Nationalist Movements of Harlem." In *Harlem USA*, edited by John Henrik Clarke, 62–71. Brooklyn, N.Y.: A&B Books Publishers, 1993.

Fitzgerald, Michael W. *The Union League Movement in the Deep South: Politics and Agricultural Change during Reconstruction*. Baton Rouge, La.: Louisiana State University Press, 1989.

Foner, Eric. *Nothing but Freedom*. Baton Rouge, La.: Louisiana State University Press, 1983.

———. *Reconstruction: America's Unfinished Revolution, 1863–1877*. New York: Harper & Row, 1988.

Forman, James. *The Making of Black Revolutionaries*. 1972. Reprint, Seattle: University of Washington Press, 1997.

Franklin, V. P. *Black Self-Determination: A Cultural History of African American Resistance*. Brooklyn, N.Y.: Lawrence Hill, 1992.

Fullinwinder, Robert K. "The Case for Reparations." *Philosophy and Public Policy* 20, nos. 2/3 (summer 2000): 1–5.

Georgakas, Dan and Marvin Surkin. *Detroit, I Do Mind Dying: A Study in Urban Revolution*. New York: St. Martin's Press, 1975.

Geschwender, James A. *Class, Race, and Worker Insurgency: The League of Revolutionary Black Workers*. Cambridge and New York: Cambridge University Press, 1977.

Gill, Gerald. *Meanness Mania: The Changed Mood*. Washington, D.C.: Howard University Press, 1980.

Height, Dorothy. "Self-Help—A Black Tradition." *The Nation* (July 24/31, 1989): 24–31.

Higgs, Robert. *Competition and Coercion: Blacks in the American Economy, 1865–1914*. Cambridge and New York: Cambridge University Press, 1977.

Hill, Walter B., Jr. "The Ex-Slave Pension Movement: Some Historical and Genealogical Notes." *Negro History Bulletin* 59, no. 4 (1996): (author will provide page numbers)

Holt, Tom. *Black over White: Negro Political Leadership in Reconstruction South Carolina*. Urbana, Ill.: University of Illinois Press, 1977.

Inikori, J. E. *Forced Migration: The Impact of the Export Slave Trade on African Societies*. New York: Africana Publishing Co., 1982.

———. *The Atlantic Slave Trade: Effects on Economies, Societies, and Peoples in Africa, the Americas, and Europe*. Durham, N.C.: Duke University Press, 1992.

Jaynes, Gerald. *Branches without Roots: The Genesis of the Black Working Class, 1862–1882*. New York: Oxford University, 1986.

Jones, Charles, ed. *The Black Panther Party Reconsidered*. Baltimore: Black Classic Press, 1998.

Jones, Elaine R. "Race and the Supreme Court's 1994–95 Term." In *The Affirmative Action Debate*, edited by George E. Curry, 146–56. Reading, Mass.: Addison-Wesley, 1996.

Kelley, Robin D. G. "An Independent Black Radical Movement Can Connect with the Rest of the World." *Ahora Now!* 6 (1998): 18–19.

——. "'But a Local Phase of a World Problem': Black History's Global Vision, 1883–1950." *Journal of American History* 86, no. 3 (December 1999): 1045–77.

——. *Yo' Mama's Disfunktional! Fighting the Culture Wars in Urban America.* Boston: Beacon Press, 1997.

Laremont, Ricardo Rene. "Jewish and Japanese American Reparations: Political Lessons for the Africana Community." *Journal of Asian American Studies* 4, no. 3 (2001): 235–50.

Leggett, John C. *Class, Race, and Labor: Working-Class Consciousness in Detroit.* New York: Oxford University Press, 1968.

Lipsitz, George. *The Possessive Investment in Whiteness: How White People Profit from Identity Politics.* Philadelphia: Temple University Press, 1998.

Litwack, Leon. *"Been in the Storm So Long": The Aftermath of Slavery.* New York: Knopf, 1979.

——. *Trouble in Mind: Black Southerners in the Age of Jim Crow.* New York: Knopf, 1998.

Loury, Glen C. "Performing without a Net." In *The Affirmative Action Debate,* edited by George E. Curry, 49–64. Reading, Mass.: Addison-Wesley, 1996.

Lumumba, Chokwe, Imari Abubakari Obadele, and Nkechi Taifa. *Reparations Yes!* Baton Rouge, La.: House of Songhay, 1993.

Magdol, Edward. *A Right to Land: Essays on the Freedman's Community.* Westport, Conn.: Greenwood Press, 1977.

Magee, Rhonda V. "The Master's Tools, From the Bottom Up: Responses to African-American Reparations Theory in Mainstream and Outsider Remedies Discourse." *Virginia Law Review* 79 (May 1993): 863–916.

Mandle, Jay. *The Roots of Black Poverty: The Southern Plantation Economy after the Civil War.* Durham, N.C.: Duke University Press, 1978.

Marable, Manning. "An Idea Whose Time Has Come." *Newsweek* (August 27, 2001): 22.

——. *How Capitalism Underdeveloped Black America.* Boston: South End Press, 1983.

——. *Race, Reform, and Rebellion: The Second Reconstruction in Black America, 1945–1990.* 2d ed. Jackson, Miss.: University Press of Mississippi, 1991.

Matsuda, Mari J. "Looking to the Bottom: Critical Legal Studies and Reparations." *Harvard Civil Rights—Civil Liberties Law Review* 22 (spring 1987): 323–99.

Monteiro, Anthony. "Review Essay: Race, Class and Civilization: On Clarence J. Munford's *Race and Reparations.*" *Black Scholar* 29, no. 1 (spring 1999): 46–59.

Munford, Clarence J. *Race and Reparations: A Black Perspective for the Twenty-first Century.* Trenton, N.J.: Africa World Press, 1996.

Muwakkil, Salim. "The Big Payback. Renewing the Call for Reparations." *In These Times* 24, no. 12 (May 15, 2000): 18.

Nieman, Donald G. *Promises to Keep: African Americans and the Constitutional Order, 1776 to the Present.* New York: Oxford University Press, 1991.

Obadele, Imari. *Foundations of the Black Nation.* Detroit: House of Songhay, 1975.

Obadele, Johnita Scott. "Reparations: Linking Our Past, Present, and Future." www. ncobra. com.

Oliver, Melvin and Thomas Shapiro. *Black Wealth/White Wealth: A New Perspective on Racial Inequality.* New York: Routledge, 1995.

Oubre, Claude. *Forty Acres and a Mule: The Freedman's Bureau and Black Land Ownership.* Baton Rouge, La.: Louisiana State University Press, 1978.

"People's Plebiscite (Election) for Reparations Set for 19 May 1999." www. ncobra. com.

Quandango, Jill. *The Color of Welfare: How Racism Undermined the War on Poverty.* New York: Oxford University Press, 1994.

Roberts, Dorothy. "The Value of Black Mothers' Work." *Radical America* 26, no. 1 (August 1996): 9–15.

Robinson, Randall. *The Debt: What America Owes Blacks.* New York: Dutton, 1999.

Rodney, Walter. *How Europe Underdeveloped Africa.* Washington, D.C.: Howard University Press, 1980.

Schrag, Peter. "Backing off Bakke: The New Assault on Affirmative Action." *The Nation* 262, no. 16 (April 22, 1996): 11–14.

Shepard, Paul. "Powerful Group to Sue for Slave Reparations." *Philadelphia Inquirer,* November 5, 2000.

Smith, Vern E. "Debating the Wages of Slavery." *Newsweek* (August 27, 2001): 20–24.

Steele, Shelby. "Or a Childish Illusion of Justice?" *Newsweek* (August 27, 2001): 23.

Steinberg, Stephen. *Turning Back: The Retreat from Racial Justice in American Thought and Policy.* Boston: Beacon Press, 1995.

Swinton, David. "Racial Inequality and Reparations." In *The Wealth of Races: The Present Value of Benefits from Past Injustice,* edited by Richard F. America. New York: Greenwood Press, 1990.

Van Deburg, William L. *New Day in Babylon: The Black Power Movement and American Culture, 1965–1975.* Chicago: University of Chicago Press, 1992.

Van Deburg, William L., ed. *Modern Black Nationalism: From Marcus Garvey to Louis Farrakhan.* New York: New York University Press, 1997.

Verdun, Vincene. "If the Shoe Fits, Wear It: An Analysis of Reparations to African Americans." *Tulane Law Review* 67 (February 1993): 597–668.

Westley, Robert. "Many Billions Gone: Is It Time to Reconsider the Case for Black Reparations?" *Boston College Law Review* 40 (1998): 429–76.

Williams, Eric. *Capitalism and Slavery*. Chapel Hill, N.C.: University of North Carolina Press, 1944.

Yamamoto, Eric K. "What's Next? Japanese American Redress and African American Reparations." *Amerasia Journal* 25, no. 2 (1999): 1–17.

5. "This Battlefield Called Life": Black Feminist Dreams

Amott, Teresa L. and Julie A. Matthaei. *Race, Gender, and Work: A Multicultural History of Women in the United States*. Boston: South End Press, 1991.

Anderson-Bricker, Kristin. "From Beloved Community to Triple Jeopardy: Ideological Change and the Evolution of Feminism among Black and White Women in the Student Nonviolent Coordinating Committee, 1960–1975." Master's thesis, Syracuse University, 1992.

Avery, Byllye Y. "Breathing Life into Ourselves: The Evolution of the National Black Women's Health Project." In *Dear Sisters: Dispatches from the Women's Liberation Movement*, edited by Rosalyn Baxandall and Linda Gordon. New York: Basic Books, 2000.

Baxandall, Rosalyn and Linda Gordon, eds. *Dear Sisters: Dispatches from the Women's Liberation Movement*. New York: Basic Books, 2000.

Beale, Frances. "Double Jeopardy." In *The Black Woman: An Anthology*, edited by Toni Cade. New York: Signet, 1970. Reprinted in Beverly Guy-Sheftall, ed., *Words of Fire: An Anthology of African-American Feminist Thought*. New York: The New Press, 1995.

Bobo, Jacqueline, ed. *Black Feminist Cultural Criticism*. Malden, Mass.: Blackwell, 2001.

Breines, Wini. "Sixties Stories' Silences: White Feminism, Black Feminism." *National Women's Studies Association Journal* 8, no. 3 (fall 1996): 101–121.

Brown, Elaine. *A Taste of Power: A Black Woman's Story*. New York: Pantheon Books, 1992.

Cade, Toni. "The Pill: Genocide or Liberation." In *The Black Woman: An Anthology*. New York: Signet, 1970.

Caraway, Nancy. *Segregated Sisterhood: Racism and the Politics of American Feminism*. Knoxville, Tenn.: University of Tennessee Press, 1991.

Carby, Hazel. *Cultures of Babylon*. London: Verso, 2000.

———. *Race Men*. Cambridge: Harvard University Press, 2000.

———. *Reconstructing Womanhood: The Emergence of the Afro-American Woman Novelist*. New York: Oxford University Press, 1987.

Caton, Simone M. "Birth Control and the Black Community in the 1960s: Genocide or Power Politics?" *Journal of Social History* 31 (1998): 545–69.

Clark Hine, Darlene, ed. *Black Women in America: An Historical Encyclopedia.* Vols. 1 and 2. Brooklyn, N.Y.: Carlson Publishing, Inc., 1993.

Clarke, Cheryl. "Lesbianism: An Act of Resistance." In Guy-Sheftall, *Words of Fire.*

Collier-Thomas, Bettye and V. P. Franklin, eds. *Sisters in the Struggle: African American Women in the Civil Rights–Black Power Movement.* New York: New York University Press, 2001.

Collins, Patricia Hill. *Black Feminist Thought: Knowledge, Consciousness, and the Politics of Empowerment.* 2d ed. New York: Routledge, 1999.

———. *Fighting Words: Black Women and the Search for Justice.* Minneapolis: University of Minnesota Press, 1998.

Combahee River Collective. "A Black Feminist Statement." In Guy-Sheftall, *Words of Fire.*

Crawford, Vicki L. "Race, Class, Gender, and Culture: Black Women's Activism in the Mississippi Civil Rights Movement." *Journal of Mississippi History* 56 (spring 1996): 1–21.

Darity, William A. and C. B. Turner. "Family Planning, Race Consciousness, and the Fear of Race Genocide." *American Journal of Public Health* 62, no. 1 (1972): 1454–59.

Davis, Angela Y. *Blues Legacies and Black Feminism: Gertrude "Ma" Rainey, Bessie Smith, and Billie Holiday.* New York: Pantheon, 1998.

———. *Angela Davis: An Autobiography.* New York: Random House, 1974.

———. *Women, Culture, and Politics.* New York: Random House, 1989.

———. *Women, Race, and Class.* New York: Random House, 1981.

Davis, Beverly. "To Seize the Moment: A Retrospective on the National Black Feminist Organization." *Sage: A Scholarly Journal on Black Women's Studies* 5 (fall 1988): 43–47.

Dawson, Michael C. *Black Visions: The Roots of Contemporary African-American Political Ideologies.* Chicago: University of Chicago Press, 2001.

De Hart, Jane Sherron. "Second Wave Feminism(s) and the South: The Difference that Differences Make." In *Women of the American South: A Multicultural Reader,* edited by Christie Anne Farnham. New York: New York University Press, 1997.

Dill, Bonnie Thornton. "Race, Class, and Gender: Prospects for an All-Inclusive Sisterhood." *Feminist Studies* 9 (1983): 131–50.

DuCille, Ann. *Skin Trade.* Cambridge: Harvard University Press, 1996.

Duggan, Lisa. "Queering the State." *Social Text* 39 (summer 1994): 1–14.

Echols, Alice. *Daring to Be Bad: Radical Feminism in America, 1968–1975.* Minneapolis: University of Minnesota Press, 1988.

Evans, Sara M. *Born for Liberty: A History of Women in America.* New York: Free Press, 1989.

———. *Personal Politics: The Roots of Women's Liberation in the Civil Rights Movement and the New Left.* New York: Knopf, 1979.

Firestone, Shulamith. *The Dialectic of Sex: The Case for Feminist Revolution.* New York: Bantam, 1970.

Foeman, Anita K. "Gloria Richardson: Breaking the Mold." *Journal of Black Studies* 26 (1996): 604–15.

Franklin, V. P. *Living Our Stories, Telling Our Truths: Autobiography and the Making of the African American Intellectual Tradition.* New York: Oxford University Press, 1996.

Freeman, Jo. *The Politics of Women's Liberation.* New York: David McKay, 1975.

Friedan, Betty. *The Feminine Mystique.* 1963. Reprint, New York: Norton, 1997.

Fuss, Diana. *Essentially Speaking: Feminism, Nature, and Difference.* New York: Routledge, 1989.

Giddings, Paula. *When and Where I Enter: The Impact of Black Women on Race and Sex in America.* New York: William Morrow, 1984.

Gordon, Vivian Verdell. *Black Women, Feminism, and Black Liberation: Which Way?* Chicago: Third World Press, 1987.

Guy-Sheftall, Beverly, ed. *Words of Fire: An Anthology of African-American Feminist Thought.* New York: The New Press, 1995.

Haden, Patricia, Donna Middleton, and Patricia Robinson. "A Historical and Critical Essay for Black Women." In Guy-Sheftall, *Words of Fire.*

Hammonds, Evelynn. "Black (W)holes and the Geometry of Black Female Sexuality (More Gender Trouble: Feminism Meets Queer Theory)." *Differences: A Journal of Feminist Cultural Studies* 6 (1994): 126–46.

Hansberry, Lorraine. "Simone de Beauvoir and *The Second Sex:* An American Commentary." In Guy-Sheftall, *Words of Fire.*

Harley, Sharon. "'Chronicle of a Death Foretold': Gloria Richardson, the Cambridge Movement, and the Radical Black Activist Tradition," in Collier-Thomas and Franklin, *Sisters in the Struggle.*

Harper, Philip Brian. *Are We Not Men? Masculine Anxiety and the Problem of African-American Identity.* New York: Oxford University Press, 1996.

Harris, Duchess. "From the Kennedy Commission to the Combahee River Collective: Black Feminist Organizing, 1960–1980." In Collier-Thomas and Franklin, *Sisters in the Struggle.*

Heacock, Maureen C. "Sounding a Challenge: African American Women's Poetry and the Black Arts Movement." Ph.D diss., University of Minnesota, 1995.

Higginbotham, Evelyn Brooks. "African-American Women's History and the Metalanguage of Race." *Signs* 17 (1992): 251–74.

Holland, Sharon P. *Raising the Dead: Readings of Death and (Black) Subjectivity.* Durham, N.C.: Duke University Press, 2000.

Holland, Sharon P. "Which Me Will Survive? Audre Lorde and the Development of Black Feminist Ideology." *Critical Matrix* 1 (1988): 2–30.

hooks, bell. *Feminist Theory: From Margin to Center.* Boston: South End Press, 1989.

———. *Ain't I a Woman? Black Women and Feminism.* 2d ed. Boston: South End Press, 1984.

———. *Talking Back: Thinking Feminist, Thinking Black.* Boston: South End Press, 1989.

Hudson-Weems, Clenora. *Africana Womanism: Reclaiming Ourselves.* Troy, Mich.: Bedford Publishers, 1995.

Hull, Gloria T., Patricia Bell Scott, and Barbara Smith, eds. *All the Women Are White, All the Blacks Are Men, But Some of Us Are Brave: Black Women's Studies.* Old Westbury, N.Y.: Feminist Press, 1981.

Hunter, Andrea G. and Sherrill L. Sellers. "Feminist Attitudes among African American Women and Men." *Gender and Society* 12 (1998): 81–100.

James, Joy. "Radicalizing Feminism." In *The Black Feminist Reader,* edited by Joy James and T. Denean Sharpley-Whiting. Oxford: Blackwell, 2000.

———. *Resisting State Violence: Radicalism, Gender, and Race in U.S. Culture.* Minneapolis: University of Minnesota Press, 1996.

———. *Shadowboxing: Representations of Black Feminist Politics.* New York: St. Martin's Press, 1999.

James, Joy, ed. *The Angela Davis Reader.* Malden, Mass. and Oxford: Blackwell, 1998.

James, Stanlie M. and Abena P. A. Busia, eds. *Theorizing Black Feminisms: The Visionary Pragmatism of Black Women.* New York: Routledge & Kegan Paul, 1994.

Jones, Charles, ed. *The Black Panther Party Reconsidered.* Baltimore: Black Classic Press, 1998.

Jones, Jacqueline. *Labor of Love, Labor of Sorrow: Black Women, Work, and the Family from Slavery to the Present.* New York: Vintage Books, 1986.

La Rue, Linda. "The Black Movement and Women's Liberation." In Guy-Sheftall, *Words of Fire.*

LeBlanc-Ernest, Angela. "'The Most Qualified Person to Handle the Job': Black Panther Party Women, 1966–1982." In *The Black Panther Party Reconsidered,* edited by Charles Jones, 305–34. Baltimore: Black Classics Press, 1998.

Lorde, Audre. "Age, Race, Class, and Sex: Women Redefining Difference." In Guy-Sheftall, *Words of Fire.*

Lorde, Audre. "Learning from the Sixties." In *The Woman That I Am: The Literature and Culture of Contemporary Women of Color,* edited by D. Soyini Madison, 454–62. New York: St. Martin's Press, 1994.

Malone-Hawkins, Sally. "Re-constructing Feminism: The Black Woman's Perspective." Ph.D diss., State University of New York at Binghamton, 1993.

Matthews, Tracye. "'No One Ever Asks What a Man's Role in the Revolution Is': Gender and Sexual Politics in the Black Panther Party, 1966–1971." Ph.D. diss., University of Michigan, 1998.

Mirza, Heidi Safia, ed. *Black British Feminism: A Reader.* London and New York: Routledge, 1997.

Munt, Sally, ed. *New Lesbian Criticism.* New York: Columbia University Press, 1992.

Murray, Pauli. *Song in a Weary Throat.* New York: Harper & Row, 1987.

Nnaemeka, Obioma, ed. *Sisterhood, Feminisms, and Power: From Africa to the Diaspora.* Trenton, N.J.: Africa World Press, 1998.

Omolade, Barbara. "Hearts of Darkness." In *Powers of Desire: The Politics of Sexuality,* edited by Ann Snitow, Christine Stansell, and Sharon Thompson. New York: Monthly Review Press, 1983.

———. *The Rising Song of African American Women.* New York: Routledge, 1994.

Ransby, Barbara. "Ella Baker and the Black Radical Tradition." Ph.D diss., University of Michigan, 1996.

Redstockings. "Manifesto." In Baxandall and Gordon, *Dear Sisters.*

Redstockings, ed. *Feminist Revolution.* New York: Random House, 1975.

Roberts, Dorothy. *Killing the Black Body: Race, Reproduction, and the Meaning of Liberty.* New York: Random House, 1997.

Robinson, Patricia and Black Sisters. "Poor Black Women." In Baxandall and Gordon, *Dear Sisters.*

Robnett, Belinda K. *How Long? How Long? African-American Women in the Struggle for Civil Rights.* New York: Oxford University Press, 1997.

Rodrique, Jessie M. "The Black Community and the Birth-Control Movement." In *Unequal Sisters: A Multicultural Reader in U.S. Women's History,* edited by Ellen Carol Du Bois and Vicki L. Ruiz. New York: Routledge, 1990.

Rosen, Ruth. *The World Split Open: How the Modern Women's Movement Changed America.* New York: Viking, 2000.

SDS Women. "To the Women of the Left." In Baxandall and Gordon. *Dear Sisters.*

Shakur, Assata. *Assata: An Autobiography.* Chicago: Lawrence Hill, 1987.

Slook, Christine Lisa. "A Black Feminist Revision of African American Women's Reproductive History." Master's thesis, University of Iowa, 1996.

Smith, Barbara. "Racism and Women's Studies." In *All the Women Are White, All the Blacks Are Men, But Some of Us Are Brave,* edited by Gloria T. Hull, Patricia Bell Scott, and Barbara Smith. New York: The Feminist Press, 1981.

——. *The Truth that Never Hurts: Writings on Race, Gender, and Freedom.* New York: Routledge, 1999.

Smith, Barbara, ed. *Home Girls: A Black Feminist Anthology.* New York: Kitchen Table—Women of Color Press, 1983.

Springer, Kimberly. "'Our Politics Was Black Women': Black Feminist Organizations, 1968–1980." Ph.D diss., Emory University, 1999.

——. *Still Lifting, Still Climbing: Contemporary Black Women's Activism.* New York: New York University Press, 1999.

Sudbury, Julia. *"Other Kinds of Dreams": Black Women's Organisations and the Politics of Transformation.* London and New York: Routledge, 1998.

The Damned (possibly Patricia Haden, Donna Middleton, and Patricia Robinson, et. al.). *Lessons from the Damned: Class Struggle in the Black Community.* Ojai, Calif.: Times Change Press, 1973.

Third World Women's Alliance. "Statement." In Baxandall and Gordon, *Dear Sisters.*

Treadwell, Mary. "An African American Woman Speaks out for Abortion Rights." In Baxandall and Gordon, *Dear Sisters.*

Wallace, Michele. *Black Macho and the Myth of the Superwoman.* 1978. New edition. London: Verso, 1990.

Warner, Michael, ed. *Fear of a Queer Planet: Queer Politics and Social Theory.* Minneapolis: University of Minnesota Press, 1993.

Weathers, Mary Ann. "An Argument for Black Women's Liberation as a Revolutionary Force." In Guy-Sheftall, *Words of Fire.*

Weber, Shirley N. "Black Power in the 1960s: A Study of Its Impact on Women's Liberation." *Journal of Black Studies* 11 (1981): 483–98.

White, Deborah Gray. *Too Heavy a Load: Black Women in Defense of Themselves, 1894–1994.* New York: W. W. Norton, 1998.

White, E. Frances. *Dark Continent of Our Bodies: Black Feminism and the Politics of Respectability.* Philadelphia: Temple University Press, 2001.

——. "Listening to the Voices of Black Feminism." *Radical America* 18 (1984): 7–25.

Wilkerson, Margaret B. "Lorraine Vivian Hansberry (1930–1965)." In *Black Women in America: An Historical Encyclopedia,* edited by Darlene Clark Hine, 524–29. Brooklyn, N.Y.: Carlson Publishers, 1993.

Williams, Maxine. *Black Women's Liberation.* New York: Pathfinder Press, 1970.

Winslow, Barbara. *Women's Liberation: Black Women, Working Women, Revolutionary Feminism.* Highland Park, Mich.: Sun Distribution International, n.d. (circa 1970s).

"Women Unite! Free the Panthers!" In Baxandall and Gordon, *Dear Sisters.*

Wright, Doris. "Angry Notes from a Black Feminist." In Baxandall and Gordon, *Dear Sisters.*

6. Keepin' It (Sur)real: Dreams of the Marvelous

Arnold, A. James. *Modernism and Negritude: The Poetry and Poetics of Aimé Césaire*. Cambridge: Harvard University Press, 1981.

Benayoun, Robert. *Le Rire des Surrealistes*. Paris: La Bougie du Sapeur, 1988.

Camacho, Jorge. "Monk Atmosphere." *Le Cerceau* 5 (Summer 1995): 6.

Carby, Hazel. *Cultures of Babylon*. London: Verso, 2000.

Césaire, Aimé. *Discourse on Colonialism*. Translated by Joan Pinkham. New York: Monthly Review Press, 1972.

———. Introduction to *Esclavage et colonisation*, by Victor Schoelcher. Paris: Presses Universitaires de France, 1948.

———. *Letter to Maurice Thorez*. Paris: Présence Africaine, 1957, 6, 7, 14–15.

Chicago Surrealist Group. "Surrealism and Blues." *Living Blues*, no. 25 (January/February 1976), 19.

Conde, Maryse. *"Cahier d'un Retour au Pays Natal": Césaire, Analyse Critique*. Paris: Hatier, 1978.

Cortez, Jayne. *Coagulations: New and Selected Poems*. New York: Thunder's Mouth Press, 1984.

———. *Somewhere in Advance of Nowhere*. New York: High Risk Books, 1996.

———. *Taking the Blues Back Home*. New York: Harmolodic/Verve CD 314 531 918-2, 1996.

Cunard, Nancy, ed. *Negro: An Anthology*. 1934. Reprint, New York: Continuum, 1996.

Davis, Angela Y. *Blues Legacies and Black Feminism: Gertrude "Ma" Rainey, Bessie Smith, and Billie Holiday*. New York: Pantheon, 1998.

Diawara, Manthia. *In Search of Africa*. Cambridge: Harvard University Press, 1998.

do Cruzeiro-Seixas, Artur. "My Escape to Africa." *Race Traitor* 9 (summer 1998): 95.

Edwards, Brent Hayes. "Black Globality: The International Shape of Black Intellectual Culture." Ph.D. diss., Columbia University, 1997.

———. "Ethnics of Surrealism." *Transition* 78 (1999): 132–34.

Fanon, Frantz. *Black Skin, White Masks*. Translated by Charles Lam Markmann. New York: Grove Press, 1967.

———. *The Wretched of the Earth*. New York: Grove Press, 1967.

Fouchet, Max-Pol. *Wifredo Lam*. 2d ed. Barcelona: Ediciones Polgrafa, 1989.

Frutkin, Susan. *Aimé Césaire: Black between Worlds*. Miami: Center for Advanced International Studies, 1973.

Garon, Paul. *Blues and the Poetic Spirit*. 1975. Reprint, San Francisco: City Lights, 1996.

"Jazz et Surrealisme: Une Possible Alliance." *Dies and Das (This and That): A Magazine of Contemporary Surrealist Interest* 1 (1984): 1–3.

Joans, Ted. *A Black Manifesto in Jazz Poetry and Prose*. London: Calder and Boyars, 1971.

------. *All of Ted Joans and No More; Poems and Collages.* New York: Excelsior-Press Publishers, 1961.

------. "Black Flower." *L'Archibras* 3 (March 1968): 10–11.

------. *Black Pow-Wow: Jazz Poems.*1st ed. New York: Hill and Wang, 1969.

------. *Double Trouble: Poems.* Paris: Revue Noire, Editions Bleu Outremer, 1992.

------. Interview with author. Dec. 15, 1995.

------. "Je Me Vois (I See Myself)." *Contemporary Authors Autobiography Series,* vol. 25. Detroit: Gale Research, 1996.

------. "Ted Joans Parle. . . ." *La Breche: Action Surrealiste* (October 5, 1963): 66.

------. *Teducation: Selected Poems 1949–1999.* Minneapolis, Minn.: Coffee House Press, 1999.

Kesteloot, Lilyan and B. Kotchy. *Aimé Césaire, L'Homme et L'Oeuvre.* Paris: Présence Africaine, 1973.

LeGrand, Gerard. *Puissance du Jazz.* Paris: Arcanes, 1953.

Leiner, Jacqueline. "Entretien avec A. C." In *Tropiques,* vol. 1, edited by Aimé Césaire. Paris: Editions Jean-Michel Place, 1978. Fascimile reproduction.

"Lettre du Lieutenant de Vaisseau Bayle, chef du service d'information au directeur de la revue *Tropiques,* Fort-de-France, May 10, 1943" and "Reponse de *Tropiques* à M. le Lieutenant de Vaisseau Bayle, Fort-de-France, May 12, 1943," signed Aimé Césaire, Suzanne Césaire, Georges Gratiant, Aristide Maugée, René Ménil, and Lucie Thesée. *Tropiques,* vol. 1, ed. by Aimé Césaire. Paris: Editions Jean-Michel Place, 1978. Documents-Annexes, xxxvi–xxxviii. Fascimile reproduction.

Miller, Eugene E. *Voice of a Native Son: The Poetics of Richard Wright.* Jackson, Miss.: University Press of Mississippi, 1990.

Moore-Gilbert, Bart. *Postcolonial Theory: Contexts, Practices, Politics.* London: Verso, 1997.

Nadeau, Maurice. *The History of Surrealism.* Translated by Richard Howard. 1944. Reprint, Cambridge: The Belknap Press of Harvard University Press, 1989.

Naum, Gellu. *L'Autre Cote: Poemes.* Translated from Rumanian to French by Annie Bentoiu and Andree Fleury. Bucharest: Cartea Romaneasca, 1991.

Ngal, M. a. M. *Aimé Césaire: Un Homme a la Recherché d'une Patrie.* Dakar: Nouvelles Éditions Africaines, 1983.

Nougé, Paul. *Music Is Dangerous.* Danville, Calif.: Soundings Magazine, 1973.

Pallister, Jane L. *Aimé Césaire.* New York: Twayne Publishers, 1991.

Richardson, Michael, ed. *Refusal of the Shadow: Surrealism and the Caribbean.* Translated by Michael Richardson and Krzysztof Fijalkowski. London: Verso, 1996.

Robinson, Cedric J. *Black Marxism: The Making of the Black Radical Tradition*. Chapel Hill, N.C.: University of North Carolina Press, 2000.

Rosemont, Franklin. "Black Music and the Surrealist Revolution." *Arsenal/ Surrealist Subversion* 3. Chicago: Black Swan Press, 1976, 17–27.

——. "Suzanne Césaire: In the Light of Surrealism." Unpublished paper in author's possession.

——. *The Forecast Is Hot! Tracts and Other Collective Declarations in the United States, 1966–1976*. Chicago: Black Swan Press, 1997.

——. "The New Argonautica." In *City Lights Anthology*, edited by Lawrence Ferlinghetti. San Francisco: Black Swan Press, 1974.

Rosemont, Franklin, ed. *André Breton: What Is Surrealism? Selected Writings*. New York: Pathfinder, 1978, 21–22.

Rosemont, Penelope, ed. *Surrealist Women: An International Anthology*. Austin: University of Texas Press, 1998.

Sawin, Martica. *Surrealism in Exile and the Beginning of the New York School*. Cambridge: MIT Press, 1997.

Schoelcher, Victor. *Esclavage et colonisation*. Paris: Presses Universitaires de France, 1948.

Senghor, L. S. "The Lessons of Leo Frobenius." In *Leo Frobenius: An Anthology*, edited by E. Haberland. Wiesbaden: Franz Steiner Verlag, 1973.

Shapiro, Norman, ed. *Negritude: Black Poetry from Africa and the Caribbean*. New York: October House, 1970, 224.

Spady, James. "Black Music: Surrealism." In *Popular Culture in America*, edited by Paul Buhle. Minneapolis: University of Minnesota Press, 1987.

Stovall, Tyler. *Paris Noir: African Americans in the City of Light*. Boston and New York: Houghton Mifflin, 1996.

Surrealist Group of France. "Murderous Humanitarianism." Reprinted in *Race Traitor—Special Issue—Surrealism: Revolution against Whiteness* 9 (summer 1998): 67–69.

Sylla, Cheikh Tidiane. "Surrealism and Black African Art." *Arsenal: Surrealist Subversion* 4. Chicago: Black Swan Press, 1989, 128–29.

Tarnaud, Claude. "Brin de Conduite." In *Jacques Lacomblez: 30 Ans d'Activité*. Paris: Musee d'Ixelles, 1983.

——. *La Forme Reflechie: Carnet de Voyage et Commentaires*. Paris: Le Soleil Noir, 1954.

Tashjian, Dickran. *A Boatload of Madmen: Surrealism and the American Avant-Garde, 1920–1950*. New York: Thames and Hudson, 1995.

Wright, Richard. *Native Son, and How Bigger Was Born*. New York: HarperPerennial, 1993.

——. *Twelve Million Black Voices*. 1941. Reprint, New York: Thunder's Mouth Press, 1988.

Young, Robert. *White Mythologies: Writing History and the West*. London: Routledge, 1990.

ACKNOWLEDGMENTS

If I thanked everyone who deserved to be thanked, the additional pages would double the size (and the price) of this book. I only hope that those I have not mentioned will understand and accept my gratitude in some other form.

First and foremost, I must thank the good people at Dartmouth College for inviting me to deliver the Martin Luther King Jr. Lecture in January 2000, notably Professors Judith Byfield and Deborah King; Ozzie Harris, director of Dartmouth's Office of Equal Opportunity and Affirmative Action; and a brilliant recent graduate named Shauna Brown. The theme that year was "Legacies of Activism/Legacies of Hate," and I decided to concentrate on the former. My lecture, which I titled "Politics and Knowledge. On the Poetry of Social Movements," planted the seeds for this book. The organizing committee for the event and the audience it attracted pushed me to think well beyond the limits of an hour-long speech. The other invited speakers raised the stakes; poet Joy Harjo, veteran radical Bill Epton (who recently joined the ancestors), and New Hampshire state representative Jackie Weatherspoon all brought powerful, compelling ideas that profoundly shaped my own thinking. I'm especially grateful to Ozzie Harris and his staff, particularly Connie Bellavance, for facilitating my visit and making my family and me feel welcome.

Thanks to the generosity of Harle Montgomery and the Montgomery Endowment, I returned to Dartmouth that summer and

omores and living in the luxurious Montgomery House on the
edge of campus. It was there that *Freedom Dreams* began to take
shape as a book. By the time I left Dartmouth half of the manuscript was complete. My family and I are so grateful to Barbara
Gerstner, director of the endowment, and her assistant, Lou Anne
Cain, for making our stay so wonderful and productive. Several
faculty members, staff, and administrators went well beyond the
call of duty to facilitate our visit: Besides those already mentioned, I express my heartfelt thanks to Alex Bontemps, Donna
and Bruce Nelson, Mary Kelley, Annelise Orleck, Leo Spitzer
and Marianne Hirsch, and Dean Jamshed J. Bharucha, for their
warmth, hospitality, and stimulating conversation.

Cedric Robinson, my mentor and author of the magnificent
book *Black Marxism: The Making of the Black Radical Tradition*,
was the other source of inspiration for this book. Eighteen years
ago he propelled me on an intellectual and political journey
that would lead to an examination of the thoughts and dreams of
Black radicals. The movement itself proved to be a third source,
particularly its recent resurgence in the form of the Black Radical
Congress and various allied organizations. I am indebted to the
entire movement for its collective knowledge and wisdom, though
I must personally thank the following activist/intellectuals whose
ideas have directly influenced this book: Amiri Baraka, Amina
Baraka, Barbara Ransby, Lisa Brock, Tracye Matthews, Manning
Marable, Leith Mullings, Abdul Alkalimat, Bill Fletcher, Fran
Beale, Jean Carey Bond and Max Bond, Sam Anderson, Joel
Washington, Cathy Cohen, Sundiata Cha-Jua, Clarence Lang,
Reverend Osagyefo Uhuru Sekou, Fanon Che Wilkins and Assata
Zerai, Horace Campbell, Gerald Horne, Komozi Woodard, Clar-
ence Lusane, Eric Mann, Liann Hurst Mann and the staff of the
Labor/Community Strategy Center, Ernest Allen, Harold Cruse,
Vicki Garvin, Michael Goldfield, Sid and Salima Lemelle, Josh
Lyons, David Roediger, Tim Schermerhorn, Akinyele Umoja,
Alan Wald, Billy Watkins, and Bob Wing.

George Lipsitz's imprint is all over *Freedom Dreams*, for he is a master at uncovering the desires and hopes of an aggrieved people. Tricia Rose always asks the hard questions, and in doing so makes us all better scholars. Farah Jasmine Griffin, Tera Hunter, and Saidiya Hartman, in their scholarship and by example, reminded me of the power of human dignity and self-possession. Ted Joans and Laura Corsiglia reminded me of the force of love. Franklin and Penelope Rosemont reminded me of the Marvelous. And Jayne Cortez and Mel Edwards reminded me that the Marvelous lies in our capacity to struggle. Indeed, without artists around me, there would be no *Freedom Dreams*. I'm especially indebted to Tracie Morris, Keorapetse Kgositsile, Sonia Sanchez, Sekou Sundiata, Geoffrey Jacques, Arno Boehler, Susanne Granzer, and my sister Meilan Carter for reminding me of the power unleashed by the imagination. Stanley Crouch, an extraordinary teacher, made me look harder at the mess we're in, yet like Robert O'Meally and Jacqui Malone, reminded me that we can (must!) swing our way out of our constrictions. The great pianist, composer, and scholar Randy Weston showed me the freedom in African culture; the love and encouragement he and his daughter Pam have given me over the last few years have left a deep mark on this book and on works to come. Henry Giroux not only infused my work with a sense of hope but invited me to Penn State to present the essential ideas from this book. He and Susan Giroux took me into their home, fed me, engaged me, and ultimately made this a better book. Harvey Kaye and his family did much the same thing in Green Bay, Wisconsin. Harvey and his students engaged my ideas with astounding energy and enthusiasm. Likewise, Marcus Rediker was kind enough to invite me to give the E. P. Thompson Lecture at the University of Pittsburgh, where I shared the basic thesis of *Freedom Dreams*. My conversations and arguments afterward sharpened my analysis. I'm also especially grateful to the late Michael Jimenez, Forrest Hylton, George Reid Andrews, Wendy Goldman, and other members of the Working-Class History Seminar. Peter Linebaugh, co-author with Marcus Rediker of *The Many-Headed Hydra*, remains a consistent source of brilliance and inspiration. That book, in many ways, was a model for *Freedom Dreams*.

Deb Chasman, my editor at Beacon Press, kept telling me how much she loved this project from its inception. Her encouragement, along with that of Tisha Hooks (my "alter" editor) rescued this manuscript from the trash heap more than once. And Joy Sobeck made my prose immeasurably more readable. Delverlon Hall provided administrative assistance, friendship, advice, and unconditional love. She is a beautiful spirit with an equally beautiful son, Devin, who will one day save us all. My graduate students contributed to this project in myriad ways, though none more than Betsy Esch. She worked as my research assistant and co-authored an article with me on Maoism and Black liberation, sections of which appear in chapter 3. My friend Judith Macfarlane provided brilliant translations of key French documents gratis; her unyielding support over the years has been implacable.

Several friends and colleagues read parts of the manuscript or just provided insights that proved crucial to this book. Given space limitations, all I can do is list their names: Angela Davis, Gina Dent, Vincent Harding, Eddie Glaude, Genna Rae McNeil, Wini Breines, Paul Buhle, MariJo Buhle, Rod and Melanie Bush, Hazel Carby, Michael Denning, Janaki Bakhle, Nick Dirks, Geoff Eley, Regina Morantz, Nell Irvin Painter, George Sanchez, Kevin Gaines, Penny von Eschen, Kyra Gaunt, Gerald Gill, Guy Ramsey, Herman Gray, Michael Honey, Wahneema Lubiano, Tiffany R. L. Patterson, Cornel West, Shane White, Cynthia Young, Anthony Foy, Peniel Joseph, Beth Coleman, Howard Goldkrand, William Loren Katz, Andrew Ross, Nikhil Singh, Veronique Helenon, Kim Butler, Sherrie Russell-Brown, Renee Green, James Spady, Marilyn Young, the staff at the Tamiment Library at New York University, especially Andrew Lee, Jane Latour, and the late Debra Bernhardt.

And then there are those folks who defy category; close friends who may or may not have read early drafts or talked with me about this book, but whose love and support has fueled a radical vision of community and sustained my family and me during the last few years. They include Michael Eric Dyson and Marcia Dyson, Denise Greene, Emir Lewis, Ayodele Greene-Lewis, Elenni Knight Davis, Michaela Angela Davis, Graham Haynes, Ezra Knight, Lem Martinez-Carroll and Judith Killen, Elsa Barkley Brown, Earl Lewis, Susan Whitlock, Jayne London, Julius Scott, Arthur Jafa, Greg Tate, Jill Nelson, Stanley Nelson, Rene Moreno, Emily Colas, Meg Williams, Kamili Anderson, Dalila Anderson, and Glenda Johnson. Maxine Gordon, who holds the unusual position of being friend, family, student, teacher, and spiritual advisor, deserves a special thanks for keeping my work and life directed. And once again, I must thank my teachers who got me here: Thelma Reyna, Jack Stuart, Leo Rifkin (rest in peace), and Jane Andrias, her husband, Richard, and their two amazing daughters, Eve and Kate.

Much gratitude to the Thelonious Monk family (Mrs. Nellie Monk, T. S., Gale, Peter Grain, Marcellus Green, everyone) for their unflinching support of my effort to write the book about the great pianist and composer, and for their patience while I take this slight detour to meditate on freedom, an idea Mr. Monk spent a lot of time thinking about. I promise, Thelonious is next!

I send infinite love to my family: my grandmothers, Carmen Chambers and Aileen Kelley; my siblings, Makani Themba-Nixon and her husband Ron Nixon, Meilan Carter, Chris Kelley, Idris Morehouse, Benjamin Kelley, Shannon Patrick Kelley, Craig Berrysmith, and all their children; my mother-in-law Annette Rohan and all of the aunts—Evelyn, Nanette (rest in peace), Dorothe, Dolores, Marie, Betsy, and Sheila; my wife's siblings Claudine, Claudius Jr., Irie; my father Donald Kelley and my late grandfather the Reverend Rafe David Kelley (rest in peace); all my cousins, but especially Kay Rodriguez who had a lot to do with this book. And, of course, I'm deeply indebted to my mother, Ananda Sattwa, who taught me everything I know about freedom and dreaming. Her importance should be evident in "When History Sleeps."

I owe Diedra and Elleza for constantly schooling me in the ways of the wise, for listening to the rantings of a scholar gone mad, and for not committing me when I began to babble on about dreams and poetic knowledge and our responsibility to make a new world. Every day they show me what love is and what a beautiful life looks and feels like. Diedra made her mark on *Freedom Dreams* in another way. She graciously allowed me to use her stunning painting *Sassa* for the cover. "Sassa," which is Ashanti for "psychic energy" or "soul," captures the book's essential message: that our spirit and imagination, those intangible resources within ourselves, constitute the most powerful creative force at our disposal. Every painting Diedra makes is a testament to what is possible, evidence of the energies of love.

Finally, I dedicated this book to three people: my sister Makani Themba-Nixon, Lisa Y. Sullivan, and Joe Wood Jr. Makani has been my role model all my life; she is a committed activist who continues to dream; she somehow retains her sense of grounding without becoming cynical. My sister worked closely with Lisa Sullivan, who shared her activism as well as her willingness to dream out loud. Lisa's entire life was driven by a dream of freedom, one that could be realized only by the struggles of ordinary people. She left us way too early, as did my friend Joe Wood Jr. Although Joe tended toward skepticism, always quick to expose and confront the problems and limitations of humanity, he taught me that change begins with how we feel, how we think, how we reconstruct our social and individual relationships. So he, too, was a dreamer of sorts. By dedicating this book to Lisa and Joe's legacies and to my sister, who continues to fight, I hope I might inspire a few more dreamers to "do" and a few more skeptics to dream.

INDEX

Library of Congress Cataloging-in-Publication Data

Names: Kelley, Robin D. G., author.
Title: Freedom dreams : the Black radical imagination / Robin D.G.
    Kelley.
Description: Twentieth anniversary edition. | Boston : Beacon Press, [2022]
    | Includes bibliographical references and index. | Summary: "Freedom
    Dreams examines the radical utopian dreams held by 19th and 20th
    century Black political movements"– Provided by publisher.
Identifiers: LCCN 2022010243 | ISBN 9780807007037 (paperback) | ISBN
    9780807007853 (ebook)
Subjects: LCSH: Black power–United States–History. | African
    Americans–Civil rights. | Civil rights movements–United
    States–History. | African American arts. | Radicalism–United
    States–History. | African diaspora. | United States–Race
    relations–History.
Classification: LCC E185 .K39 2022 | DDC 323.1196/073–dc23/eng/20220615
LC record available at https://lccn.loc.gov/2022010243